A Critique of
Feminist Biblical Interpretation

GENDER ROLES AND THE BIBLE:
Creation, the Fall, and Redemption

A Critique of
Feminist Biblical Interpretation

GENDER ROLES AND THE BIBLE:
Creation, the Fall, and Redemption

Jack Cottrell, Ph.D.

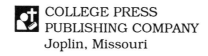 COLLEGE PRESS
PUBLISHING COMPANY
Joplin, Missouri

Library of Congress Catalog Card Number: 93-74946
International Standard Book Number: 0-89900-678-7

TABLE OF CONTENTS

INTRODUCTION 11

  I. Definitions 11

  II. Types of Feminism 13
    A. Secular Feminism 13
    B. Goddess Feminism 14
    C. Liberal Christian Feminism 16
    D. Biblical Feminism 18

  III. About This Work 20
    A. The Common Ground 20
    B. The Focal Point 21
    C. Motivation 22
    D. The Plan of This Study 24

CHAPTER ONE:
FEMINISM AND BIBLICAL
INTERPRETATION 27

  I. The Problem: "The Hard Passages" 27
    A. "Hard" at Specific Points 28
    B. "Hard" in Their Overall Teaching 30

  II. The Rules of Interpretation 31
    A. The Two Horizons of Interpretation 31
    B. The Importance of the Context 32
    C. "Scripture Interprets Scripture" 33
      1. Transcultural Versus Cultural 35

2. Doctrinal Versus Practical. 36
3. General Versus Specific 37
4. Clear Versus Unclear. 37
5. Systematic Versus Incidental. 38
6. Didactic Versus Historical. 38
D. Applying the Principles 38

III. Letting Scripture Interpret Scripture 40

IV. Prescriptive Versus Descriptive 41
A. Transcultural Versus Cultural 43
B. Doctrinal Versus Practical. 44
C. General Versus Specific 46
D. Clear Versus Unclear. 53
E. Didactic Versus Historical. 54
F. Systematic Versus Incidental. . . . . . . ·. . . 56

V. Conclusion. 57

CHAPTER TWO:
FEMINISM AND CREATION 63

I. Genesis One. 63
A. Points of Agreement 64
1. Both Male and Female Are
in the Image of God. 64
2. Both Male and Female Have Equal
Dominion over the Earth 67
B. Points of Disagreement 68
1. Male and Female Were Created
Simultaneously 69
2. Maleness and Femaleness Define the
Image of God 70
C. Conclusion Concerning Genesis One 77

II. The Relation Between Genesis One
and Genesis Two. 78

III. **Genesis Two**. 80
   A. The Male Is Central in the Narrative. 80
   B. The Male Was Created First 83
   C. The Woman Was Created from the Man 88
   D. The Woman Was Created for the Man 90
   E. The Man Named the Woman 94
   F. Conclusion 99

IV. **The Decisive Point: The New Testament**
   Commentary 99

CHAPTER THREE:
FEMINISM AND THE FALL. 107

  I. **The Sin** 108
   A. Why Did Satan Choose Eve? 109
     1. The Feminist Explanation. 109
     2. Critique of the Feminist Explanation . . 113
   B. Was Eve More Responsible for the First
     Sin Than Adam? 119
   C. Adam's Responsibility and Male Headship. . 124

  II. **The Curse**. 126
   A. The Feminist Understanding of the Curse
     on the Woman 126
   B. A Non-Feminist View of the Curse. 129
     1. The Pivotal Nature of Genesis 2 129
     2. The Curse as the Corruption of
       Created Headship 130
     3. The Curse Is a True Curse. 132

 III. **The Restoration** 134
   A. Feminism and the New Creation. 135
   B. Critique of the Feminist Concept of
     Restoration 137
     1. Christ and the Curse 138
     2. When Is the Curse Lifted? 139

3. Galatians 3:28 and the Reversal of
the Curse 142
4. Conclusion. 143

CHAPTER FOUR:
FEMINISM AND JESUS CHRIST 149

I. **Gender and the Incarnation** 150
A. How Feminists Explain the Male
Incarnation 150
1. A Concession to the Culture of
Patriarchal Judaism 150
2. Jesus was Anthrōpos, Not Male. 151
3. Jesus Was both Male and Female 152
B. Critique of Feminism's Approach to the
Gender of Christ 155
1. A Concession to Culture?. 155
2. The Meaning and Use of Anthrōpos . . . 156
3. Is Christ both Male and Female?. 160
C. Scripture and the Maleness of Christ 166

II. **Christ's Encounters with Women** 169
A. The Feminist View. 169
1. Mary and Martha, Luke 10:38-42 171
2. The Samaritan Woman, John 4:5-42. . . 172
3. Conversation with Martha,
John 11:20-27. 173
4. The Women with Jesus, Luke 8:1-3 and
Mark 15:40-41 173
5. The Women at the Tomb, Matthew 28:8-10
and John 20:17-18 174
6. Miscellaneous. 175
B. A Non-Feminist Response 176
1. Exaggerated Radicalness. 177
2. Feminist Hyperexegesis 181
3. Conclusion. 188

III. **Christ's Teachings About Women** 188

A. The Feminist View of Jesus' Teaching. 189
B. Response to the Feminist View of
     Christ's Teaching. 192
     1. The Frequency of Jesus' References
          to Women 193
     2. Comparison of the Male and Female
          Roles in Jesus' Teaching 196
     3. Conclusion. 202

IV. Why Were There No Female Apostles? 203
A. The Feminist Explanation 203
B. Analysis of the Feminist Arguments 205

V. Conclusion 211

CHAPTER FIVE:
FEMINISM AND GALATIANS 3:28 217

I. Galatians 3:28 and the Work of Christ 221
A. Does Galatians 3:28 Reverse the Curse? . . . 223
B. Does Galatians 3:28 Replace the First
     Creation Order? 230
C. Does Galatians 3:28 Refer to Distinctions in
     the Law of Moses? 236

II. The Jewish Prayer 236
A. Feminist Claims 237
B. Response. 238

III. Is Galatians 3:28 a Baptismal Formula? . . . 240

IV. Galatians 3:28 and Other Gender Texts . . . 246
A. The Feminist Approach. 246
B. Evaluation of the Feminist Approach 250
     1. Unwarranted Assumptions 252
     2. A Consistent Approach 257

V. **The Meaning of Galatians 3:28 in Its Context** 258
    A. Analysis of Feminist Approaches. 259
    B. The Law of Moses 267
    C. The Metaphor of Inheritance 272
    D. The Place of Galatians 3:28 in Paul's Argument 283

CONCLUSION 303

BIBLIOGRAPHY. 305

INTRODUCTION

This work is about feminism. In a secondary sense it is about gender roles, but primarily it is about feminism. Most specifically, it is about Biblical feminism's use of the Bible. It is an examination and evaluation of how Biblical feminism interprets and uses the Bible to support its view of gender roles.

I. DEFINITIONS

We must first define some terms that frequently occur in this context. The first is *sexism*. This is the idea that one sex is in some way superior while the other is inferior. The term is almost always used to connote the belief that the male gender is superior while the female is inferior. Feminists speak of it as a "fundamentally male ideology" that results in "gender privilege of males over females."[1] It is always used in a pejorative sense.

Hierarchicalism is the view that reality in general and the human race in particular are by nature ordered in a kind of hierarchy, with some categories being ranked above or below others in accord with some criterion or purpose. In reference to the human race, it is the belief that there are inherent differences between the sexes that go beyond anatomy. These differences are such that it is natural or intended for certain leadership roles to be restricted to men. Thus some role distinctions are determined according to gender, including certain roles of authority and submission (such as husband and wife). Whether or not this term is used in a pejorative sense depends on who is using it. For most non-feminists it carries no negative connotations, since the non-feminist view is basically hierarchical. To feminists, however, the concept is anathema, since they view it as equivalent to sexism.

Androcentrism literally means "man-centered" or "male-centered." It is a term used by feminists to describe the sexist philosophy that males are central in importance because they are superior to women, and that society should be ordered so that men are dominant. It is obviously a pejorative term with negative and condemnatory overtones. The adjective *androcentric* can describe a book, a philosophy, or a religion. For example, feminists would say that traditional non-feminist hierarchicalism is an androcentric philosophy.

Patriarchalism means "the rule of the fathers." Whereas androcentrism is a philosophy or way of thinking, patriarchalism (or patriarchy) is a social-cultural system based on that philosophy. It is the actual state of affairs in a religion, church, or society where androcentrism or male hierarchicalism is the reigning philosophy. A patriarchal society or religion is one controlled by men for the sake of men, and in which men of power dominate everything and everyone else, including and especially women. From the feminist perspective this is the ultimate obscenity.

Egalitarianism is essentially the opposite of hierarchicalism and expresses the basic philosophy of feminism. It is the belief in the fundamental and total equality of the sexes. Except for biology men and women should be regarded as having equality in every way: equal worth; equal value of their work, and therefore equal pay; equal opportunity to pursue whatever vocational or economic goal they desire; equal access to all social, political, and religious roles. All role distinctions based on gender, especially relationships of authority and submission, must be abolished. (Most hierarchicalists accept every aspect of this agenda except for the abolition of all role distinctions.)

Feminism is often used as a synonym for egalitarianism, though strictly speaking it is a sociological movement whose basic goal is to promote the egalitarian philosophy. It is more than just belief in egalitarianism; it is belief plus action. As one feminist says, "Feminism is not just a theoretical world view or perspective but a women's liberation movement for social and ecclesiastical change."[2] This connotation of political and social activism is how the term *feminist* differs from *female*, which refers to biological characteristics; and *feminine*, which refers to culturally defined roles and characteristics.

II. TYPES OF FEMINISM

In the study of feminism one quickly learns that all feminists are not alike. Beyond a certain small core of beliefs and goals, their worldviews and methods diverge considerably. Here we shall give a brief description of four of the major types of feminism so that it will be clear what Biblical feminism is not.[3]

A. Secular Feminism

Secular feminists are those who have abandoned all religious belief as having any positive relation to feminist philosophy. Their concerns are based purely on human philosophy and humanistic theories of social justice. They have concluded that society as such is patriarchal, with men having power over women and women having only secondary and subservient roles. The goal of secular feminism is to set women free from the bondage of male domination in the context of a secular worldview with secular motives, secular goals, and secular means of reaching these goals. As a social-political movement it seeks full equality for women in education, in the work-place, in government, and in society in general.

Some of the basic goals of the secular feminist movement appear to be quite moderate and reasonable, and find little opposition in principle in even the most conservative Christian circles. These include such things as equal pay for equal work, equal access to educational programs, and equal opportunity in the job market. However, secular feminism usually does not limit itself to such relatively modest goals. Its total agenda has often included many radical elements that are objectionable both to Christians and to many non-Christians alike. Examples are full reproductive freedom (i.e., abortion on demand), independence from men (including lesbianism as a valid or even preferred lifestyle), and a total obliteration of distinctions between the sexes. Its ultimate goal is a gender-free or unisex society.

Secular feminism has certainly been one of the most successful social movements of all time. It is difficult for Christians to view this success positively, however. While some of the social changes it has brought about are good and beneficial to women, as a whole secular feminism is an enemy of Christian faith and an enemy of women's true welfare.

The very fact that it is *secular* feminism in itself points to its basic contrast with the Bible. In the Biblical worldview God and the supernatural are real, and the norms by which we live originate with God through his revealed Word. The secular worldview, as seen in the very meaning of the word *secular*, says that this natural world is the totality of being. There is no God, no supernatural. All moral "norms" arise from within the world and are relative; each individual ultimately writes his or her own moral code. Secular feminism is almost altogether the product of women who accept this secular worldview.

B. Goddess Feminism

Secular feminism is by definition all politics and no spirituality. Its agenda and its methods are truly political, in the broad sense of using power in the public arena in order to influence policy. Since it is secular, however, its activities are divorced from any spiritual or religious framework.

Some women have not been satisfied with this approach to feminism. They agree with the politics of secular feminism; they wholeheartedly endorse its agenda and pursue its goals. But they feel that something is lacking; they feel the need for a spiritual connection or spiritual basis for themselves *as feminists*.

This presents a problem. While they do not see any conflict between feminist politics and spirituality as such, many of these women *do* believe that feminism is incompatible with the formal traditional religions of the world today, *especially* those based on the Bible. They regard the Biblical tradition as "irredeemably sexist."[4] Where can a feminist turn, then, to find spiritual fulfilment? Many are finding it in old traditions that remained underground until occultism became culturally respectable in the 1960s, namely, the variety of neo-pagan religions that worship "the Goddess," especially witchcraft.[5] Thus this category of feminism is appropriately called Goddess feminism.

The thesis of Goddess feminism is that feminist goals can best be achieved through a "return to the Goddess." This theme is based on a reconstruction of the last several thousand years of world history. It begins with the idea that Goddess worship was the original nearly-universal religion and that it fostered a matriarchal culture. But then, beginning about five thousand years ago, the Goddess was overwhelmed and replaced by male gods such as the Biblical Yahweh; and the original matriarchal culture was replaced by patriarchal cultures that have oppressed women.

Thus according to this view the only hope for the world is a return to the Goddess, i.e., a return not only to Goddess worship but also to a matriarchal or at least a partnership culture. This is the scenario which has caused many feminists to become an active part of the current revival of neo-pagan religions and witchcraft. They see it as a chance to destroy patriarchy and demote males from their false thrones, and to reclaim the power stolen from women thousands of years ago.

When Goddess feminism is evaluated from the standpoint of the Bible, the result is every bit as negative as the judgment upon secular feminism. In almost every way it stands in direct opposition to the Biblical worldview. It rejects the Creator-creature distinction and embraces a kind of pantheistic monism. It rebels against the idea of absolute truth and absolute moral law. The very ideas of sin and guilt are denied. All laws regarding sexual morality in particular are regarded as the perverted creations of patriarchal religion, especially that of the Old Testament. Complete sexual freedom and the absolute "right" to abortion are fundamental aspects of the creed of Goddess feminists. They embrace the golden rule of feminism: *women's experience is the highest norm.*

Goddess feminism is self-consciously antibiblical, the self-proclaimed enemy of Biblical faith. In its reconstruction of world history, portraying the overthrow of Goddess religion by patriarchalism, one of the main villains is the Hebrew people and especially the Hebrew priests, who allegedly helped dethrone the Goddess and subject women to thousands of years of degradation and oppression.

Christianity, with its central doctrines of sin and salvation, are also rejected as the antithesis of Goddess spirituality. Jesus Christ is repudiated because he is a man; Goddess feminists want nothing to do with a male Redeemer who is the son of a deity perceived as male.

C. Liberal Christian Feminism

The third major type of feminism is liberal Christian feminism. This type shares the same general goals of secular and Goddess feminism, but it pursues these goals from within the Christian framework and seeks to apply them to Christendom as well as to society as a whole. For this reason one of the main items on its agenda is equal access for women to all forms of religious and ecclesiastical leadership positions.

Liberal Christian feminists reject the secular view that religion is no longer relevant for women as they struggle for freedom. They affirm the need for religious symbols and rituals and communities to undergird and express their feminist experience. In this way they agree with Goddess feminists.

However, the liberal Christian feminists strongly disagree with their Goddess sisters about the use of the Bible and Christianity for the women's movement. While granting that the Bible is mostly androcentric and patriarchal, they decline to abandon it altogether and to give up their connection with Jesus Christ. Thus they take the view that the Biblical message can still be a force for feminism, despite its patriarchy.

This explains why this version of feminism is called *Christian*, but why is it called *liberal*? This has to do with its view of the nature of the Bible. Even though it accepts the Christian heritage and seeks to come to terms with the Bible's message about women, liberal Christian feminism does not accept the Bible as the revealed and inspired Word of God nor as any kind of canonical authority. Thus the term *liberal* means "liberal Christian" as opposed to "conservative or evangelical Christian."

If the Bible is not the authoritative norm for faith and practice, what is? The answer is simple: *women's experience*. This includes women's experience as victims of patriarchal oppression and their experience of liberation therefrom, but even more fundamentally it includes the basic inner feminist conviction of the full and unqualified equality of women with reference both to ontological essence and to societal roles. This is a point on which liberal feminism is in complete agreement with secular and Goddess feminism: women's experience is the ultimate criterion of all truth. The experience of women replaces the Bible as the canon or standard or criterion by which everything else is judged—including the Bible itself.

Liberal feminists thus assert that women's experience is the key to determining what any given text means in today's world. This means that when women do exegesis they must look for a meaning that speaks to their specific needs and is consistent with their unique experience as victims of male domination. In this way many texts can be creatively and imaginatively reinterpreted so as to proclaim a liberating feminist message, whether that was the original intention of the author or not.

Thus while Goddess feminists see themselves as liberating the deity itself from patriarchalism, liberal feminists think of themselves as also liberating the Bible therefrom. The latter affirm that for the most part the Bible *can* be thus liberated through the process of feminist hermeneutics; therefore Scripture can be used by women today. In one very crucial area, however, it would appear that there is no essential difference between Goddess feminism and liberal Christian feminism. This is the fact that they both accept the same ultimate authority and norm, namely, women's experience. As long as this is the case, many of the differences between them are formal only.

D. Biblical Feminism

The last category is Biblical feminism, which will be the main focus of the rest of this work. It might well be called evangelical Christian feminism, since it has developed and intensified within modern American Evangelicalism since about 1970. It could also be called conservative Christian feminism, as opposed to liberal Christian feminism. But the expression *Biblical feminism* is appropriately descriptive, because most of those who hold this view (1) accept the final authority of the Bible and (2) believe that feminism is the Bible's authentic teaching.

Biblical feminists are distinguished from all other types by their views of Biblical authority and Biblical interpretation. Regarding the former, no other form of feminism accepts the Bible as the final authority in matters of faith and practice. Secular and Goddess feminists openly repudiate the Bible and make no attempt to relate positively to it. Liberal feminism does use the Bible, but not as its final authority. The ultimate standard for the other forms of feminism is women's experience of struggle for liberation from male dominance. Biblical feminism, in contrast, does accept the Bible as the inspired Word of God and as the final authority.

Biblical feminism also differs from the other forms of feminism in that it interprets the Bible as consistently teaching an egalitarian view of women. All of the other forms say that the Bible is totally or at least partially patriarchal.

How do Biblical feminists relate to other evangelicals? In the first place, all conservatives, feminists and non-feminists alike, declare their acceptance of the final authority of the Bible. It is true that a few conservative feminists have taken positions that reflect a shaky view of Biblical authority.[6] For the most part, however, there is agreement here, with most of the main participants on both sides of the issue subscribing even to the inerrancy of the Bible in its original text.

Also, conservative feminists and non-feminists both attempt to honor the Bible's originally intended meaning as hermeneutically normative. They acknowledge the existence of the "two horizons" of Biblical interpretation, i.e., that of the writer and that of the interpreter; but they generally agree that the former is decisive in determining the meaning of a text.

What, then, is the main point of difference between Biblical feminists and their non-feminist fellow conservatives? In a word, it is *hermeneutics*, or Biblical interpretation. How to *interpret* the Bible is the key issue. Biblical feminists believe that the Bible, correctly interpreted, consistently teaches egalitarianism. Their non-feminist brothers and sisters believe that it consistently teaches hierarchicalism. In some cases this may involve differences

19

in hermeneutical principles themselves. In most cases, however, it is a disagreement over what a particular word or passage actually means, usually involving very different applications of the accepted general principles. Either way, the problem ultimately centers around the question of the proper interpretation of certain key passages of Scripture.

It should be noted that all egalitarians do not agree among themselves concerning how broadly the application of the principle should be applied. Some apply it comprehensively to all roles in the home and in the church. Others would apply it to the church but not to the home. For our purposes a feminist[7] is anyone who applies it at least to the church. That is, anyone who believes that all ecclesiastical offices and functions (including preaching and the eldership) may be filled by any qualified man or *woman* is a feminist.[8] At the same time, those who believe that certain hierarchical relationships based on gender are still normative within the church are non-feminists.[9]

III. ABOUT THIS WORK

As indicated above, this work will concentrate almost exclusively on the subject of Biblical feminism. More specifically, it will focus on the issue of Biblical interpretation, and the differences between evangelical feminists and non-feminists on this point. How this subject is approached herein will now be explained.

A. The Common Ground

The only type of feminism that is a serious option to anyone who holds to a high view of Scripture is Biblical feminism. Though the first three types must be taken seriously because of their impact on modern society and their influential role in contemporary culture, evangelical faith will reject them from the outset because they do not accept the Bible's absolute and final authority in all things, including gender roles. Biblical feminism, though, is a quite different matter. It *does* operate with an expressed acceptance of the full authority of the Bible.

On this point I fully agree with the Biblical feminists. This is my own perspective on the Bible. I view it as most of these feminists do, namely, as the inspired and inerrant Word of God and as the final authority on all matters. On this point we stand upon the same solid ground, the inspired Scriptures whose nature is described in John 10:35 and 2 Timothy 3:16. This is our common starting point. We agree that whatever the Bible teaches will be normative.[10]

B. The Focal Point

The specific subject of this book is Biblical interpretation, i.e., how the Bible should be interpreted with respect to its teaching on the subject of gender roles. Does it teach hierarchicalism, or does it teach egalitarianism? Feminists interpret it as teaching the latter. They declare that egalitarian faith and practice represent the Bible's true teaching and thus the revealed will of God. Applying all the tools of Biblical scholarship with great zeal, they immerse themselves in the task of exegesis in order to demonstrate a Biblical basis for feminism. The zealousness and seriousness with which they go about this must be respected, and their efforts cannot be lightly dismissed by their fellow Bible believers.

I have personally made a very serious attempt to understand the feminists' interpretation of Scripture. As a result I think I understand the basic egalitarian ethic which most of them believe is taught in the Bible: 1) In the home, husband and wife have a mutual partnership, with neither being the leader or the one in authority. 2) In the church, gender has nothing to do with who fills any particular role; there should be NO role distinctions between men and women. Whatever qualified men can do, qualified women can do also. This includes preaching, teaching men, and holding the office of elder in the local church.

Also, I have tried to understand not just the general position of feminists but also the intricacies of the exegesis with which they attempt to support their view. I have found that this is not an easy task, since feminist literature is filled with what has been called "hermeneutical oddities" and "technical ingenuity." So many new exegetical trails are being blazed that it is difficult to keep up with them all.

No one can take this debate seriously without facing the question, are the feminists correct? Does the Bible indeed teach egalitarianism? As for myself, I was reared and educated in the milieu of non-feminist hierarchicalism. Feminism and its exegetical rationale were not a part of my heritage. Thus in my study of this issue I have been forced to ask this question: *does* the Bible support feminism? Is feminism's interpretation of Scripture the correct one?

This is the focal point of this work, the specific question to be answered. What is correct Biblical interpretation on this subject? When properly interpreted, does the Bible teach egalitarianism or hierarchicalism? Does it support feminism or non-feminism?

C. Motivation

I will state here in the very beginning that after examining the exegetical evidence for feminism, I am still very much a non-feminist. I have not been convinced to abandon my traditional stance on the issue. I also want to make it clear that in and of itself, egalitarianism would be perfectly acceptable to me. I have no personal agenda that would cause me to resist the trend toward partnership-style marriages and toward women preachers, elders, priests, or whatever. I resent the constant accusations that the "patriarchal powers that be" continue to resist feminism from selfish motives, especially the desire to preserve male power structures in home, church, and society. I will state unequivocally that this is not an issue for me.

There is only one issue that really matters in relation to this or any other such subject, namely, *what does the Bible teach about it?* Thus my primary motive for making this study is concern for the integrity of Biblical teaching on the subject of gender roles. When I consider the many specific Biblical interpretations designed to support the egalitarian philosophy, the result is usually a sense of aggravation, frustration, and at times even outrage. Why? Not because my "patriarchal power" is being threatened. Rather, it is because I am convinced that the feminist interpreters are simply not being fair and responsible in their handling of Scripture.

This is my motivation. I see passage after passage of the Word of God being twisted and distorted to fit a precon-ceived viewpoint. I see interpretations being confidently affirmed when there is absolutely no basis for them. I see unsubstantiated speculations subtly and without warning being transformed into established truths. I see unusual word meanings being substituted for accepted ones with little reason beyond ideological necessity. I see the contexts of crucial passages being ignored. I see theologically-impor-tant conclusions being based on assertions that are simply and clearly contrary to fact.

Some would say that the real issue here is justice. Feminists say it is a matter of justice for women. I.e., justice demands that women be treated in exactly the same way as men, with no distinctions being made on the basis of gender. I agree that it is a matter of justice. But even more important than justice for women—or men—is justice in our treatment of the Word of God. I.e., justice demands that we be fair and objective in our interpretation of it.

My basic thesis may be summed up in the statement that the feminist interpretation of Biblical texts relevant to the subject of gender roles is faulty to an extreme. This study is an attempt to establish this thesis. Once this has been accomplished, it will be clear that the only way to claim a Biblical basis for feminism is to misuse Scripture.

D. The Plan of This Study

This study is divided into two main parts, to be published in two separate volumes. After a general survey of the hermeneutical issues that are at stake, this first volume focuses on texts that have to do with the Biblical themes of creation, Fall, and redemption. This includes examinations of Genesis 1 and 2 (the creation), and of Genesis 3 (the Fall). These are followed by a study of Jesus and the Gospels, and their relevance for a Biblical understanding of the role of women. The final study is of Galatians 3:28, taken by many as the capstone of the creation-Fall-redemption theme as it applies to gender roles.

These texts have one important thing in common: they are the main texts used by feminists as they try to make a positive case for Biblical egalitarianism. The creation texts are interpreted as teaching an original egalitarian relationship between men and women; Genesis 3 is interpreted as the introduction of hierarchicalism, via the Fall and the curse; and the work of Christ is interpreted as reversing the curse and restoring egalitarianism. Thus an analysis of the details of the feminist interpretation of these texts is crucial.

The projected second volume of this study will deal with texts related to male headship and female submission in the home and in the church. Much attention will be given to Ephesians 5:21-33 and other texts that deal with husband-wife relationships. Also examined closely will be texts that speak of women's role in the church, such as 1 Timothy 2:12 and 1 Corinthians 14:34-37. Also included will be an analysis of texts that speak of specific women who served with distinction within the people of God, such as Miriam, Priscilla, and Phoebe.

Many of the texts discussed in the second volume are what feminists call the "hard passages," i.e., texts that seem to contradict the basic egalitarian philosophy. A major purpose of this part of the study will be to examine the unusual hermeneutical expediencies employed by feminists in an effort to make these texts compatible with their ideology.

ENDNOTES

[1]Rosemary Radford Ruether, *Sexism and God-Talk: Toward a Feminist Theology* (Boston: Beacon Press, 1983), p. 165.

[2]Elisabeth Schüssler Fiorenza, *Bread Not Stone: The Challenge of Feminist Biblical Interpretation* (Boston: Beacon Press, 1984), p. 5.

[3]For a detailed study of these types of feminism, see my book, *Feminism and the Bible: An Introduction to Feminism for Christians* (Joplin, MO: College Press, 1992).

[4]Ruether, *Sexism*, p. 268. Because of this, and because many feminists in this category at one time were active within Christianity or Judaism, this type of feminism is sometimes called postchristian or postbiblical.

[5]On the connection with witchcraft see Margot Adler, *Drawing Down the Moon: Witches, Druids, Goddess-Worshippers, and Other Pagans in America Today*, rev. ed. (Boston: Beacon Press, 1986), chapter 8.

[6]See Cottrell, *Feminism and the Bible*, pp. 243-248.

[7]From this point on the terms *feminism* and *feminist*, unless otherwise qualified in the text, will be used to refer to Biblical feminism.

[8]There is some ambiguity here, because some Bible believers accept egalitarianism as such but do not apply it consistently or completely. For example, they may argue for the elimination of role distinctions everywhere except the eldership of the church. Whether they are "feminists" or not becomes a matter of semantics. In the final analysis the label itself is just a semantic convenience. What matters is the extent of one's commitment to the principle of egalitarianism.

[9]In reality most feminists reject hierarchy in both the home and the church, and most non-feminists reject egalitarianism in both.

[10]The English version of the Bible quoted in this book will be the New American Standard Bible, unless otherwise noted.

FEMINISM AND BIBLICAL INTERPRETATION

As stated in the Introduction, the ultimate factor that separates Biblical feminists from non-feminist Bible believers is *Biblical interpretation*, or hermeneutics. What is at stake is the proper interpretation of a whole host of passages that speak directly or indirectly to the issue of gender roles.

Our intention is to examine these passages in some detail, and to evaluate the specific interpretations of them set forth by feminists in conformity with their egalitarian philosophy. But before we begin our discussion of individual subjects and texts, we will first examine the subject of Biblical interpretation in general. This will show that in the final analysis the problem with feminism is not its interpretation of this text or that text in particular, but rather its whole approach to the task of interpretation, its *methodology* of interpretation.

I. THE PROBLEM: "THE HARD PASSAGES"

Feminists have particular difficulty with certain passages of Scripture which do not seem to agree with egalitarianism, but which seem rather to put certain restrictions on the role of women in the home and in the church. These include especially 1 Corinthians 11:2-16; 14:34-37; and 1 Timothy 2:9-15. Sometimes Genesis 3:16; Ephesians 5:22-24; and 1 Peter 3:1-7 are included as well. Feminists often refer to such texts as "hard passages," "problem passages," or "problem texts."[1]

A. "Hard" at Specific Points

Why are these texts considered to be problematic, difficult, or hard? This concept may be understood in two ways. First, they are "hard passages" because they raise certain specific exegetical questions that are difficult to answer, whether one is an egalitarian or otherwise. Hull says there are "literally *dozens* . . . of exegetical problems yet to be solved" in 1 Corinthians 11:2-16; 14:33-36; and 1 Timothy 2:8-15 alone.[2]

Examples of such "exegetical problems" are the nature and purpose of the head covering in 1 Corinthians 11:5-10, the meaning of "because of the angels" in 1 Corinthians 11:10, the meaning of "the Law" in 1 Corinthians 14:34, and the meaning of 1 Timothy 2:15. It is true that scholars continue to disagree over the meaning of these and other specific points of exegesis within the "hard passages."

Does this mean, however, that it is impossible to know what the passages *as a whole* are trying to say? This is the conclusion of some feminists. Gundry, for example, says concerning 1 Timothy 2:11-15 that no one can be sure what verse 12 means because "virtually no scholar claims to understand the last part of the passage." She attacks non-feminists for claiming that verse 12 limits women's ministry roles while admitting uncertainty about the meaning of verse 15.

> Such snatch-and-chop proof-texting violates sound interpretive principles. One cannot justify isolating a verse or two from an obvious problem context and using the isolated portion dogmatically. We simply do not know what the *whole* is trying to say. . . . We cannot be dogmatic in insisting part of the passage is something we are sure about and the rest a mystery. The verses are linked together in meaning, whatever the meaning may be.[3]

Hull carries this a step further when she says that since scholars cannot agree on what these passages mean, "it would therefore be most unwise to try to use these particular passages as definitive guides to male-female relationships." Also, "Until we have a better grasp of the exact meaning and context of these three passages, as well as better understanding of their relationship to all of Scripture, we must avoid the pitfalls of selective exegesis."[4]

We must admire these feminists for devising such a convenient method of ridding themselves of these bothersome passages, i.e., the principle that if you cannot understand everything about a text, then you cannot understand any of it well enough to apply it to daily life. Though such an idea may at first sound plausible, a little reflection reveals it to be completely unreasonable and in the end devastating to the whole enterprise of Biblical interpretation.

It is unreasonable because it is a version of the fallacy that incomplete knowledge is false knowledge. If this principle were applied consistently it would make human knowledge as such impossible, because we are finite beings who can *never* have *complete* knowledge about anything. But this realization should not lead us to embrace total agnosticism. Because knowledge is incomplete does not necessarily prevent it from being true and usable. This is the case with our knowledge of God, for instance. As finite creatures we can never know him completely, but we can have true and usable knowledge of him.

Thus for some feminists to tell us that we cannot use 1 Timothy 2:12 in developing our doctrine of gender roles because we do not completely understand verse 15 is quite unreasonable. It is like trying to persuade an enemy to put down his gun because he does not understand every part of its mechanism, or like trying to convince one's teenaged son that he should not drive the family car because he does not completely understand how the engine works. This kind of argument is not very convincing.

Such a principle is also devastating to the whole enterprise of Biblical interpretation, since many passages contain specific parts that are difficult to understand. Are feminists willing to apply this principle to *all* such passages? This is not likely. In 1 Corinthians 15, for example, the perennial difficulty of interpreting verses 28-29 does not prevent us from understanding the overall teaching of the chapter concerning the ascension of Jesus and the resurrection of the dead. Uncertainty about the meaning of 1 Corinthians 11:30 does not prevent us from understanding the rest of what Paul says about the Lord's Supper in this passage. Knowing the exact meaning of the "man of lawlessness" in 2 Thessalonians 2:3 is not a prerequisite for using the passage as a whole to enrich our knowledge of the second coming of Jesus. In short, as a general hermeneutical principle the idea is patently absurd. Only if the particular exegetical difficulties in a passage were central and vital to the passage as a whole would it make any sense. Trying to apply it to the passages most problematic to egalitarianism sounds suspiciously like a case of special pleading.

B. "Hard" in Their Overall Teaching

This leads us to the second sense in which these texts are called "hard passages." They are hard or difficult not just because of specific problems of exegesis within them, but primarily because what appears to be their main point or overall thrust concerning the role of women is difficult if not impossible to reconcile with egalitarianism. This is what feminists usually mean when they talk about the "hard passages." They are hard to take at face value because they do not seem to support feminist ideology. They are difficult to interpret within the context of feminism because ordinary, common-sense interpretation leads to non-feminist conclusions.

This becomes more clear when we stop to consider the fact that the problem of "hard passages" is exclusively a feminist problem. These passages are not hard for non-feminists, because they are in every way consistent with hierarchicalism. At the same time non-feminists do not have the sort of trouble with the usual feminist "prooftexts" that feminists have with the non-feminist texts. I have never seen a non-feminist refer to Galatians 3:28 and Romans 16:1-7 as "hard passages," simply because it is *not* hard to interpret these and other such texts within a hierarchical framework.

The question to be addressed now is *why* this problem of "hard passages" arises for feminists. The fact is that the difficulty is created by feminists themselves as a result of faulty hermeneutical method, or an improper approach to Biblical interpretation. My contention is that feminists violate some of the most basic rules of hermeneutics in order to build a Biblical case for egalitarianism, in the process creating the problem of "hard passages" and making it necessary to resort to the most innovative sorts of interpretation in order to make these passages conform to egalitarian philosophy.

II. THE RULES OF INTERPRETATION

Evangelicals in general agree on the validity of certain basic hermeneutical principles, certain basic rules of interpretation. In themselves these rules are partial neither to egalitarianism nor to hierarchicalism. They are enumerated in the writings of feminists and non-feminists alike. In this section we shall briefly describe them.

A. The Two Horizons of Interpretation

In recent discussions of hermeneutics a major subject is the "two horizons" of interpretation. This is the idea that the interpreter of Scripture must take account not only of the intended meaning of the original writers ("what it meant") but also of his own preconceived worldview and biases ("what it means"). The issue is which of these "horizons" should be the primary norm for interpreting Scripture today.

The modern trend in liberal theology in general is to give priority to the second horizon. In other words, what a text *means* for today, as determined by the interpreter, is more important than what it *meant* when written, as determined by the author. This approach is justified by concepts of the cultural relativity of the writers and an inescapable subjectivity of the interpreter. The primary result of this approach is a skepticism concerning our *ability* today to know what the original writers really meant. The ultimate result is that modern "exegetes" feel free to interpret the Bible to mean whatever they want it to mean. It is fair to say that this is in general how liberal Christian feminists approach the Bible. As Elisabeth Fiorenza says, Biblical scholarship "can no longer articulate as its unqualified goal the intention to declare with scientific certainty what the text *meant,* because this is virtually an epistemological impossibility."[5]

Evangelical scholars in general reject this approach. They continue to emphasize the context and intention of the author as the determiner of meaning for Biblical texts. This is true of feminists as well as non-feminists, and it is a major point of difference between liberal Christian feminists and Biblical feminists. As the evangelical feminist Alvera Mickelsen says, the first question for any interpreter is this: *"What was the Bible saying through God's human servant to the first hearers or readers of that message? What did they think was the meaning?"*[6] Non-feminists have no quarrel with this as a basic rule of interpretation.

B. The Importance of the Context

Another basic hermeneutical principle is that an understanding of the broader context of a statement in Scripture is vital for understanding what the author meant in that particular statement. We must not isolate a verse from its context and interpret it as if it had no connection with some specific situation or a larger point or argument which the author is trying to make. Such a practice creates the probability that the second horizon — the subjectivity of the interpreter — will take precedence in the interpretive process.

This applies particularly to the *literary* context of a statement. That is, a statement takes its meaning from the purpose of the whole book of the Bible in which it occurs, or at least from the purpose of the general section of which it is a part. Gundry lists this as the first principle of interpretation: "Always interpret a verse in agreement with its context (its surrounding verses or chapters). That is, the meaning of the part must be consistent with the whole."[7]

This rule also ties interpretation to the *historical* context in which a statement is made. This is the point of Gundry's third principle: "When interpreting a passage, consider the customs and events taking place when it was written."[8]

Grant Osborne states this principle thus: "Passages must be interpreted in the light of their context." Then he makes this important comment: "This cannot be overemphasized, for the historical and literary contexts of any passage are crucial to an understanding of the author's intention."[9]

C. "Scripture Interprets Scripture"

Non-feminists heartily concur with the rule about the importance of the context, as they do with this next principle: Scripture interprets Scripture. This rule is based on the belief that the whole Bible is ultimately in some real sense the product of a single mind, the mind of God. Thus its contents are marked by a unity and a consistency of the whole. Not only will one passage not contradict another, but the meaning of any one passage will be illuminated by whatever else the Bible has to say on that subject. Thus the interpretation of a passage must take into account all other

Scripture on the same subject. Two of Gundry's principles relate to this point: "Interpret a passage in the light of all other Scripture," and "Do not interpret a passage in such a way as to make it deny what we know to be true of God from other Scripture."[10]

This principle in particular calls our attention back to the problem of "hard passages." This is true because the "Scripture interprets Scripture" rule is usually invoked when we encounter a passage that appears to us to be difficult for any reason. The proper course of action in such a case is to compare such a passage with other passages on the same subject. Often this is all that is necessary to clear up the difficulty.

At times, however, comparing Scripture with Scripture seems only to compound the problem, since the meaning found in one text (or group of texts) on a particular subject may not be immediately obvious in others on the same subject, and may in fact seem to point in a completely conflicting direction. This is how some, especially feminists, regard the whole body of texts about gender roles; and this is how the whole concept of "hard passages" arises.

How may such an apparent conflict be resolved? One main approach is to make a distinction between those passages that speak of conduct that is still binding today, and those that speak of conduct that is not binding for some reason. A common way of representing this distinction is through the terms *prescriptive* and *descriptive*. A prescriptive statement is one which prescribes or requires certain conduct as a general rule, while a descriptive statement is merely describing such things as the author's own fallible feelings or preferences, what is required by a certain localized situation, or what is required in the interest of cultural accommodation.

Once the distinction between prescriptive and descriptive has been made, the "Scripture interprets Scripture" principle is modified to read, "Prescriptive Scripture interprets descriptive Scripture." I.e., the passage that is prescriptive takes precedence over that which is merely descriptive. In the case of an apparent conflict, the former is binding while the latter is not.

This leaves just one question, namely, how can we determine which texts are prescriptive and which are descriptive? I.e., when Scripture is compared with Scripture and two different kinds of conduct seem to be indicated, which is prescriptive and which is descriptive? What emerges at this point is a whole list of supplementary principles designed to show which passage takes precedence over the other in a case where two seem to be saying different things. Though these supplementary rules are sometimes treated as separate and distinct from the "Scripture interprets Scripture" rule, they are in fact just versions or extensions of it.

These supplementary rules are stated in various ways, all of which are invoked by feminists at one point or another. These should be covered in the listing that follows.

1. Transcultural Versus Cultural

One of the most common versions of the "Scripture interprets Scripture" principle is that what is transcultural takes precedence over what is culturally determined. This acknowledges the fact that in the Bible some texts refer to behavior that is cultural and therefore limited in application, and some transcend cultural limitations and are therefore normative for all times and places. David Diehl says that "the *cultural* factor in biblical interpretation" is "one of the giant questions of biblical hermeneutics today," the one that overarches all the others. "How do we distinguish between culturally directed applications of biblical principles and the transcultural biblical principles themselves?"[11]

Even though a satisfactory answer to this question is notoriously difficult to find, almost everyone acknowledges this as a legitimate approach to Biblical interpretation. Common examples of culturally-limited commands are those having to do with footwashing and the holy kiss. In reference to women, many would argue that the instructions concerning headcovering in 1 Corinthians 11 were occasioned by the cultural practices in the Middle East in the first century and are not intended to be permanently binding. In this sense they are descriptive, not prescriptive for today.

In view of the general acceptance of this rule that the transcultural takes precedence over the cultural, is it possible that it might be applied to other aspects of Biblical teaching on gender roles? Is the command regarding women's silence culturally limited? Are the prohibitions against women teaching and having authority over men also cultural?

2. Doctrinal Versus Practical

Another version of the "Scripture interprets Scripture" rule is that doctrinal statements must take precedence over references to the practical applications and social implementation of doctrinal principles. Though not everyone agrees, the usual idea is that doctrinal statements are prescriptive while the practical or social statements are merely descriptive. The latter must always be interpreted in terms of the former. As Gundry's seventh principle says, "Interpret social teaching in line with doctrinal teaching."[12]

As Scanzoni and Hardesty have stated this principle, "Passages which are theological and doctrinal in content are used to interpret those where the writer is dealing with practical local cultural problems."[13] Stating it in a slightly different way, Mollenkott contrasts passages "which are associated with individual church problems" or "addressed to very specific cases" with passages that are "in a fully theological context" and thus set forth "God's ideal for all times and places."[14]

3. General Versus Specific

A third version of the "Scripture interprets Scripture" rule is that the general interprets the specific. As usually applied, the rule suggests that Biblical teaching dealing with specific problems in specific churches or areas is more likely to be culturally limited and thus descriptive in nature. On the other hand, normative or prescriptive texts tend to be more general in their treatment of a subject.

This rule calls attention to the fact that most New Testament epistles seem to be *occasional*, i.e., they were occasioned by the need to address specific questions and problems in the early church. Osborne reminds us that "each of the epistles was written to meet a specific problem in the first-century Church." Thus we can look for "a temporary application to a specific problem."[15]

Willard Swartley gives this rule: "The interpreter should give priority to theological principles and basic moral imperatives rather than to specific counsel on particular topics when these two contradict."[16] Or as some would put it, when these two *appear* to contradict. In this connection Robert Johnston correctly notes, "Feminists have tended to emphasize the broader affirmations of the gospel" while non-feminists have "centered on specific passages of advice."[17]

4. Clear Versus Unclear

Still another version of this principle is that "clear passages are used to determine the meaning of unclear passages."[18] Two of Gundry's principles state this in other words: "Do not use an obscure passage to disprove one with clear and obvious meaning," and "Interpret the unknown in accordance with the known."[19]

5. *Systematic Versus Incidental*

A fifth contrast invoked to help Scripture interpret Scripture is the rule that systematic teaching on a subject takes precedence over incidental references to that subject. In cases where harmonization is difficult, the former is prescriptive, the latter descriptive. Kassian states it this way: "Verses which mention a topic in passing (incidentally) should not override passages in which the topic is specifically addressed (didactically)." Also, "The didactic passage must interpret the incidental, not vice versa."[20]

As Scanzoni and Hardesty have said, "Passages which deal with an issue systematically are used to help understand incidental references elsewhere." This gives priority to "the *locus classicus*, the major biblical statement, on a given matter," rather than "isolated proof texts."[21] Agreeing with this, Osborne says, "To take a mere allusion to a teaching as constituting the developed doctrine would be to read in too much of one's own theology."[22]

6. *Didactic Versus Historical*

A final version of this general principle, as stated by Osborne, is that "didactic passages must be used to interpret historical events." This refers not only to the historical sections of the New Testament (such as Acts), but also "to historical problems reflected in the epistles." The latter is especially crucial for the question of feminism, he says.[23]

D. Applying the Principles

As we have indicated, the issue of Biblical interpretation is what ultimately separates feminist from non-feminist Bible believers. Johnston has stated it this way: "Behind the apparent differences in approach and opinion regarding the women's issue are opposing principles for interpreting Scripture — i.e., different hermeneutics. Here is the real issue facing evangelical theology as it seeks to answer the women's question."[24]

This assessment is only partially correct. It may be true that feminists and non-feminists disagree on some aspects of a few of the supplementary rules discussed in the previous section, as we shall see later. But for the most part, feminists and non-feminists do *not* have different hermeneutics in the sense of "opposing principles for interpreting Scripture." Rather, they appear for the most part to have the *same* hermeneutics, with both sides being in general agreement with all of the main principles discussed above and most of the supplementary ones as well.

What, then, is the problem? The problem is that *someone is simply not applying the rules correctly*. Someone is affirming agreement with the rules but then is proceeding to violate them in reference to the Bible's teaching on women. As might be expected, each side accuses the other of doing this very thing. Each accuses the other of allowing his or her preconceived ideology to determine what is found in the text, rather than allowing the text to speak for itself.

While acknowledging that feminists think this is exactly what non-feminists do, I must state my strong conviction that the opposite is the case: in their interpretation of the Bible's teaching on the role of women, feminists do not follow their own stated rules; they do not apply the agreed-upon hermeneutical principles correctly. This is true to a degree of all three of the general rules discussed above, but it is especially true of the "Scripture interprets Scripture" principle in all its versions. Herein lies the fundamental difficulty with Biblical feminism. The next two sections will explain this in detail.

III. LETTING SCRIPTURE
INTERPRET SCRIPTURE

We have discussed the feminists' concept of "hard passages" and have suggested that this whole problem arises out of a faulty hermeneutical method, one which begins by selecting only those texts which lend themselves to an egalitarian interpretation, and then draws this interpretation from them while weaving them into the feminist ideological pattern. The problem is that these selected passages are initially considered in isolation from the "hard passages," the crucial texts from 1 Corinthians and 1 Timothy especially. These latter texts are simply left out of the picture, in a kind of limbo, until the feminist philosophy has been set into place; then they are addressed as "problem passages" because they do not fit this philosophy.

This is faulty hermeneutical methodology because it violates the basic "Scripture interprets Scripture" principle. The so-called "hard passages" are not allowed to help determine the meaning of the other texts dealing with women's roles. Feminist interpreters draw egalitarian conclusions concerning the meaning and application of very general Biblical doctrines and principles, while leaving out of consideration some of the most important Biblical data concerning how these general doctrines should be applied in specific cases. The texts most patently relevant to the whole subject are left to be dealt with as a footnote.

Setting these two sets of passages over against one another instead of using them to interpret each other distorts both sets. On the one hand it permits feminists to read into the so-called egalitarian texts an ideology that is *not* inherent in them and is not necessitated by them. The fact is that egalitarian conclusions are not the only conclusions warranted by such texts as Genesis 1:26-28; Romans 16:1-7; Galatians 3:28; and various passages in the Gospels. Such conclusions may be *possible*, to be sure, in the absence of any relevant texts pointing toward some other interpretation; but they are not the only conclusions warranted by these texts in and of themselves. These passages are perfectly consistent with hierarchicalism, and may properly be interpreted in this sense if so warranted by other relevant texts.

Now the question is, *are* there other relevant passages that might justify or even require that texts such as Genesis 1:26-28 and Galatians 3:28 be interpreted in ways consistent with hierarchicalism? Of course. The obvious fact is that texts such as 1 Corinthians 11:2-16; 1 Timothy 2:9-15; and 1 Peter 3:1-7, when placed into the total picture from the beginning, do indeed point toward a coherent non-feminist interpretation of Biblical teaching as a whole. When placed within the total picture, as proper hermeneutical procedure requires, these texts show us that the other set of texts should never have been interpreted as teaching egalitarianism in the first place.

Now on the other hand, failing to use these two sets of passages to interpret each other distorts the feminists' perception of the "hard passages" as well. In fact, this is what causes them to be thought of as "hard" in the first place. Once egalitarianism has been artificially established by using the other set of Scriptures in isolation from these passages, it is no wonder that the latter do not fit in when taken at face value. If they are indeed *difficult texts*, this difficulty has in a large measure been artificially created. Texts that were intended to be a part of a hierarchical worldview must now be explained so that they fit into an egalitarian worldview. Texts that are naturally consistent with one viewpoint must now be skewed in an unnatural way. Certainly this is difficult to do, and it is no wonder that feminist interpretations of these texts are often so tortuous.

IV. PRESCRIPTIVE VERSUS DESCRIPTIVE

The rule that "Scripture interprets Scripture" includes the idea that no one text or group of texts can be interpreted without taking into consideration all the Bible has to say on a given subject. Our contention is that feminists are able to find egalitarianism in the Bible only because they violate this basic principle. In the previous section we explained how this is true in a general sense. In this section we shall see how it is true in reference to each of the specific supplementary rules designed to help us apply the general principle.

In the final analysis, the basic feminist justification for beginning with the so-called "egalitarian texts" and leaving the "problem texts" aside is that the former are *prescriptive*, while the latter are only *descriptive* in some sense. As noted earlier, this distinction in itself is valid. Everyone agrees that some Biblical references are descriptive only, i.e., they are not normative or binding for faith and practice today. The crucial question is, how do we decide whether a given passage is meant to be descriptive or prescriptive?

What makes this question even more crucial is the fact that, as Clark Pinnock says, "certain passages in the New Testament, to say nothing of the Old, cannot be feministically interpreted."[25] I.e., they do not support feminism *if they are considered to be prescriptive for today*. Thus the general approach or rule of thumb for feminists seems to be this: any passage that supports hierarchicalism and goes against egalitarianism must be *descriptive*, and is not binding as eternal truth.

How is this procedure justified? What hermeneutical basis is given for treating the hierarchical passages as descriptive? Here is where the supplementary rules of interpretation discussed earlier are pressed into service. The specific rules designed to show when one passage must take priority over another in the interpretive process are applied thus: the "egalitarian passages" are found to be normative, doctrinal, general, clear, systematic, and/or didactic — and thus prescriptive; the "hierarchical passages" are seen as cultural, practical, specific, unclear, incidental, and/or historical — and thus descriptive.

My contention is that this is where feminists most often

42

violate accepted hermeneutical principles. Good and sound rules of interpretation are twisted and misapplied. Distinctions are made and texts are labeled according to ideology, not according to rational analysis. Brief specific explanations of how this is the case will now be given, as a kind of preview of the more detailed discussion that will follow in the main body of this work.

A. Transcultural Versus Cultural

The distinction between transcultural and cultural is valid, and it is proper to call the former prescriptive and the latter descriptive. As such it is a distinction almost universally invoked by feminists in order to explain away the "problem passages." Crucial aspects of the teaching included in them are assumed to reflect only the cultural beliefs or circumstances of the New Testament world regarding women, and thus are regarded as not being prescriptive or normative for today. Some consider them to be expressions of Paul's own cultural bias, absorbed from his rabbinical training and not yet fully expurgated by the egalitarian gospel. Others consider these texts to be accommodations to the cultural expectations of the day, such being necessary in order to avoid creating a stumbling block to the acceptance of the gospel in general.

Several problems with this approach must be pointed out. First, it involves the unexamined assumption that *no* aspects of a particular culture will *ever* correspond to eternal truth. But this premise is not self-evidently true. Just because a particular practice or idea can be shown to be a common aspect of Jewish culture or Greco-Roman culture does not in itself mean that such an item is not eternally valid. Is it not possible for individual cultures occasionally to come up with something that overlaps the divine will? Does the fact that the rabbis taught hierarchicalism make it a false doctrine, *ipso facto*? To think so is quite presumptuous.

What is needed, then, apart from the simple presence of an idea or practice in a particular culture, is some way to distinguish cultural elements that are in tune with eternal truth from cultural elements that are not. Identifying the guidelines that help us make this distinction has proved to be exceedingly difficult. Sometimes the suggested guidelines simply beg the question or state the obvious. For example, Osborne declares that "what we need is a series of covering laws to distinguish the eternal core from the cultural application in all the commands of Scripture and *then* apply these to the sections on women in the Church." Here is one of his proffered "covering laws": "Teaching that transcends the cultural biases of the author and his readers will be normative." Here is another: "If a command is wholly tied to a cultural situation that is not timeless in itself, it will probably be a temporary application rather than an eternal norm."[26] But such guidelines are not at all helpful, simply because they do no more than restate the problem. *How* to identify teaching that transcends cultural biases, or *how* to tell if a command is wholly tied to a cultural situation, is the very thing we are trying to decide.

In the final analysis the issue will not be decided in terms of the transcultural versus the cultural as such, but will depend more on how the other supplementary rules are applied. In a sense these other rules may be thought of as the specific ways to distinguish the cultural from the noncultural. It is in the handling of these other rules that the weaknesses of feminist Biblical interpretation are most clearly seen.

B. Doctrinal Versus Practical

Feminists commonly equate doctrinal or theological teaching with the prescriptive, and teaching about practical issues with the descriptive. As noted above, Scanzoni and Hardesty have declared that doctrinal passages must interpret those dealing with practical local problems. Then they proceed to divide the New Testament references thus: "Except for Gal. 3:28, all of the references to women in the New Testament are contained in passages dealing with practical concerns about personal relationships or behavior in worship services."[27] They cite this same opinion later in order to blunt the significance of 1 Timothy 2:12: "Of all the passages concerning women in the New Testament, only Galatians 3:28 is in a doctrinal setting; the remainder are all concerned with practical matters."[28]

For another example, in discussing the role of culture with reference to Biblical interpretation, Tucker and Liefeld say, "The issue here is whether the role of women is a purely theological matter, like faith and justification, or whether in the ancient world the way women appeared and what they did in public had a social significance that doctrines per se did not." Then two sentences later, without trying to justify their decision, they proclaim, "There is a qualitative distinction between the doctrines of faith and justification and the social role of women."[29]

Whether or not this principle itself is valid, deciding which passages belong in which category is not as clear-cut as it seems. Especially in Paul's writings, the doctrinal and the practical are often intertwined. It may be true that the role of women is not a *purely* theological matter, but this does not mean that it has no theological implications and connections at all. In fact, in two of the so-called "practical" passages (1 Cor. 11 and 1 Tim. 2), Paul clearly relates the subject to the doctrines of creation, the nature of man, and the Fall. To exclude such passages from the category of the doctrinal is quite arbitrary. On the other hand, such doctrines as justification and faith are not *purely* theological either, as if they had no social significance for the ancient and modern worlds. Feminists themselves acknowledge this point when they vehemently insist that Galatians 3:28 (their premier doctrinal passage) contains within itself all the necessary social application concerning women's roles.[30]

Johnston has some very perceptive thoughts and questions about the hermeneutical distinction we have been discussing. He says,

> What is dangerous in such a procedure, though it admittedly works in many cases, is the implied epistemological claim that objective, impersonal statements are of a somehow higher order of trustworthiness than the more personal and relational aspects of Scripture. Do we need systematic argument in order to be fully confident of the meaning of God's revelation? Is it not true that Paul's "purely" theological insights are, on closer inspection, responses to the cultural crises and life situations of young churches facing concrete problems, and that his "purely" practical advice has within it a theological dimension? Paul neither "did theology" in an abstract, academic manner nor "proffered advice" devoid of theological undergirding. Both his "systematic theology" and his "practical theology" are more accurately part of his one and the same "church theology."[31]

In the final analysis, because of the very nebulous nature of the categories, it is simply not possible to make an unqualified equation between the practical and the descriptive, especially in reference to the Bible's teaching about women's roles. To invoke such a rule to negate the force of the "problem passages" is just poor hermeneutics.

C. General Versus Specific

The supplementary rule that *general* statements and principles must always take precedence over teaching about *specific* issues and problems is probably the one most abused in feminist Biblical interpretation. The misuse of and violation of this rule is seen in several important ways.

One serious problem in this connection relates to the *occasional* nature of the epistles. In the context of this discussion feminists usually find it necessary to remind us that each epistle was occasioned by a specific problem (or problems) which the writer felt needed to be addressed. We have noted Osborne's statement that "each of the epistles was written to meet a specific problem in the first-century church."[32]

Now, granted that this is the case, what are the implications of this fact? Here is where feminist hermeneutics becomes problematic. It is assumed that if an epistle is addressing a specific problem, then the application of that specific teaching must be limited to that particular first-century situation. Osborne, for example, says that this occasional nature of the epistles is one of the "considerations that argue for a recognition of cultural application" of the material.[33] The pattern of thinking is as follows: if it is occasional, it is specific; and if it is specific, it is only descriptive and not prescriptive. Thus a statement within an occasional letter such as 1 Timothy (e.g., 2:12) must have been dealing with a specific problem and therefore must be descriptive only.

A very common formal fallacy seems to have intruded at this point. It is called "the simple conversion of a universal affirmative." In essence it declares, "All A is B, therefore all B is A." With reference to our hermeneutical problem it takes the form, "All descriptive statements are specific, therefore all specific (i.e., occasional) statements are descriptive." But this simply is not true. We cannot just assume that teaching dealing with specific problems is descriptive only. Even if we grant that each epistle was occasioned by specific problems, this does not in itself mean that those problems were culturally or locally unique. The problem of division in Corinth, for example, called for some very practical instruction from Paul, specifically applied in 1 Corinthians. Very few would doubt that it is intended to be normative for the whole church, however.

Fee and Stuart begin their discussion of cultural relativity with a reference to *historical particularity*, which means first of all that "the Epistles are occasional documents of the first century, conditioned by the language and culture of the first century, which spoke to specific situations in the first-century church." This leads them to suggest "that the recognition of a degree of cultural relativity is a valid hermeneutical procedure and is an inevitable corollary of the occasional nature of the Epistles."[34] But this will lead to fallacious thinking if this "inevitable corollary" concept is applied to *every* specific statement and practical application in these epistles just because they are occasional. The occasional nature of the epistles makes the presence of descriptive, non-normative statements within them possible, but not necessary, and certainly not all-inclusive.

In other words, it is a fallacy to assume that a command occasioned by a specific historical situation is not binding outside that situation. A specific situation may well occasion the reciting of a general principle. It depends on what is occasioning the command. It may not be a cultural or locally unique problem at all, but something involving inherent right and wrong. To equate cultural or descriptive with occasional begs the question and prejudices the argument in favor of feminism.

A second problem comes when feminists begin to apply the "general versus specific" rule, as they understand it, to the various passages dealing with the role of women. As we would expect, they unanimously treat Galatians 3:28 as a general principle which is therefore prescriptive, and 1 Timothy 2:12 as a specific teaching for a local situation and therefore as descriptive of a unique first-century situation only. But this raises a very serious question. Assuming the validity of the distinction between general and specific, is it really so clear-cut that 1 Timothy 2:12 obviously belongs in the latter category and Galatians 3:28 just as obviously belongs in the former? Is this assumption not open to serious challenge? I believe that it is.

First Timothy is certainly an occasional letter, and it addresses certain specific problems. But it is fallacious to think that because of this every specific command in the letter is historical or cultural and thus limited in application to Ephesus or the first century alone. The bulk of the general context of 1 Timothy 2:12 (chapters 2 and 3) is certainly intended to be universally applied. The immediate context (2:8-15) does have elements that most would take to be only culturally required (e.g., 9b). But verse 12 does not fit that pattern. It is not at all specific but is indeed quite general: "I do not allow a woman to teach or exercise authority over a man." None of the terms has qualifiers; it is as general as a general principle can be. Also it is very doctrinal or theological in nature, as indicated by its connection with the creation and the Fall in verses 13-14. It is not an incidental remark, but is a vital part of the instruction Paul sets forth in verses 9-15. The proper spiritual adornment for women making a claim to godliness, he says in verse 10, is good works. One of these godly good works is to accept the role described in verse 12.

Galatians, on the other hand, is just as much an occasional letter as is 1 Timothy. Osborne has reminded us that "each of the epistles was written to meet a specific problem in the first-century Church," but when discussing Galatians 3:28 feminists somehow forget this point and treat Galatians as an exception to this rule. But it is not. In this epistle Paul speaks specifically to the Galatians ("You foolish Galatians" — 3:1) in their historical situation. He is specifically addressing the problem of the Judaizers and their perversion of the gospel of grace, along with the very practical result of this perversion, namely, the insistence on circumcision as a requirement for being a Christian.

Thus we can see what an arbitrary decision it is when Bartchy, for example, distinguishes between "normative" texts and "problematic" texts (the latter dealing with "special problems"), and assigns Galatians 3:28 to the former while demoting 1 Timothy 2:12 to the latter.[35]

A final problem related to the "general versus specific" principle is the very validity of the rule in itself. According to the rule, general doctrinal statements and moral principles take precedence over teaching dealing with specific problems. The latter must yield to the former in deciding what is normative; the latter must always be interpreted in terms of the former. One reason for saying this is that the general statements are often equated with what is clear, while what are called specific statements are thought of as unclear.

This is the pattern followed almost universally by feminists. One of the most common approaches is to cite the three crucial stages in the general history of mankind — creation, Fall, and redemption, and to fit the philosophy of egalitarianism into this framework on the basis of certain very general Biblical statements such as Genesis 1:26-28; Matthew 20:25-28; 2 Corinthians 5:17; and Galatians 3:28. An example of this is the article by Ronald Heine cited earlier in this chapter, "The Bible and the Role of Women in the Church." Another example, with the historical drama expanded into five acts, is the article by Mary Stewart Van Leeuwen, "Life After Eden."[36]

An excellent example of this methodology is Hull's book, *Equal To Serve*. In discussing the "hard passages" she says that "we must put them aside and concentrate on the larger truths that are clear to us." She says specifically that this is how we should treat 1 Corinthians 11:2-16; 14:33-36; and 1 Timothy 2:8-15. And Colossians 3:18; Ephesians 5:22-24; 1 Peter 3:1-6; and Genesis 3:16 could also be added to the list, since "for some these passages do appear to teach a secondary place for women."[37] Then she says,

> But over and against those texts are the passages we have explored together in this book, passages that show that women are fully redeemed, women are equal ambassadors for Christ, and women do serve God equally and are commended by the text for doing so. Paul assures us in Galatians 3:28 that in Christ there is no male or female and tells us in 2 Corinthians 5:17 that in Christ all believers are now new, in complete harmony with John 1:12, which proclaims that all who believe are given the power to become God's children. Finally, Romans 8:17 adds that His children are now His heirs. *All these clear teachings add up to the larger truth of the equality of all believers, and we do not ever throw that out.*[38]

This is Hull's approach throughout the book. Her case for feminism is based on the most general of Biblical teachings, with special attention being given to Galatians 3:28 and to 2 Corinthians 5:17-21, the latter passage being seen as bestowing upon men and women equally the "ministry of reconciliation" and the role of "ambassadors for Christ." These, she says, are the "clear teachings"; and we must not allow the hard (i.e., unclear) passages "to cancel out truth that *is* clear."[39]

For feminists, very much depends on the validity of this method of interpretation. In a large measure the whole case for egalitarianism rests upon it, since most of the proof texts for this philosophy are of a very general nature. But the fact is that this particular principle (that the general interprets the specific) cannot stand as a universal rule of interpretation. Sometimes the reverse is and has to be the case: *the specific sometimes has to interpret the general.*

This is true more often that we might think. The Bible has many general doctrinal statements and general moral principles, and we do not and cannot always know how they must be applied in specific situations. Thus we often depend on the more specific teachings revealed in the Bible to show us the proper and sometimes the improper applications of the general. This is the very point of Jesus' teaching in Matthew 5:21-48, for example. Here he takes general ethical principles and shows us some of the specific ways they must be applied. Another example is Matthew 19:9, where Jesus says divorce is wrong except in a case of sexual immorality. We might think this were the *only* exception if the inspired Apostle Paul had not added another in 1 Corinthians 7:15, thus requiring us to interpret the general command in terms of the specific teaching. Still another example is the sixth commandment, "You shall not murder" (Exod. 20:13). Many have tried to conclude from this most general commandment that capital punishment is wrong, but this is impossible in light of the specific teaching in other texts, such as Exodus 21:12-17.

These examples show how wrong it is to assume that general statements and principles are always clear and can be applied without our being guided by the Bible's own specific applications and qualifications of them. It is true that their meaning *as general principles* may be clear, but *how to apply them* will not necessarily be clear without further teaching. This is definitely true of the very passages feminists use as prooftexts. Genesis 1:26-28 may teach that both men and women are created in the image of God; but whether or not this general fact demands egalitarianism regarding gender roles is pure speculation unless God himself gives us further light on that specific subject. To declare that it requires egalitarianism is as fallacious as assuming (as some do) that creation in God's image automatically rules out capital punishment, which is *exactly the opposite* of God's own specific application of the general truth (Genesis 9:6).

This reversal of the "general interprets the specific" rule also applies to Galatians 3:28. There does seem to be a general principle here — "for you are all one in Christ Jesus," and it does relate to the male-female relationship — "there is neither male nor female." But *how* it applies to male-female relationships in all situations simply cannot be deduced from this text alone. To declare that it demands an egalitarian philosophy of gender roles is pure speculation and cannot be decided either way without further light on the subject. To declare that it does require egalitarianism would be as fallacious as an Israelite's assuming that God's words at Sinai, "You shall be to Me a kingdom of priests" (Exod. 19:6), automatically qualified every person of both genders in all tribes to be priests.

The fact is that God *has* given further light that relates to and qualifies the general teaching in passages such as Genesis 1:26-28 and Galatians 3:28. That further light is found in the specific teaching of the so-called "hard passages," which are not nearly so hard when one uses them to interpret the general statements rather than vice versa.

D. Clear Versus Unclear

Another way that feminists violate the rules of interpretation is by using unclear passages to negate teaching that is clearly stated elsewhere. We have already seen that feminists commonly think of the general Scriptures as the ones that are clear, but that this simply is not necessarily true with regard to specific applications. With regard to Galatians 3:28 Mary Kassian makes the following comments:

> Galatians chapter 3 does not clearly address the question of role distinctions between male and female. Yet there are other passages in the Bible where the relationship between men and women *is* clearly addressed. Galatians 3:28, which is at best "fuzzy" in terms of addressing social roles, must be *subordinate* to clear passages which teach the submission of wives to husbands and the prohibition of women to the office of elder. To view the Galatians 3:28 verse, which is unclear about social roles, as holding greater weight than those passages which clearly address the topic is hermeneutic error.[40]

Kassian is correct in pointing out how feminists err by applying the terms *clear* and *unclear* to the wrong passages.

Another example of this same erroneous procedure is the use of the references to Phoebe (Rom. 16:1-2), Junias/Junia (Rom. 16:7), and Euodia and Syntyche (Phil. 4:2-3) to qualify and negate the teaching of 1 Timothy 2:12. Feminists often assert, dogmatically and unqualifiedly, that these texts describe Phoebe as a deacon or an elder, the woman Junia as an apostle, and Euodia and Syntyche as evangelists who preached the gospel alongside Paul. The fact is that these women *could* have been all these things, *if* no other Biblical teaching precludes it, since the passages in question are just ambiguous enough to allow for such possibilities. But that is just the point: they *allow* for such possibilities, but do not at all require them. In this sense we have to say that these passages simply are *not clear* with regard to the exact roles filled by these women in the early church.

First Timothy 2:12, on the other hand, is a much more clear and straightforward statement of what kinds of roles are *not* permitted for women in the church. Thus good hermeneutical procedure requires us to use the 1 Timothy passage to interpret the unclear ones in Romans and Philippians. As Susan Foh says, in reference to Junia in Romans 16:7, "Hermeneutically, it would be improper to interpret a brief, unclear reference as an example of a female apostle in disagreement with a relatively clear command supported by theological arguments (1 Tim 2:12-14)."[41] Improper or not, this is exactly what feminists do.

E. Didactic Versus Historical

The rule that the didactic (i.e., having to do with *teaching*) should be used to interpret the historical is valid, but feminists often violate it and misapply it. They violate it by constantly citing historical references and using them to interpret and qualify the didactic message of 1 Timothy 2:12.

The main example of this faulty methodology has to do with individual women whose names are recorded in the New Testament along with a brief description of their role in the church or of a single act of service they performed. Included here are the historical accounts of the Samaritan woman (John 4), and of the women who came to the tomb and took the message of the resurrection back to the other disciples (Matt. 28; John 20). Also included are the brief reference to Priscilla's and Aquila's private conference with Apollos (Acts 18:26), and the references to the various women in Romans 16:1-7 and Philippians 4:2-3, as mentioned above. Feminists use these references to historical events and situations to establish the general theological principle of the propriety of women in roles of preaching, teaching of men, and authoritative leadership.

But what about 1 Timothy 2:11-15, a didactic passage (i.e., containing authoritative apostolic teaching) which establishes a general truth about women's roles on theological grounds, and which contains not one overt reference to any particular historical person or situation in New Testament times? Does it not clearly prohibit women from any leadership roles that involve teaching men or having authority over men? Does not the hermeneutical principle require us to use this didactic passage to interpret what was really involved in the historical references named above? Yes, it should; but feminists at this point violate the rule and use the historical to limit and qualify the didactic. It cannot mean what it appears to mean, they say; or it must be merely descriptive and not prescriptive. In this case, when comparing Scripture with Scripture, the didactic is twisted to conform to historical references which in themselves are ambiguous and unclear with regard to the very issue at stake (as noted in the previous section).

How are feminists able to do this without acknowledging that they have violated the "didactic versus historical" principle? Because they have broadened the definition of *historical* beyond what is intended by the principle itself. It is intended to apply to truly descriptive statements that refer to historical persons and events and situations without necessarily approving them and without giving theological commentary on them. These are the kinds of historical references that cannot be used to negate or contradict the content of passages that are didactic in nature.

Feminists have confused the issue, however, by using the term *historical* to include any teaching which they believe has been *occasioned by historical circumstances.* As Osborne says, "Didactic passages must be used to interpret historical events. This must relate both to the gospels or Acts as interpreted by the epistles *and to historical problems reflected in the epistles. The latter is especially crucial to the problem at hand.* "[42] This redefinition is crucial for feminists, because it enables them to classify as "historical" *any* passage in the epistles that is not consistent with their egalitarian philosophy, since (as Osborne himself notes) every epistle was written to meet a specific problem in the early church.

We must insist that this is an invalid connotation of the term *historical* in this context. The distinction between didactic and historical is valid if the historical is limited to records of and references to historical *events*. But the *teaching* occasioned by historical events and historical problems is by definition didactic, not historical; and it should be assumed to be prescriptive unless there is a good and clear reason to think otherwise. Indeed, the local problems of the churches of apostolic times are responsible for most if not all of the epistolary instruction in the New Testament, and we readily acknowledge its universal application in almost all cases. If any of this teaching is intended to be limited, such must be determined on some other grounds. It cannot be established simply by its connection with the particular circumstances of a specific time and place.

We conclude, then, that feminists violate and misapply the "didactic versus historical" rule in their effort to find a Biblical basis for egalitarianism.

F. Systematic Versus Incidental

The final principle that explains how Scripture interprets Scripture, valid in itself but frequently violated by feminists, is the rule that the systematic must interpret the incidental. An example of how feminists sometimes do just the opposite is the weight given to the incidental reference to Junias (or Junia) in Romans 16:7, from which it is concluded that a woman served as an apostle in the early church, and that women can therefore hold any leadership role that exists in the church today. "Yet," says Kassian, "elsewhere when the subject of church leadership is directly addressed, women are clearly forbidden to hold authority over men. Feminists, however, give more weight to the *incidental* example (which may or may not be valid) than to the *didactic* passage."[43]

Another example of how feminists violate this principle lies at the very heart of their whole Biblical case for egalitarianism, namely, their treatment of Galatians 3:28. We have already noted how they do not do justice to the occasional nature of this epistle, thus trivializing their own insistence on the importance of historical context in the hermeneutical process. Our point here is that they take even less account of the literary context in which Galatians 3:28 appears. That is to say, they do not seem to realize that when seen in its total context of chapters 3 and 4, Galatians 3:28 is much more an incidental reference to women than a systematic treatment of the subject (just as 1 Timothy 2:12 is much more systematic than incidental).

Tucker and Liefeld say that "the biblical teachings about women are not disembodied truths suspended, as it were, above the real world in some timeless abstract proposition."[44] *But this is exactly how all feminists tend to view Galatians 3:28* — as a disembodied truth suspended above the real world as a timeless abstract proposition. They ignore the context, the progression of Paul's argument, and the place of 3:28 in that argument, as we will demonstrate later in this volume. We will also show that contextually there is absolutely no justification for considering Galatians 3:28 to be any kind of systematic statement concerning gender roles. And there is no justification for using it to nullify the clearly systematic hierarchical teaching of passages like Ephesians 5:22-24; 1 Timothy 2:12; and 1 Peter 3:1-6. To do so is to transgress a recognized rule of Biblical interpretation.

V. CONCLUSION

In this chapter we have briefly examined the basic rules for interpreting the Bible acknowledged by feminists and non-feminists alike. My contention is that, even though they accept the validity of these rules, feminists do not actually follow them in their interpretation of the Biblical passages about women's roles. This is true especially of the fundamental principle that Scripture must be allowed to interpret Scripture. Feminists do not follow this rule in general, nor do they follow the specific supplementary rules that explain how to apply it in particular cases. Nor do feminists always follow the basic principle of interpreting a passage according to its context, especially in reference to their favorite text, Galatians 3:28.

The question must be asked, *why* do feminists so consistently violate these generally accepted rules? One answer, of course, is that this is the only way the egalitarian philosophy can be extracted from the Bible. But even though I am absolutely convinced that this answer is true, it is not the only answer. To leave it at that might suggest that feminists are here being accused of deliberately going against the rules and knowingly misinterpreting Scripture. But I do not believe this is the case.

Thus we must look for another answer, on a deeper level; and I believe it is as follows. Feminists violate the "Scripture interprets Scripture" rule in all its forms, and they violate the rule about context, because from the very beginning they also violate the most basic rule of all, namely, that the true meaning of Scripture is determined by the horizon of the writer and not that of the interpreter. Though they certainly do not do so consciously, I am firmly convinced that the feminists' interpretation of passages about women is more influenced by the second horizon than the first. They read into the Bible the desires of their hearts rather than seeing there what its authors intended.

Liberal feminists contend that objectivity in Biblical interpretation is impossible, and that the second horizon will thus always prevail. Sometimes even conservative writers seem to want to agree with this idea, but most rightly do not. There is no doubt that the interpreter's horizon is an ever-present factor in the hermeneutical process, but it is simply not true that its influence is so strong that the intended meaning of the Bible can never be objectively discerned.

But even though objectivity is possible, the fact is that the second horizon, the context of the interpreter, often is the stumbling block to a correct interpretation of Biblical texts. This is true, I believe, of feminism. In my judgment this is the reason why feminists tend to violate the other hermeneutical principles in so many ways. Though to a lesser degree than is true of liberal feminists, Biblical feminists have never been able to escape the seductive power of *women's experience*. Passages that can be interpreted in a way that is consistent with this experience are brought together and given that interpretation and labeled doctrinal and prescriptive from the outset, while passages that are contrary to the experience are labeled cultural or descriptive or incidental or whatever, and are set aside from the beginning. The rules are simply adapted to justify these moves. It is a case of "hermeneutical ventriloquism," to use Pinnock's marvelous phrase.[45]

The rest of this book, along with the volume to follow later, is a much more thorough discussion of the many examples of feminist Biblical interpretation cited in this chapter, and of material not cited here as well. All in all the thesis of this chapter will be thoroughly established in what follows.

ENDNOTES
CHAPTER ONE

[1]Patricia Gundry, in her book *Woman Be Free: The Clear Message of Scripture* (Grand Rapids: Zondervan, 1977), devotes chapter 5 to "Those Problem Passages." Likewise Gretchen Gaebelein Hull, in *Equal To Serve: Women and Men in the Church and Home* (Old Tappan, NJ: Revell, 1987), calls them the "hard passages" or "problem passages" (pp. 183-187). An appendix lists the "Exegetical Difficulties in the 'Hard Passages'" (ibid., pp. 251-266). In the midst of his discussion of the subject Ronald Heine says, "Let us now turn our attention more specifically to the problem passages in Paul" ("The Bible and the Role of Women in the Church," *Christian Standard* [Sept. 24, 1978], 113:6).

[2]Hull, *Equal To Serve*, p. 186.

[3]Gundry, *Woman Be Free*, p. 75.

[4]Hull, *Equal To Serve*, pp. 183-184.

[5]Elisabeth Schüssler Fiorenza, *Bread Not Stone: The Challenge of Feminist Biblical Interpretation* (Boston: Beacon Press, 1984), p. 148.

[6]Alvera Mickelsen, "An Egalitarian View: There is Neither Male Nor Female in Christ," *Women in Ministry: Four Views*, ed. Bonnidell and Robert G. Clouse (Downers Grove: InterVarsity Press, 1989), p. 177.

[7]Gundry, *Woman Be Free*, p. 58.

[8]Ibid.

[9]Grant R. Osborne, "Hermeneutics and Women in the Church," *Journal of the Evangelical Theological Society* (December 1977), 20:339.

[10]Gundry, *Woman Be Free*, pp. 58-59.

[11]David W. Diehl, "Theology and Feminism," *Gender Matters: Women's Studies for the Christian Community*, ed. June Steffensen Hagen (Grand Rapids: Zondervan, 1990), p. 44.

[12]Gundry, *Woman Be Free*, p. 59.

[13]Letha Scanzoni and Nancy Hardesty, *All We're Meant To Be: A Biblical Approach to Women's Liberation*, 1st ed. (Waco: Word Books, 1974), p. 18.

[14]Virginia Mollenkott, "A Conversation with Virginia Mollenkott," *The Other Side* (May-June 1976), p. 73.

[15]Osborne, "Hermeneutics," pp. 338-339.

[16]Willard M. Swartley, *Slavery, Sabbath, War, and Women: Case Issues in Biblical Interpretation* (Scottdale, PA: Herald Press, 1983), p. 230.

[17]Robert K. Johnston, *Evangelicals at an Impasse* (Atlanta: John Knox Press, 1979), p. 49.

[18]Mary A. Kassian, *Women, Creation, and the Fall* (Westchester, IL: Crossway Books, 1990), p. 150.

[19]Gundry, *Woman Be Free*, p. 59.

[20]Kassian, *Women*, p. 150.

[21]Scanzoni and Hardesty, *All We're Meant To Be* (1974), p. 18.

[22]Osborne, "Hermeneutics," pp. 338-339.

[23]Ibid., p. 338.

[24]Johnston, *Evangelicals*, p. 50.

[25]Clark H. Pinnock, "Biblical Authority and the Issues in Question," *Women, Authority and the Bible*, ed. Alvera Mickelsen (Downers Grove: InterVarsity Press, 1986), p. 56.

[26]Osborne, "Hermeneutics," pp. 338-340.

[27]Scanzoni and Hardesty, *All We're Meant To Be* (1974), pp. 18-19.

[28]Ibid., p. 71. This same quotation also appears in the third edition of this book, *All We're Meant To Be: Biblical Feminism for Today* (Grand Rapids: Eerdmans, 1992), p. 101.

[29]Ruth A. Tucker and Walter L. Liefeld, *Daughters of the Church: Women and Ministry from New Testament Times to the Present* (Grand Rapids: Zondervan, 1987), p. 444.

[30]"Paul laid the groundwork for social change in Galatians 3:28," say Scanzoni and Hardesty in *All We're Meant To Be* (1992), pp. 315-316.

[31]Johnston, *Evangelicals*, p. 65.

[32]Osborne, "Hermeneutics," p. 338.

[33]Ibid.

[34]Gordon Fee and Douglas Stuart, *How To Read the Bible for All Its Worth* (Grand Rapids: Zondervan, 1982), pp. 65-66.

[35]S. Scott Bartchy, "Power, Submission, and Sexual Identity Among the Early Christians," in *Essays on New Testament Christianity: A Festschrift in Honor of Dean E. Walker*, ed. C. Robert Wetzel (Cincinnati: Standard Publishing, 1978), pp. 57-59, 70ff.

[36]In *Christianity Today* (July 16, 1990), 34:19-21. She adds Pentecost and final renewal as the fourth and fifth stages of the drama.

[37]Hull, *Equal To Serve*, p. 188.

[38]Ibid. Italics in the original.

[39]Ibid.

[40]Kassian, *Women*, pp. 156-157.

[41]Susan T. Foh, "A Male Leadership View: The Head of the Woman Is the Man," *Women in Ministry: Four Views*, ed. Bonnidell Clouse and Robert G. Clouse (Downers Grove: InterVarsity Press, 1989), p. 103.

[42]Osborne, "Hermeneutics," p. 338. Italics added.

[43]Kassian, *Women*, p. 150.

[44]Tucker and Liefeld, *Daughters*, p. 444.

[45]Pinnock, "Biblical Authority," p. 57.

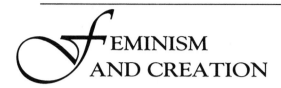

FEMINISM AND CREATION

In the feminism debate the significance of the proper interpretation of Genesis 1-3 cannot be overestimated. Radical feminists of all types usually write this portion of Scripture off as hopelessly patriarchal at best and the root of all sexist evil at worst.

But since Biblical feminists are committed to the authority of the Bible, they cannot just dismiss this passage; and since they contend that the Bible consistently teaches feminism, they must interpret Genesis 1-3 as being compatible with egalitarianism. In fact they go much further than this. They interpret this passage as not merely compatible with egalitarianism, but as aggressively teaching it. They have made a particular understanding of the two main events described in this passage — the creation and the Fall — crucial to the feminist gospel.

In this chapter we shall focus on the meaning of the creation account in Genesis 1 and 2. We shall see how feminists try to interpret Genesis 1:26-28 as positively teaching egalitarianism, and how they seek to refute the traditional non-feminist interpretation of Genesis 2.

I. GENESIS ONE

Genesis 1:26-28 gives the following concise description of the creation of the human race:

> 26 Then God said, "Let Us make man in Our image, according to Our likeness; and let them rule over the fish of the sea and over the birds of the sky and over the cattle and over all the earth, and over every creeping thing that creeps

on the earth."

27 And God created man in His own image, in the image of God He created him; male and female He created them.

28 And God blessed them; and God said to them, "Be fruitful and multiply, and fill the earth, and subdue it; and rule over the fish of the sea and over the birds of the sky, and over every living thing that moves on the earth."

A. Points of Agreement

Feminists stress certain points in this text with which we may heartily agree, while at the same time they find meanings here with which we must strongly disagree. The points of agreement are as follows: (1) both male and female are created in the image of God, and (2) both male and female are given equal dominion over the earth.

1. Both Male and Female Are in the Image of God

Feminists and non-feminists alike understand Genesis 1:26-28 as affirming that both men and women are created in the image of God. This is seen specifically in God's statement of intention in verse 26, "Let Us make man in Our image." The Hebrew word translated "man" is 'ādām, which sometimes means the male but which is also used generically to include both males and females. It is generally agreed that in verse 26 it has the latter sense, because the following clause refers back to it with a plural verb, "and let them rule," and because of the specific reference to male and female in the following verse. This would seem to be confirmed in the summary statement in Genesis 5:1-2, "In the day when God created man ['ādām], He made him in the likeness of God. He created them male and female, and He blessed them and named them Man ['ādām] in the day when they were created."

It is widely assumed that verse 27 is also an explicit affirmation that both male and female were created in

God's image: "And God created man in His own image, in the image of God He created him; male and female He created them." Feminists take for granted that "man" in verse 27 is identical with "man" in verse 26, and that in each case it is the generic "humankind."[1] Elaine Storkey says without qualification, "'Man' in the Genesis account stands for 'humanity' and not for a person with a specific gender attribute."[2] Alvera Mickelsen says, "The Hebrew word *'ādām* is sometimes used in the sense of humankind, as in these verses."[3] Spencer translates verse 27 as "God created the Adam." Then she says, "'The Adam' is a 'they.' The clause 'he created him' is parallel to the following clause 'he created them' indicating that the 'him' is synonymous with the 'them.' 'The Adam' is a 'male and female.' Thus 'the Adam' could be translated 'Human' or 'humanity.'" She concludes, "Thus, if 'Adam' is made in the image of God then 'male and female' have been made in the image of God."[4] Gretchen Gaebelein Hull unequivocally says, "The text specifically states that within humankind (*adam* in Hebrew) both male and female were made in the image of God."[5]

We agree that both men and women were created in the image of God, but the textual basis for this conclusion is not as clear-cut as the preceding quotations imply. The fact is that the only specific basis for concluding that both male and female are in God's image is the statement of intention in verse 26, where God says "Let Us make man [*'ādām*] in Our image." Here the word *'ādām* can reasonably be understood in the generic sense of "humankind." However, a significant change is made in verse 27. In the statement, "and God created man in His own image," the term for "man" is *hā'ādām*, with the definite article [*hā-*]. This change is not incidental. To assume that *hā'ādām* in verse 27 is the same as *'ādām* in verse 26 is poor exegesis; it completely ignores the way *ha'ādām* (*'ādām* with the definite article) is used throughout these chapters of Genesis.

From Genesis 1:26 through 4:1 *'ādām* is used twenty-seven times in three forms. Twenty-two times it appears with the article as *hā'ādām*: 1:27; 2:7 (twice), 8, 15, 16, 18, 19 (twice), 20, 21, 22 (twice), 23, 25; 3:8, 9, 12, 20, 22, 24; 4:1. Three times it appears with a preposition, *le'ādām*: 2:20; 3:17, 21. Only twice, in 1:26 and 2:5, does it appear simply as *'ādām*, where it most likely has the generic sense of "humankind."

Here is the point that must be stressed: in the twenty-one instances (besides Genesis 1:27) where *'ādām* appears with the definite article as *hā'ādām*, the context shows that it unequivocally refers to Adam the male.[6] Therefore consistent exegesis requires us to understand *hā'ādām* in 1:27 in the same way, namely, as a reference *only* to Adam the male. This is the only explanation for the fact that the article is added in verse 27, whereas it is omitted in verse 26. To ignore this difference or to treat it with indifference is inexcusable, especially when so much is at stake.

This changes significantly our understanding of verse 27. Its first clause should read, "And God created Adam the male in His own image." This meaning is reinforced by the second clause, "in the image of God He created *him*." Here the object of the verb is singular and masculine, referring back to Adam the male. Thus the first two clauses are synonymous parallelism. The third clause then adds the fact that "male and female He created them." Here the form is parallel to the second clause but the content is not; thus the last two clauses are complementary parallelism.

This means that Genesis 1:26-28 does not *explicitly* state that both male and female are created in the image of God. This conclusion can be drawn only if *hā'ādām* in verse 27 means the generic "humanity," but sound exegesis shows that it does not. Certainly the truth that both male and female are created in God's image is *implicit* in God's statement of intention in verse 26, where *'ādām* is most likely generic and the plural verb is used. Our purpose here is not to dispute this fact, but to point out that the actual textual basis for it is not as clear and specific as feminists usually assume.

What is the theological significance of the fact that both

genders are created in God's image? It means that both
male and female have the same essential being and therefore have *ontological equality.*[7] It means, in Letha
Scanzoni's words, that men and women are "alike in their
dignity and worth before God."[8] Or as Hull says, "Because
God created both sexes in His image, both have equal
worth and value."[9]

2. Both Male and Female Have
Equal Dominion over the Earth

Another point from Genesis 1 about which feminists and
non-feminists agree is that God gave the male and the
female equal or joint dominion over the rest of creation.
This joint rulership is affirmed in verse 26: "Let Us make
man in Our image, according to Our likeness; and let them
rule over" the other creatures. Here "man" (*'ādām*) means
"mankind," and the plural verb refers to both male and
female. Verse 28 specifically gives the same mandate to
male and female: "Be fruitful and multiply, and fill the
earth, and subdue it; and rule over" the other creatures.
Here there is no question concerning the joint rulership,
power, and authority shared by men and women over the
creation.

This truth is strongly reaffirmed by feminists in general.
Commenting on these verses, Spencer says that "male and
female share in power and authority, even as they share in
dignity."[10] Hull agrees: "Genesis 1:26-30 tells us that as
originally created, both men and women were to rule the
earth mutually and cooperatively."[11] Van Leeuwen echoes
this point: "*Both* the man and woman are told to fill the
earth and subdue it; *both* are told to be fruitful and multiply; *both* are told they have dominion over every other
living thing."[12]

We agree completely with such statements; they are
true to the text and cannot be disputed. But it must be
pointed out that the fact of equal dominion is neither a

support for egalitarianism nor a threat to hierarchicalism. It is completely compatible with both. This equal rulership has to do with the relationship of the human race, both male and female, to the rest of creation; it says nothing about the relationship of the male and the female to each other. This chapter is silent on the latter point.

Gilbert Bilezikian tries to turn this silence to the advantage of egalitarianism by advancing the claim that since Genesis 1 intends to "meticulously define" every aspect of the hierarchical organization of the universe, the omission of any reference to such a relationship between Adam and Eve is proof that none was intended. "It is inconceivable that the very statement that delineates the organizational structure of creation would omit a reference to lines of authority between man and woman, had such a thing existed," he says. "The fact that no reference is made to authority roles between man and woman in a text otherwise permeated with the concept of hierarchical organization indicates that their relationship was one of mutuality in equality."[13]

The fallacy of this argument is the totally unsupported premise that Genesis 1 is "permeated with the concept of hierarchical organization," and that it intends to "meticulously" define "the organizational structure of creation." There is absolutely no reason to interpret this chapter in such a sense.

Since male and female are both created in God's image, they enjoy not only an ontological equality in relation to one another, but also an ontological uniqueness and superiority in relation to the rest of the visible creation. This is the basis of their joint dominion over the earth. Whether or not there is an intended functional hierarchy within the ontological equality cannot be decided from Genesis 1.

B. Points of Disagreement

Genesis 1:26-28 is a favorite text of feminists, but their

reliance upon it for support of egalitarianism is sorely misplaced. Two of their main emphases, discussed in the previous section, have no inherent feminist implications and are equally acknowledged by non-feminists. At the same time, two other significant feminist claims based on Genesis 1 must be firmly rejected simply because they are not warranted by the text. These points of disagreement are as follows: (1) the male and the female were created simultaneously, and (2) maleness and femaleness *define* the image of God.

1. Male and Female Were Created Simultaneously

Some feminists have argued that Genesis 1:27 teaches that the male and female were created at the same time. The nineteenth-century radical feminist, Elizabeth Cady Stanton, said that the texts of Genesis 1 "plainly show the simultaneous creation of man and woman."[14] Scanzoni and Hardesty repeat this idea: "In Genesis 1 male and female are said to be created simultaneously by God as the culmination of creation."[15] Jewett agrees,[16] as does Mollenkott when she refers to "the statement in Genesis 1 that male and female were created simultaneously."[17]

Why should these feminists want to make this point? The answer is clear. By denying that the man was created before the woman, they can negate the argument for male headship based on temporal priority in creation. As Stanton said, simultaneous creation shows that "all those theories based on the assumption that man was prior in the creation, have no foundation in Scripture."[18] This is the implicit agenda behind all claims of simultaneity.

Such an idea, however, must be emphatically rejected. Indeed, it is a mystery how anyone could so boldly assert that Genesis 1 actually teaches it as something that should be obvious to all. What does Genesis 1:27 say? "And God created man in His own image, in the image of God He created him; male and female He created them." Stanton says this verse *plainly shows* simultaneous creation; Scanzoni and Hardesty assert that in this verse male and female *are said to be* created at the same time; Mollenkott labels it *the statement* that they were created simultaneously. But such claims are totally absurd. As anyone can plainly see, the statement "male and female He created them" is *absolutely silent* about the *order* of the creation. It is a summary statement that asserts the bare fact that God created both the male and the female. Neither simultaneity nor priority is asserted or even implied in it. There is absolutely nothing in the text to warrant the idea of simultaneous creation.

If Genesis 1 does teach the simultaneous creation of the male and the female, then two consequences follow. First, it puts Genesis 1 in conflict with Genesis 2, which clearly teaches that the male was created first. Radical and liberal feminists have no qualms about asserting such a contradiction,[19] but those who hold to a more conservative view of Biblical authority must struggle with this point and usually conclude that Genesis 2 is some kind of symbolic poetry.[20] Second, the idea of simultaneity puts Genesis 1 in conflict with the teaching of the Apostle Paul, who on two occasions affirms the temporal priority of the creation of the male (1 Cor. 11:8-9; 1 Tim. 2:13). It is extremely difficult if not impossible to hold to the doctrine of simultaneous creation and still accept the divine inspiration and authority of Paul's teaching.

2. Maleness and Femaleness Define the Image of God

Another false conclusion that feminists draw from Genesis 1:26-28 is that maleness and femaleness are part of the very definition of the image of God in which mankind is created. Jewett points out that Karl Barth was the first major theologian to expound upon this idea, though he did not draw feminist conclusions therefrom. Jewett summarizes Barth's view and accepts this explanation of Genesis 1:27.[21]

The basic assumption here is that the third clause of verse 27 ("male and female He created them") is to be equated with the first two clauses, especially as a parallel exposition of the second clause ("in the image of God He created him"). The idea is that the second and third clauses are saying the very same thing in two different ways. To be created in the image of God *means* to be created male-and-female. As Bilezikian says, "That man comes as male and female is the reflection of an essential aspect of the Trinity within the being of God." That is to say, "because the product had to conform to the specifications of the divine image, 'man' inevitably came as male and female."[22]

Now, how do feminists apply this idea to the interests of egalitarianism? They do so in several ways. First, they claim that the male-female relationship mirrors the relationship between the persons of the Trinity. The duality of male and female reflects the plurality of the Godhead, and the relationships within each are equivalent.[23] Since the intertrinitarian relationships are those of equality, mutuality, and partnership, the relationships between the sexes must be the same.

Mutuality is the feminists' term for total role equivalence between men and women. Imaging the Trinity is supposed to result in mutuality, or partnership. As Mollenkott says, "The type of relationship that suggests itself when both partners are godlike is mutuality."[24] "One of the hallmarks of that image," says Gottfried Oosterwal, "is that it constitutes a partnership, a reflection and a representation of God himself."[25]

A second application of the idea of the male-female definition of God's image is that the very essence of God embraces within itself the equivalent of maleness and femaleness. God is not just "male" but is "female" as well, insofar as he can be thought of as either. As Donald Bloesch says, even though "the living God transcends sexuality," nevertheless "he encompasses masculinity and femininity within himself. Indeed, we are created in his image as male and female."[26]

This idea is repeated over and over by feminists. Because the image of God includes both male and female, says Rolf Aaseng, "what God is encompasses both sexes."[27] God did not create woman just for Adam's sake, says Bilezikian. Actually, "the creation of the woman stemmed from ontological necessities rooted in the very nature of God. Femaleness was also an aspect of the *imago Dei*."[28] Karen and Leif Torjesen endorse this "gender-inclusive way of understanding God." Both male and female traits, as culturally developed, "are found *together* in the Trinitarian doctrine of personality in God."[29] "God is neither male nor female, but incorporates both 'masculine' and 'feminine' traits into an irreducibly social nature," says Van Leeuwen.[30]

Including both maleness and femaleness within the nature of God is important to feminists because it enables them to "demasculinize" God, i.e., to stop thinking of God in exclusively masculine images. By including the feminine element in God's very nature they are able to assert the full equality of male and female, which they believe rules out any form of hierarchy between the sexes.

A third feminist application of the alleged male-female definition of the image of God has to do with the ordination of women to ministry. The idea is that since God includes both male and female, then both males and females are needed to adequately represent God. As Aaseng says, "We need the opposite sex to help us form an image, faint though it may be, of God."[31] The Torjesens say, "Thus the image of God in humanity, first mentioned in Genesis 1:27, cannot be reflected by the male alone or the female alone. It is reflected only by male and female together in their common humanity as a reflection of what God is in the totality of God's own self."[32]

Spencer makes the specific application of this idea to the Christian ministry. Because the image of God is a double image, she says, "there is no possibility . . . that Adam, the male, could by himself reflect the nature of God. Neither is it possible for Adam, the female, by herself to reflect God's nature. Male and female are needed to reflect God's nature."[33] Therefore "females as well as males are needed in positions of authority in the church to help people better to comprehend God's nature. God's image needs male and female to reflect God more fully. The biblical text also guards against excluding either females OR males from the task of ministry."[34]

What shall we say to this typical feminist understanding of the image of God as consisting of maleness and femaleness? Our basic and conclusive criticism of the idea is simply that the alleged textual basis for it is non-existent. As with some of the previous points, the idea is drawn from a misreading of Genesis 1:27. It depends upon the notion that the second clause, "in the image of God He created him," is parallel in both form and content with the third clause, "male and female He created them." That this verse is in poetic style, and that the *form* of these two clauses is parallel may be granted. But the crucial assumption that the *content* of these clauses is parallel cannot be established for two reasons.

First, as we have seen, the first two clauses of 1:27 are referring only to Adam the male. They affirm that God created Adam the male in his own image. The third clause is not added simply to repeat the content of the second clause or to provide an exposition of it (contrary to Jewett[35]), but rather to add a completely new thought, i.e., that God created not only Adam the male but *also the female*. That the female is also created in God's image is implied but not specifically stated. The specific reference to the female in this verse is not necessitated by any desire to explain the nature of the image of God, but to prepare the way for what follows in verse 28, namely, the command to be fruitful and multiply.

The second reason why the content of the third clause cannot be established as parallel to the content of the second clause is because the nature of Hebrew poetic parallelism does not require it. It *allows* it, but does not *require* it. Thus even if we recognize that clauses two and three are

parallel in *form*, this in itself is not evidence that they are parallel in *content*. In Hebrew poetry the second clause of a couplet may have content that is equal to, opposite to, or simply different from the first clause. In Genesis 1:27 the content of the last two clauses (a couplet) is simply different. An example of this type of parallelism is the very first verse of the Psalms, where the three clauses of the triplet (in this case) speak of walking, standing, and sitting. These are obviously not identical activities. Another example is the second verse of the familiar Twenty-third Psalm,

> He makes me lie down in green pastures;
> He leads me beside quiet waters.

The form is parallel, but the content is obviously not.

Thus we must conclude that Genesis 1:26-28 provides no textual basis for the idea that maleness and femaleness are part of the very definition of the image of God. Hebrew poetic style makes such an idea possible, but does not require it; whether or not the second clause of a couplet is simply repeating the content of the first clause must be determined on grounds other than simple parallelism of form. In the case of Genesis 1:27, that the last two clauses are not parallel in content is shown by other textual considerations, especially the fact that the second clause is limited in its reference to Adam the male.

The most obvious reason for including two separate and distinct ideas in verse 27 (creation in God's image; creation in two genders) is the reference to the two separate and distinct categories of mandates in verse 28 (be fruitful/multiply/fill the earth; and subdue/rule over the earth and all its other creatures). Mankind is created in God's image and thus is uniquely qualified to rule the creation; mankind is also created male and female in order to multiply through sexual procreation.

A second major criticism of this feminist equation of the image of God with maleness-femaleness is that such a view of the image of God is never hinted at anywhere else in Scripture. In Genesis 1:26-28 itself the idea most obviously connected with the image of God is the one mentioned in the previous paragraph, i.e., the qualification of mankind to rule over the rest of creation. Ephesians 4:24 and Colossians 3:10 connect the image with "righteousness and holiness of the truth," and with "true knowledge." James 3:9 relates the image of God to the unique preciousness of human personhood (as does Genesis 9:6). Thus this statement by Jewett is totally unwarranted: "Being in the divine image and being male and female, though not synonymous, are yet so closely related that one cannot speak biblically about the one without speaking also about the other."[36]

If maleness and femaleness are the very essence of the image of God, it follows that no individual male or female fully possesses the image. This is explicitly affirmed by those feminists who say that both genders are needed to adequately represent God, especially in the role of minister. But there is absolutely nothing in Scripture to suggest that the image of God is thus fragmented and incomplete in any individual, male or female. In fact, the opposite is the case. Individuals are spoken of as being in God's image not partially or incompletely but fully; the individual in and of himself has all that is involved in being created in God's image. Thus it is wrong to murder a man or curse a man, since each man is made in the image of God (Gen. 9:6; Jas. 3:9). Speaking of the male specifically, 1 Corinthians 11:7 says that "a man ought not to have his head covered, since he is the image and glory of God." These references show how misguided it is to say that male and female together are needed to reflect God's image.

A third criticism of the idea that maleness and femaleness define the image of God is the fact that if this were true, then most animals would also at least in part be in God's image, since most animal species consist of these two genders. For example, Genesis 6:19; 7:3, 9, 16 use for animals the same words for "male and female" that are used for humankind in Genesis 1:27. But the idea that animals might be in God's image in any sense shared by human beings goes against the whole purpose of mankind's being made in God's image in the first place. Bearing the image of God is what makes human beings unique and distinct from animals, not like them.

A fourth criticism is that even if it were true that maleness and femaleness define the image of God, this would not necessitate egalitarianism, since all intertrinitarian relationships are *not* mutual or reciprocal. A hierarchical relationship of subordination exists within the persons of the Trinity. Some say this is an intrinsic, eternal relationship, in which the Son eternally is subordinate to the Father.[37] In my opinion this view is difficult to sustain exegetically. However, a relationship of subordination within the so-called economical Trinity cannot be denied. The Bible clearly teaches that God the Son in his functional role as Redeemer took upon himself the form of a servant and placed himself within an authority-obedience relationship to the Father (1 Cor. 11:3; Phil. 2:7; Heb. 10:7). God the Son as the incarnate Redeemer is thus functionally subordinate to the Father while at the same time being ontologically equal to him. Thus even if maleness and femaleness were required to portray the relationships within the Trinity, this would not rule out hierarchicalism.

Our main point, though, is that the whole idea that maleness and femaleness at least in part constitute what it means to be in the image of God is unwarranted speculation and is completely foreign to Scripture. A proper interpretation of the text shows that this was never intended to be the point of Genesis 1:26-28.

This is not to deny that women are made in the image of God, a point which may be reasonably concluded from Genesis 1:26. Both men and women are made in God's image, and each completely so. Their ontological equality is all the more affirmed by seeing the image as complete and unfragmented in each gender.

C. Conclusion Concerning Genesis One

We conclude that Genesis 1 teaches neither egalitarianism nor hierarchicalism; it is consistent with both views. There is no way to confirm either on the basis of Genesis 1 alone. Thus to say that "the Bible teaches that woman and man were created for full and equal partnership"[38] is simply not the case. It is true that no distinctions are made between men and women in Genesis 1, but this is not the same as saying that Genesis 1 *teaches* that there are no distinctions between men and women. This chapter is silent on whether role distinctions should or should not exist. Inferences from a supposed simultaneous creation and from an alleged male-female image of God are without foundation. There is *nothing* here to provide a basis for egalitarianism with regard to roles.

The only equality that can be established from chapter 1 is ontological equality, from which no inferences can be made regarding interrelationships between the sexes. Ontological equality does not rule out relationships of subordination. This is true within the divine nature itself; it is also true of angels, which are certainly equal in essence but among which a hierarchy exists. I.e., some are archangels or ruling angels (1 Thess. 4:16; Jude 9). Within the human realm, all are equal in nature yet some groups have a God-appointed authority over other groups, e.g., parents over children and civil rulers over citizens.

At the same time we acknowledge that Genesis 1 does not teach hierarchicalism. Non-feminists do not claim that it does; rather they insist that it is neutral on the subject. This is probably why they "largely ignore chapter 1," as Mickelsen says accusingly.[39] If they seem to do so, it is probably because they realize that there is nothing there that will decide the issue one way or the other.

Relationally, the main point of Genesis 1:26-28 is the comparison or contrast of the human race *in general* with other living creatures, i.e., the animals. Whatever the point of contrast, it applies equally to male and female. The basis for the contrast is that only human beings (males *and* females) are made in God's image. The main point is that humankind as such is qualitatively superior to animals. The presence of role distinctions within the human race is neither affirmed nor denied. Relationships *within* humankind is a subject not addressed here at all.

II. THE RELATION BETWEEN GENESIS ONE AND GENESIS TWO

Before we turn to look specifically at the second chapter of Genesis, we must raise the question concerning the relationship between it and chapter one. Radical and liberal feminists usually say that these chapters portray two different creation accounts that contradict one another. Some borderline evangelical feminists agree that Genesis 1 and Genesis 2 contradict *if* both are taken literally. Thus in order to avoid the stigma of openly acknowledging contradictions within the Bible, they usually say that Genesis 2 is some type of poetry or mythology.[40]

Most Biblical feminists, however, take a literal approach to both chapters and accept both as true. They are also convinced that both teach total role equality between the sexes in ministry and marriage. For example, Hull sees "a completeness and a mutuality in the male-female relationship" in Genesis 2 no less than in Genesis 1.[41] "One of biblical feminism's most important contributions," she says, "has been to reclaim the Bible truth that Genesis 2:18-24 teaches that a woman's place is as man's social equal."[42]

On the other hand, non-feminists generally see Genesis 1 and Genesis 2 as complementing each other. Genesis 1 is seen as a general survey of the whole of creation to show how mankind fits into the total scheme. A major point is mankind's dominion over the creation. Both the male and the female, who are ontological equals, have co-authority over the universe. But since this chapter is silent on specific relationships between the male and female,

Genesis 2 is added to give a more detailed account of how they are supposed to relate to each other.

In broad terms, non-feminists see Genesis 2 as continuing the idea of the essential or ontological equality of the sexes. This is seen, for example, in the way woman relates to man as contrasted with the way the animals relate to man. But in addition to this ontological equality, individual yet complementary roles begin to be made clear in chapter 2. Thus the sexes are revealed to be "equal but different," to use Stott's expression.[43] As Kassian says, "Genesis 1 shows the uniqueness and equality of human beings, while chapter 2 balances the equality with role distinctions."[44] Further, non-feminists see these role distinctions as involving a hierarchical relationship of male headship and female submission. This hierarchy is seen to be implicit throughout Genesis 2 and is found in such facts as the male's priority in creation, the female's being created out of the male, the purpose of the creation of the female, and the male's naming of the female.[45]

If hierarchy is only implicit in Genesis 2 and is not explicitly stated, why do non-feminists seem so confident that this is indeed the proper interpretation of the chapter? Mainly because of the New Testament commentary on the passage, especially in 1 Corinthians 11 and 1 Timothy 2. If the Apostle Paul under the inspiration of the Holy Spirit sees headship and submission implied by the facts and events of Genesis 2, then so should we.

Because Genesis 2 is used so much by non-feminists, it is very important for feminists to try to show why the hierarchical arguments drawn from it are not valid. Thus their main exegetical efforts with respect to this second chapter are directed toward the traditional hierarchical interpretations of it, as the next section will show.

III. GENESIS TWO

The issues in Genesis 2 mostly revolve around the arguments used by non-feminists to show that a hierarchical relationship between men and women was part of God's original creation plan. Non-feminists do not believe, of course, that this chapter was written only to emphasize this point. It is well understood that the primary emphasis in this passage is on the unity and the relatedness of the man and the woman in their essential equality with each other and their common superiority to the animal kingdom.

But even though male headship[46] is not the *main* point of Genesis 2, non-feminists insist that the concept is present there as the underlying assumption of the entire narrative. The theological implications of all the facts and events recorded therein are hierarchical in nature, a conclusion that is clearly warranted by the New Testament commentary on the passage.

In this section we shall set forth five arguments or lines of thought from Genesis 2 that support a hierarchical view of gender roles. In the process we shall see how feminists respond to these arguments. The bulk of feminists' exegetical work in this chapter is devoted to this response; by examining it we shall gain some insight into the nature of feminist hermeneutics.

A. The Male Is Central in the Narrative

The first line of evidence for male headship is that the male is the center and the subject of the entire narrative.[47] All the action and events revolve around the man. He is the subject; all else is brought into the story in relation to him. He is the "headliner," the "star"; he occupies center stage. Everything else, including the woman, has a supporting role.

The male (*hā'ādām*) is the first to be created (2:7). The garden is prepared for him, and he is placed within it (2:8).

The male, not the female, is given the name — the generic name — borne by the human race as a whole: Adam, or Man (2:5; see 1:26 and 5:2). The male is the one to whom God speaks in the narrative (2:16); he is the first to receive divine revelation and instruction. The animals are brought for naming to the male, not the female (2:19-20). The woman is made from the man, not the man from the woman (2:22). The woman is also made for the man and brought to him, not vice versa (2:18, 22). Afterward it is the man who speaks and makes a theological comment upon the woman's creation, not vice versa (2:23). It is the male who names the female, not vice versa (2:23).

Thus viewed from every possible angle, the whole narrative in Genesis 2 is the story of how God created *the man* and provided in every way for his well-being.[48] The man is the central character — central not just in the narrative as if this were a mere literary device, but central in the historical drama of creation itself. When God came to the point where he created the human race, he placed the man squarely in the center of his creative work. The other activities recorded in Genesis 2 are all relative to the man's existence, nature, and needs. This includes the creation of the woman. This chapter simply cannot be read in any other way.

Understanding that the male is the center and subject of the narrative answers an argument feminists sometimes make from 2:24, where it is said that "a man shall leave his father and his mother, and shall cleave to his wife." Some see this as a sign of the subordination of the man to the woman, since it is the man who has to pull up roots and join his wife's family. This suggests "a matrilocal family model rather than the patriarchal one which prevailed in the Old Testament," say Scanzoni and Hardesty.[49] Mary Evans agrees: "It is interesting to note that far from supporting patriarchalism, Genesis 2:24 sees the man, rather than the woman, leaving home to 'cleave' to his wife."[50]

The problem in this whole approach is that it fails to

take account of the simple fact that the entire narrative of Genesis 2 centers around the male. The *man* is the one who "leaves and cleaves" simply because he, not the woman, is the central subject of the narrative. The whole chapter is about the man and his activities; everything revolves around him. The statement in 2:24 is made about the man simply because the man is the one being discussed. In all probability, if the story had been centered around the woman, the same would have been said of her, since in actuality when a man and a woman form a new home they *both* leave their original homes and cleave to each other. Neither matriarchy nor patriarchy is implied by the statement. The fact that it is made about the man is just one more indication that he, not the woman, is the center of the narrative.

As far as I know, Biblical feminists have done little or nothing to respond to this particular argument for male headship from Genesis 2. Indeed, there is not much that can be said, since the facts of the story speak for themselves; the man *is* the subject throughout. But is it proper to infer from this that male leadership is normative? In discussing the God-given mandate to subdue the earth, Van Leeuwen says, "Nor is there any indication in the creation accounts that the man was to take the lead in this process."[51] But when we read Genesis 2 with the consciousness that it is indeed talking about the man, is it not clear that this *does* constitute an indication that the man was to take the lead in fulfilling this mandate?

Perhaps if this were the only such indication, it would be a fairly weak inference; but it is not the only one. When added to the further arguments now to be discussed, the leading role of the male in the narrative is a strong argument for the leadership role of the male in God's plan as such.

B. The Male Was Created First

One of the oldest and most venerable arguments for male headship is the priority of the male in the order of creation: Adam was created first, then Eve. The form of the argument goes something like this:

> First premise: priority in creation within the human race is indicative of headship.
> Second premise: priority in creation is given to the male.
> Conclusion: headship belongs to the male.

Feminists usually respond to this argument by attacking one or the other of the two premises.

We have already seen that some feminists deny the truth of the second premise. They deny that the male was created first by asserting that the male and the female were created simultaneously. This can be done, of course, only by denying that Genesis 2 is intended to be taken literally. But there is absolutely no basis anywhere in Scripture for positing a simultaneous creation, as noted earlier; and there is no indication that Genesis 2 was meant to be just nonliteral poetry. Faithful, common-sense exegesis of this chapter leaves the second premise intact.

The more common feminist approach is to deny the truth of the first premise. While acknowledging that the male was created first, feminists argue that such priority has no theological meaning or implications with respect to headship. As Mary Hayter states it, "There remains no ground for the argument that temporal priority of creation in itself signifies superiority of either being or function." [52] According to this view, the order of creation is irrelevant.

Feminists belittle the argument from priority by attempting to make the principle apply not just to the human race within itself but to the whole scope of creation. This is done in two ways. First, it is said that if temporal priority in creation implies headship, then animals must be head over or superior to human beings, since animals were created before human beings. Hull says, "If someone says

GENDER ROLES AND THE BIBLE: CREATION, THE FALL, AND REDEMPTION

that the first-formed creature should take priority, then animals (and the most primitive animals at that!) should take precedence over human beings."[53] Van Leeuwen agrees: "The argument from primacy . . . founders on the fact that, to be consistent, we would now have to say that the animals are superior to *both* male and female, since they were created before both."[54]

Second, feminists remind us that the order of creation in Genesis 1 is from lower to higher life forms, wherein those created *last* — human beings — are superior to all that preceded them. Then they ask why this principle of an ascending scale of creation found in Genesis 1 should not be extended to the separate account of creation recorded in chapter 2. This would establish the woman as superior to the man since she is created *after* the man. Jewett says, "If one were to infer anything from the fact that the woman was created after the man, it should be, in the light of the first creation narrative, that the woman is superior to the man."[55] Hull sums it up thus:

Clearly the traditionalists' position involved special pleading. Those who wanted to teach that the last-formed life form (humankind) was the culmination of creation, while teaching that within that life form the first-formed would take precedence, wanted it "both ways." They could only have it "both ways" by imposing the presupposition of male supremacy upon the text, because — if anything — the supposed order of creation would indicate female supremacy.[56]

We should note that feminists do not seriously press either of these lines of thought. They are not trying to argue either for animal supremacy or female supremacy. They argue these points only to show what they believe should be the logical conclusion *if* the order of creation is used *at all* to establish any kind of headship. Their main point is that priority of creation is actually irrelevant with regard to such a consideration. As Joy Fleming says, "Temporal priority implies nothing about relative worth or authority."[57]

84

In response we must insist that these criticisms are invalid and do not succeed in overturning the argument from priority in creation. The only way these criticisms can be valid is under two conditions: first, if Genesis 1 and 2 are one uninterrupted creation account; and second, if priority in creation *per se* establishes a headship/submission relationship. But *neither* of these premises is true, and hierarchicalists reject them both.

In the first place, Genesis 1 and 2 are *not* one continuous creation account and cannot be treated as such, even though the feminist argument leaves the impression that this is so. But this is an unfair and invalid way of arguing, since they know that neither feminists nor non-feminists claim that these two chapters are a single uninterrupted account. It is obvious that the purpose and form of each separate account are different, and we cannot impose a purpose or form on one just because it is present in the other.

It seems reasonable to interpret the general order of creation in Genesis 1 as progressing from the lesser to the greater. But suggesting that the order of creation in Genesis 1 and the order in Genesis 2 must have the same significance or none at all ignores the different purposes of the two descriptions of creation. Genesis 1, the overview of the totality of creation, is complete in itself and moves to an obvious climax. But Genesis 2 is a more detailed description of what is merely summarized in Genesis 1:27; it is a simple narrative, with no indication that it is arranged so that it builds to some kind of climax. The literary form and structure of the two chapters are simply not the same, just because the purpose of the second narrative is not the same as that of the first.[58] Thus it is invalid to suggest that whatever we say about the order of creation in chapter 1 must be applied to chapter 2 also.

In the second place, and even more significantly, the non-feminists' argument from temporal priority does *not* claim that priority in creation *in itself* is what establishes a relationship of headship and submission. The premise is *not* "Priority in creation confers headship," but rather "Priority in creation within the human race is indicative of headship." This is not meant to be a general principle, as if it applied to created things as such. And even with regard to males and females within the human race, the relationship between priority in creation and male headship *is not causal*. The male is not the leader *because* he was created first, any more than in Genesis 1 the human race has dominion over other creatures *because* it was created last. The human race has dominion because by God's appointment human beings were created in his own image. It has no inherent relationship to the climactic order of the creation in that chapter. Likewise the male is the leader and head of the female *by divine appointment*; it has no inherent relationship to his priority in creation.

The fact is that, in the abstract, nothing can be learned from the simple fact of priority in creation. We could speculate as to what it might mean, but we could never come to any certain conclusions about it on the basis of reason alone. Why, then, do non-feminists dogmatically insist upon the truth of the premise, "Priority in creation within the human race is indicative of headship"? Because *divine revelation* has confirmed it to be so. Man is established as the head of the woman by God's appointment, and the order of creation reflects this divinely-established order (1 Cor. 11:3-9). Women are prohibited from teaching and from exercising authority over men, "for it was Adam who was first created, and then Eve" (1 Tim. 2:12-13).

Divine revelation never says that priority in creation as such is indicative of headship; it limits this relationship to the human male and the human female. Also, divine revelation never says that priority in creation *confers* headship to the male. At best it reveals or points to such headship, but does not cause it. If there is a causal relationship between them, it is the other way around: male headship is the reason why the man was created first. It is a reflection of God's intention concerning male-female relationships.

In the final analysis the decisive factor in the validity of the argument from priority in creation is the New Testament revelation concerning the matter. Feminists will often discuss this argument and offer their criticisms as outlined above *without once referring to this divine commentary on Genesis 2.*[59] Sometimes the New Testament references will be noted, then cavalierly dismissed. For example, Mary Evans makes the following amazing comment: "There is no indication in Genesis 2 itself that temporal priority is of any particular significance. . . . It is true that Paul in 1 Tim. 2:13 refers to the fact that Adam was created before Eve; *although Paul himself does not draw out the implications of this.*"[60] Such a statement says volumes as to how great an influence ideology can have upon Biblical interpretation.

There is one other problem with the feminists' criticisms of the argument from priority in creation, namely, it is invalid to assume that whatever is true of the relationship between the human sexes must also be implied in the broader comparison of animals with the human race. This is what is sometimes called a "category mistake," the fallacy of mixing categories. This fallacy can be illustrated by comparing forms of transportation. In reference to general development we can say that there has been an advance from lesser to greater forms, e.g., from walking to horse-drawn wagons to automobiles. The order is climactic. But when we compare different brands of automobiles, this does not apply; otherwise we would have to say that Geos and Hyundais are functionally superior to Cadillacs and Mercedes. But we recognize immediately that this would be an invalid move because it assumes that what applies to units within a category must also apply to the sub-units as well, when in reality these sub-units form a totally different category. But in their efforts to undermine the validity of the argument from priority of creation, feminists make the same invalid move when they suggest that the climactic order of creation in Genesis 1 should extend into chapter 2 as well.

Our conclusion is that the feminist attacks on the argument for male headship based on priority of creation are completely without effect. They involve false logic, an invalid reading of Genesis 1 and 2, and a disregard of the New Testament commentary on the subject. Thus the argument is shown once again to be valid, and the principle of male headship is shown to be revealed by the facts recorded in Genesis 2.

C. The Woman Was Created from the Man

The third line of evidence for male headship is the fact that the man is the source of the woman; the woman is derived from the man. There is no way that this fact can be denied if the narrative is taken to be literal at all: "The Lord God fashioned into a woman the rib which He had taken from the man" (2:22). This is another element of Genesis 2 that hierarchicalists take as indicative of the divine will that the man should function as the head of the woman.

Feminists offer two responses to this argument. First, they say that if the source or derivation of the woman from the man means anything, it establishes a relationship of *equality* between the two. It shows that the woman is of the very same substance as the man. The position paper, "Men, Women and Biblical Equality," states: "The Bible teaches that the forming of woman from man demonstrates the fundamental unity and equality of human beings."[61] Mickelsen says, "Adam recognized that Eve was 'made of the same stuff' as he and therefore could be the equal that God knew he needed to share responsibilities in the world."[62]

Second, feminists attack this argument as they did the last one, by trying to extend the scope of the comparison to include elements of creation outside the human race itself. I.e., if being made out of something indicates subordination to it, then the man must be subordinate to the dust because that is what he was made from (2:7). Jewett says, "That subordination does not follow from derivation can be seen from this very same narrative where it is said (Gen. 2:7) that the man was formed 'out of' the ground . . . . Who would argue that the man is subordinate to the ground because taken from it?"[63]

Feminists thus reject the argument from derivation, saying that it has no implications regarding headship and submission.

How do hierarchicalists respond to the feminist critique of this argument? First, we can agree that the female's being formed from the male is proof of a fundamental equality between the two. It constitutes another dimension of the *ontological* equality between the sexes in addition to the one based on their both being made in God's image. However, the feminist fallacy again is to think there is an inseparable link between ontological equality and functional equality, which there is not. The equality of being or essence established by Genesis 2:22 is perfectly consistent with the hierarchy of functions indicated thereby.

Second, man's origin from the dust is not analogous to woman's origin from the man because the two events are not parallel. In the first case the only things taken from the dust were the physical elements that went into Adam's body. Even after these elements were shaped into a body, that body was not yet alive; it became a living human being only after God breathed the breath of life into it (2:7). The life that made him a human person thus came from God, not from the dust.[64] Through this second stage of the creation of Adam, God removed him decisively from the category of dust. Eve, on the other hand, was made from the living body of the living human being, Adam. A more appropriate analogy to this would be the way a living baby is born to a living human mother. The source and the product are qualitatively the same from the beginning.

Third and finally, the feminist criticism of this argument assumes that non-feminists are positing a causal relationship between the male as the *source* of the female and the male as the *head* of the female. But such is not the case. Thus the basic problem here is similar to that in the previous point, and our response is basically the same. That is, the female's being derived from the male does not necessarily, in and of itself, confer headship upon the male. We would not know that such derivation is an indicator of male headship except for divine revelation, which we have in 1 Corinthians 11:3-8, where Paul links the two together: "For man does not originate from woman, but woman from man" (11:8). In his decision to bring woman into existence out of the essence of man, God established an appropriate and everlasting symbol of his intention for man to exercise headship over the woman and for the woman to exist in a relationship of dependence upon the man.[65]

Again, the New Testament commentary is the decisive factor in this argument. We know it is a valid argument because the inspired Apostle Paul himself uses it. When feminists reject it, they are arguing against Paul, and ultimately against the Holy Spirit who inspired him.

D. The Woman Was Created for the Man

The fourth argument from Genesis 2 that supports male headship is the fact that the woman was created for the man. Not only was she created *from* him; she was also created *for* him. Though the man was created first, he was not intended to exist alone for very long. As God himself declared, "It is not good for the man to be alone; I will make him a helper suitable for him" (2:18). Thus the female was brought into existence for the express purpose of meeting the needs of the already-existing male, and to enable him to lead a fulfilled life. The woman was created for the man; the man was not created for the woman.

Non-feminists have traditionally used this as an argument for male headship. At times they have focused on the term used for the woman in verse 18, "a helper suitable for him" (or "a help meet for him," KJV). That the woman is called a help or a helper has been taken by some to be an indication of her subordinate role. Adam is the leader and

Eve is his assistant, and thus must it ever be.

The feminists' response to this argument focuses on the proper translation and theological implications of the expression "a helper suitable for him." Their main point is that the Hebrew term translated "helper" (*'ēzer*) carries no inherent connotations of subordination; therefore hierarchicalists are simply wrong when they cite this term as a proof of their view. The fact is that the feminists are correct about this and are justified in celebrating a genuine hermeneutical victory with regard to *'ēzer*. The problem is that they lay much more weight upon this victory than it is able to bear, as if clarifying this point about a single Hebrew term in some way proves egalitarianism.

Their argument proceeds thus. First and most important is the insistence that nothing in the term *'ēzer* implies subordination or implies that the helper should be viewed as a kind of apprentice or assistant. As Mollenkott says, "The powerful associations of the word *ezer*, picked up from the way the word is utilized elsewhere, deny any subordinationistic intent in the Genesis narrator's use of the word."[66] Though it is used twenty-one times in the Old Testament, it is never used of someone in a subordinate role. "Three times it refers to vital human assistance in moments of extreme need; sixteen times it speaks of God's direct assistance to human beings; and twice it is applied specifically to Eve."[67]

The fact that the term is used mostly of God to describe how he helps us is emphasized triumphantly by feminists. "God is hardly secondary or subordinate to us," says Mickelsen.[68] As Mollenkott points out, "Obviously, a word that is used sixteen times concerning divine action is an exalting and glorious word that carries no connotations of secondariness."[69] "If being 'one who helps' inherently implies subordination, then, in that case, God would be subordinate to humans!" declares Spencer.[70]

Feminists are not content just to point out that *'ēzer* does not imply a subordinate position for Eve. They go further and assert that the term implies equality and partnership. Spencer says that the context in no way implies "that Eve's duties as 'one who helps' are different from the one she helps. . . . To 'help' here means 'to share the same tasks.'" Their similar tasks in subduing the earth required the work of equals. Thus the point is "male and female equality, joint rulership, and interrelationship."[71] This is reinforced by the term translated "suitable for him," which means one who is like him, one who is his counterpart and complement, one who is his equal — unlike the animals. The term "emphasizes appropriateness or suitability, and thus implies equality."[72] The best translation of the expression, says Fleming, is "partner corresponding to him," since this "probably serves best to convey equality and mutuality."[73]

Thus do feminists respond to the argument that male headship is implied by the fact that the woman was created for the man. Not only do they deny that the term for "helper" has connotations of subordination; they also argue that the entire expression "a helper suitable for him" actually shows the equality of the man and the woman.

How shall we evaluate these attempts to undermine this argument for male headship? First, as noted earlier, we must concede their point about the meaning of the term *'ēzer*. Non-feminists can no longer say that the term as such implies a subordinate role for women.[74] But second, and more importantly, the non-feminists' case here does not rest upon the meaning of a single word, but upon the implications of the event as a whole, namely, that the woman was in fact *made for the man*. Stephen Clark says it well:

> The observation about the word *ezer* is only a first step in looking at the phrase in which it occurs. Indeed, to focus on the word by itself, without considering its context in the phrase and in the passage, is not very helpful. The actual phrase says that God created woman to be a help for man; that is, the purpose of her creation was to be a help to the man. Taken in its context, there is clearly some sort of subordination indicated by the phrase as a whole. . . .[75]

The attempt to negate the force of the context by pointing out that the term *'ēzer* is used mostly of God is a red herring; it involves a *non sequitur*. Because a term is used of God does not give it connotations of superior rank. Whether a helper is superior to, equal to, or subordinate to the one who is helped is a matter to be determined only by the context, not by the word itself. What does the context reveal? Piper and Grudem point out that the context of Genesis 2 "makes it very unlikely that 'helper' should be read on the analogy of God's help, because in Genesis 2:19-20 Adam is caused to seek his 'helper' first among the animals."[76] That is, it was not inappropriate to look for "help" among those creatures of a lower nature, even though none was to be found there comparable to Adam himself. Again appealing to the point being made in the context, Hicks and Morton point out that the alleged parallel between God and the woman is a "false analogy" because "God was not created to be our helper."[77]

That the woman was created for the man and not vice versa is only what we would expect in view of the point made earlier, that the man is the center and subject of the whole narrative and everything else happens relative to him.

Thus the whole context of Genesis 2 implies that woman's being created for man involves her subordinate relationship to the man. But this connection is not just an implication of the circumstances in the text; it is confirmed by Paul's teaching in 1 Corinthians 11:9. Here, as a proof of male headship (verse 3), Paul declares, "For indeed man was not created for the woman's sake, but woman for the man's sake." This New Testament commentary is decisive, and it simply cannot be ignored or explained away. In an attempt to mute the hierarchical force of Genesis 2, Owen Crouch says, "She was 'for' him. But no more than he was 'for' her."[78] But such a comment trivializes the whole account and is a blunt denial of what Paul says, namely, that man *was not* created for the woman's sake. That the woman was created for the man's sake and *not* vice versa shows that God intended a relationship of subordination between the man and the woman and that he did not intend for it to be reciprocal.

That God describes the woman as a helper *suitable for* or corresponding to the man does reflect the ontological equality between the sexes, but in no way does it require functional equality. It shows that in her essential being woman, unlike the animals, is on an equal plane with man; but it does not negate the role of subordination established by God when he created the woman *for the man,* i.e., for the sake of the man or as a helper for the man.

E. The Man Named the Woman

A fifth argument for male headship from Genesis 2 is the fact that the man gave the woman her name (2:23). The naming process began with the animals, when God "brought them to the man to see what he would call them; and whatever the man called a living creature, that was its name. And the man gave names to all" the animals (2:19-20). It is argued that the very act of a person's giving a name to something or someone establishes his authority over that other person or that thing. Thus Adam's naming of the animals is an indication of his position of authority over them. But then, when God brought the newly-formed woman to Adam, he named her as well: "She shall be called Woman, because she was taken out of Man" (2:23). Thus this very act of naming the woman shows his authority over her; Adam "stresses his rule over her in that he assigns her a name."[79]

In their response to this argument feminists usually do not deny that the Old Testament considers naming to be an act of authority. As Trible says concerning the naming of the animals, "Through the power of naming, the animals are subordinated to the earth creature [*hā 'ādām*]. They become inferiors, not equals." This "repeated emphasis on naming underscores the subordination of the animal world to the earth creature."[80] However, says Trible, the same is not true regarding the naming of the woman, because the full formula for authoritative naming is not used in this case. The complete formula must include both the verb *call* and the noun *name* (as in 2:19-20). "This complete activity of *calling the name* becomes the way in which the earth creature establishes power over the animals. The verb *call* by itself does not mean naming; only when joined to the noun *name* does it become part of a naming formula."[81] But this full formula is not used in the naming of the woman in 2:23. "The noun *name* is strikingly absent from the poetry. Hence, in calling the woman, the man is not establishing power over her but rejoicing in their mutuality."[82]

These conclusions of Trible are often repeated by feminists. For example, Van Leeuwen attempts to refute the argument from naming by declaring that "the classic Hebrew naming formula (the one used by Adam when he 'named' the animals) consists of *calling* a person, an animal or a place *by name*. Upon seeing Eve for the first time, Adam does not 'call her by name' — he merely calls or recognizes her as 'woman.'" Van Leeuwen then quotes Trible.[83]

As feminists see it, even though Genesis 2:23 does *not* constitute a naming incident, Genesis 3:20 does. This verse says, "Now the man called his wife's name Eve, because she was the mother of all the living." This is significant because it occurs only after the Fall and after the pronouncement of the curse in Genesis 3:16, "And he shall rule over you." In other words, when Adam really did get around to naming Eve in the sense of claiming authority over her, he was doing so illegitimately in his fallen state as an expression of his corrupted patriarchal mentality.[84] Walter Liefeld notes that Adam "did not *name* her 'Eve' until *after the Fall*. If there is any control it follows the terrible effect of man assuming dominion over the woman (Gen 3:16)."[85]

What is the result of these arguments and counter-arguments? Basically, while feminists accept the idea that naming signifies authority over, they deny that Genesis 2:23 is an incident of authoritative naming. Many hierarchicalists, on the other hand, agree that naming signifies authority over, and continue to claim that Genesis 2:23 *is* an incident of authoritative naming. For example, H. Wayne House says, "When Adam named her — a prerogative in the Old Testament of one having authority — he demonstrated his authority over her."[86] Susan Foh says, "But there is another clue that Adam is to be regarded as having authority over the woman. Adam named her. . . . To name someone is associated with authority over that person."[87]

But how can non-feminists continue to assert this in view of the feminists' criticisms of this argument? Several points can be made. First, the whole idea that "*called the name of*" is the Old Testament formula indicating the authority of the namer over the named is simply not true. The naming of a person, place, or thing is equally significant when described either by the verb *call* with the noun *name*, or by the verb without the noun. Examples of both are abundant, and a study of them shows that no special significance seems to be involved when *name* is used as opposed to when it is not used. For example, God sometimes personally applies a name to a person or a thing. On some occasions both noun and verb are used (e.g., Gen. 17:5; Isa. 43:1; 45:3-4; Jer. 11:16; 20:3); on other occasions just the verb is used (e.g., Gen. 1:5, 8, 10; Isa. 62:4). Either way the authority is not conveyed by the formula but is inherent in the one calling the name. For another example of how the "formula" seems inconsequential, sometimes both models (with and without either *call* or *name*) are used in the same verse (Gen. 17:5; 35:18)[88] or in the same immediate context (Gen. 16:14-15; Deut. 3:13-14; Judg. 15:17, 19). Examples of how both models are used in the same general context are abundant (e.g., Num. 11:34 and 13:24; Judg. 18:12 and 18:29; 2 Sam. 5:9 and 5:20; 2 Kings 14:7 and 18:4; 1 Chron. 13:11 and 14:11).

Other considerations also suggest that "called the name of" is not a formula by which the namer asserts authority over the named. In Genesis 16:13, Hagar gave a name to

96

Yahweh using the so-called formula. The mother of the Messiah will "call His name Immanuel" (Isa. 7:14). Surely these are not assertions of authority over Yahweh and the Messiah.[89] In Exodus 16:31 the Israelites called the name of the heavenly food "manna," but this did not give them power over it.

All in all there simply is no consistent pattern of the use of a specific naming formula to indicate authority over the named. If naming is sometimes an act of authority, such must be concluded on grounds other than the particular words used to describe the act. Where Phyllis Trible got the idea that the use of certain terms constitutes an authoritative naming formula is a mystery to me. In any case evangelical feminists would do well to stop quoting Trible and one another on this point, and instead study the actual Old Testament texts that have to do with naming.

Second, the description of Adam's naming the animals (2:19-20) is itself not couched in words suggesting a formula. Although both the verb *call* and the noun *name* are used, the text does not say Adam "called their names" anything at all. No specific names are given, whereas in passages usually cited as examples of the "naming formula," the specific name is included, e.g., Genesis 4:17; 4:25; 4:26. Also in verse 19 the terms *call* and *name* are not really used together as we would expect them to be in a "formula." It says, "Whatever the man called a living creature, that was its name." The fact that the two words are used here does not in itself constitute a formula. Verse 20 does use the so-called formula, but again without any specific names being mentioned. In other words, even if Adam's naming the animals is a sign of dominion, it is clear that such an event did not have to be described in some specific formula.

Third, the fact that the word *name* is not used in 2:23 in the naming of the woman is easily explained by the fact that it is a direct quotation and not a narrative description like 2:19-20. A parallel is Ruth 1:20-21, where Naomi says, "Do not call me Naomi; call me Mara." She could have said,

"Do not call my name Naomi; call my name Mara"; but this would have been superfluous. The same is true in Genesis 2:23, where Adam is speaking specifically and directly (and emphatically) about the woman: "She shall be called woman."

Fourth, whatever the meaning of the naming of the animals, it would seem that the naming of the woman would have the same significance simply because of the proximity of these two events and their obviously important connection in the narrative.

Fifth, the idea that Adam's calling his wife's name Eve in Genesis 3:20 is a reflection of the "terrible effect" of the Fall is totally unfounded speculation. There is absolutely nothing at all in the text to suggest that this act of naming has anything whatsoever to do with the Fall. To assume that the one is the cause of the other is to commit the fallacy that logicians call "*post hoc, ergo propter hoc*," or "after this, therefore on account of this." The text does not even hint at such a causal connection, nor does it give any reason to think that Adam was naming his wife in order to assert sinful dominion over her. Rather, it indicates that Adam's giving her the name was a way of honoring and exalting her: "The man called his wife's name Eve, because she was the mother of all the living." If formulaic naming is an authoritative act, then Genesis 3:20 is such an act; and it is done without the slightest stigma whatsoever.

Having made these points, we must conclude that if indeed naming someone establishes a kind of headship or authority over the person named, then both Genesis 2:23 and 3:20 indicate the authority of the man over the woman. I state this as a conditional sentence because I am personally not convinced that Adam's act of naming the woman in Genesis 2:23 (or 3:20, for that matter) is a really solid argument for male headship. I say this because, according to the general practice of applying names in the Old Testament, such an act did not necessarily always imply an assertion of authority. (See again, for example, Genesis 16:13 and Isaiah 7:14.) Nevertheless in Genesis 2 the act of

naming is certainly consistent with the fact of male headship, and it is without doubt one of the main ways in which
the male is central in the narrative and in the drama of
creation itself. Because of this latter fact alone we may
speak of it as a proof of male headship at least in an indirect sense, even if it is not so in a direct sense.

F. Conclusion

In this section we have seen that there are at least four
and perhaps five good reasons for reading Genesis 2 as
establishing hierarchicalism, i.e., male headship, as the
original order of creation. These are (1) the man is central
in the drama and the narrative of creation; (2) the man was
created first; (3) the woman was created out of the man; (4)
the woman was created for the man; and (5) the man
named the woman. Since God was certainly in sovereign
control of the whole creation event, we must conclude that
these specific facts and arrangements were not incidental
but were deliberately chosen by God to convey to our minds
his own appointment of the male to the role of leadership.

In this section we have also examined the hermeneutical
attempts of feminists to blunt or even reverse the force of
these arguments, but we have seen that their arguments
are truly without any textual basis. Most significantly, we
have also seen that they contradict the specific New
Testament commentary on this passage, which affirms
male headship.

IV. THE DECISIVE POINT:
THE NEW TESTAMENT COMMENTARY

Speaking specifically of Genesis 2, Jewett says that
"sexual hierarchy must be read into the text; it is not
required by the text."[90] Clark, on the other hand, speaking
of both Genesis 2 and 3, says that "the most normal read-

ing of the account would indicate that the woman is subordinate to the man throughout."[91] In my opinion, anyone who gives thoughtful and objective consideration to the text would have to agree with Clark.

The decisive point in all of this, however, is not what Jewett thinks or what Clark thinks or what I think, but what the Holy Spirit thinks as represented in the inspired references to Genesis 2 that occur in the New Testament. Whether it be called the "normal reading" or "reading into," the New Testament does it: it sees hierarchy in the text of Genesis 2. Even if Jewett is right, that hierarchy must be read into the text, still it is no one less than the inspired Apostle Paul who is doing this; so how can we presume to do anything else? If Paul through the Spirit is reading hierarchy into the text, it is because it is already latent there, and not because it is somehow contrary to its teaching.

I have read many feminist discussions of Genesis 1 and 2, and what amazes me, as noted earlier, is that so many of them will carry the analysis through to the feminist conclusions explained above *without once mentioning 1 Corinthians 11:8-9 and 1 Timothy 2:13.* For example, in her exposition of the egalitarian view of women's roles in the symposium edited by Clouse and Clouse, Alvera Mickelsen has a section entitled "What Does the Creation Account Tell Us?" She spends over five pages setting forth the feminist party line concerning Genesis 1-3, responding especially to the non-feminist arguments from Genesis 2, *and never once refers to the New Testament commentary on the subject.* Her opening comment is this: "Interpretation of Genesis 1-3 forms a classic illustration of how faulty principles of interpretation may be used to support what we want the Scriptures to say."[92] But there could not be a better example of this very fact than her own work! To be more precise, her biggest problem is not so much following a faulty principle of interpretation as ignoring one of the universally-accepted primary principles, namely, that Scripture must be used to interpret Scripture.

In this same section Mickelsen also makes the following

remarkable statement: "Many foreign ideas have been 'read into' the account of Genesis 2. Some interpreters say, for example, that because Adam was created first, he was created to have some kind of supremacy, headship or authority over Eve. This 'order of creation' argument has been used for hundreds of years."[93] Yes, it has — for over nineteen hundred years, as a matter of fact, and by an interpreter no less than the Apostle Paul! But Mickelsen chooses to ignore this fact, which shows that the real problem with the interpretation of Genesis is not what hierarchicalists "read into" the text but what feminists "unread out of" the text.

Mickelsen is far from atypical among feminists in her treatment of the creation texts. Another example is Gretchen Hull. In her book *Equal To Serve* she introduces and discusses the Genesis texts on several occasions (pp. 77ff., 152ff., 180ff.), yet *never once* does the New Testament commentary enter into her discussion. In a separate section ("The 'Hard Passages'") she dismisses 1 Corinthians 11:2-16 and 1 Timothy 2:8-15 with the generality that since there are so many points in these passages on which scholars disagree, it would be unwise to try to use them for understanding male-female relationships.[94] In still another section she mentions the fact that non-feminists sometimes appeal to "Paul's references to Genesis in 1 Corinthians 11:2-16 and 1 Timothy 2:8-15," but she makes no attempt to discuss their relevance other than to say that "his arguments are not completely clear to us."[95]

This does not mean that feminists ignore these passages which comment on Genesis 2. In fact they discuss them in excruciating detail when those passages themselves are the main point of attention. And as we shall see later in our own discussions of these passages, feminists are very careful to find interpretations of them which make Paul's references to Genesis 2 completely irrelevant as guides to understanding that Old Testament text. Why? Because feminists understand that, taken at face value, this New Testament commentary points to just one unequivocal and irrevocable conclusion, namely, that Genesis 2 affirms a hierarchical relationship between man and woman as God's intention from the beginning.

That feminists go to such extreme lengths to construct a defense against this inevitable conclusion, despite and in the face of the New Testament commentary, illustrates the truth of my contention at the end of the previous chapter. There I suggested that feminists are controlled more by the second horizon of Biblical interpretation than the first. What they see in the text is dictated by the necessities of feministic experience rather than by what the author originally intended.

ENDNOTES
CHAPTER TWO

[1]See Phyllis Trible, *God and the Rhetoric of Sexuality* (Philadelphia: Fortress Press, 1978), pp. 15ff. Trible is not a Biblical feminist but is widely quoted by those who are.

[2]Elaine Storkey, *What's Right with Feminism* (Grand Rapids: Eerdmans, 1985), p. 153.

[3]Alvera Mickelsen, "An Egalitarian View: There Is Neither Male Nor Female in Christ," *Women in Ministry: Four Views*, ed. Bonnidell Clouse and Robert G. Clouse (Downers Grove: InterVarsity Press, 1989), p. 182.

[4]Aida Besançon Spencer, *Beyond the Curse: Women Called to Ministry* (Nashville: Thomas Nelson, 1985), p. 21.

[5]Gretchen Gaebelein Hull, "In the Image of God: Women and Men as Social Equals," *ESA Advocate* (November 1990), 12:14.

[6]This is true also of the three times it is used with the preposition.

[7]Susan T. Foh, "A Male Leadership View: The Head of the Woman Is the Man," *Women in Ministry: Four Views*, ed. Bonnidell Clouse and Robert G. Clouse (Downers Grove: InterVarsity Press, 1989), p. 72.

[8]Letha Scanzoni, "The Feminists and the Bible," *Christianity Today* (Feb. 2, 1973), p. 11.

[9]Gretchen Gaebelein Hull, *Equal To Serve: Women and Men in the Church and Home* (Old Tappan, NJ: Revell, 1987), p. 80.

[10]Spencer, *Beyond the Curse*, p. 23.

[11]Hull, *Equal To Serve*, p. 80.

[12]Mary Stewart Van Leeuwen, *Gender and Grace: Love, Work and Parenting in a Changing World* (Downers Grove: InterVarsity Press, 1990), pp. 41-42.

[13]Gilbert Bilezikian, *Beyond Sex Roles: What the Bible Says About a Woman's Place in Church and Family* (Grand Rapids: Baker Book House, 1985), p. 25. See also p. 41.

[14]Elizabeth Cady Stanton, in *The Woman's Bible*, Part I (New York: European Publishing Company, 1895), p. 15.

[15]Scanzoni and Hardesty, *All We're Meant To Be: Biblical Feminism for Today*, 3rd ed. (Grand Rapids: Eerdmans, 1992), p. 29.

[16]Paul K. Jewett, *Man As Male and Female: A Study in Sexual Relationships from a Theological Point of View* (Grand Rapids: Eerdmans, 1975), p. 122.

[17]Virginia Ramey Mollenkott, *Women, Men, and the Bible*, revised ed. (New York: Crossroad, 1988), p. 83.

[18]Stanton, *The Woman's Bible*, I:15.

[19]See ibid., pp. 20-21.

[20]See Mollenkott, *Women*, p. 83. See her letter to the editor, *Christianity Today* (June 4, 1976), pp. 24-25. See also Jewett, *Man*, p. 122.

[21]Jewett, *Man*, pp. 33-48.

[22]Bilezikian, *Beyond Sex Roles*, p. 23.

[23]"Male and female reflect the plurality of God as Trinity. The interrelationship between male and female symbolizes the interrelationship

within God" (Spencer, *Beyond the Curse*, p. 21). See Jewett, *Man*, p. 43.

[24]Mollenkott, *The Divine Feminine: The Biblical Imagery of God as Female* (New York: Crossroad, 1983), p. 5.

[25]Gottfried Oosterwal, "Dialogue," *Gospel in Context* (April 1979), 2:22.

[26]Donald G. Bloesch, *The Battle for the Trinity: The Debate over Inclusive God-Language* (Ann Arbor: Servant Publications, 1985), pp. 32-33.

[27]Rolf E. Aaseng, "Male and Female Created He Them," *Christianity Today* (Nov. 20, 1970), p. 6.

[28]Bilezikian, *Beyond Sex Roles*, p. 216, n. 7.

[29]Karen and Leif Torjesen, "Inclusive Orthodoxy: Recovering a Suppressed Tradition," *The Other Side* (December 1986), pp. 15-16.

[30]Van Leeuwen, *Gender*, pp. 39-40.

[31]Aaseng, "Male and Female," p. 6.

[32]Torjesen, "Inclusive Orthodoxy," p. 16.

[33]Spencer, *Beyond the Curse*, p. 21.

[34]Ibid., p. 29.

[35]Jewett, *Man*, p. 33.

[36]Ibid., p. 46.

[37]For an example see Robert Letham, "The Man-Woman Debate: Theological Comment," *Westminster Theological Journal* (1990), 52:68-69.

[38]"Men, Women and Biblical Equality," section 2 under "Biblical Truths," in *Priscilla Papers* (Fall 1989), 3:12.

[39]Mickelsen, "An Egalitarian View," p. 182.

[40]See Mollenkott, letter to *Christianity Today* (June 4, 1976), p. 25; and Jewett, *Man*, p. 122.

[41]Hull, *Equal To Serve*, p. 80.

[42]Hull, "In the Image of God," p. 14.

[43]John Stott, *Involvement, Volume II: Social and Sexual Relationships in the Modern World* (Old Tappan, NJ: Revell, 1984), p. 139.

[44]Mary A. Kassian, *Women, Creation, and the Fall* (Westchester, IL: Crossway Books, 1990), p. 15.

[45]These are the four main arguments for hierarchy in Genesis 2 as summed up by Mary J. Evans, *Woman in the Bible* (Downers Grove: InterVarsity Press, 1983), p. 14.

[46]Male headship is *not* the same as woman's "inferiority to the man," a concept which non-feminists reject but which feminists continue to introduce into the discussion (see Jewett, *Man*, p. 126) even though it is a false and misleading characterization of the hierarchical view.

[47]See Stephen Clark, *Man and Woman in Christ* (Ann Arbor: Servant Books, 1980), pp. 24-25.

[48]The male continues to be the central and leading figure in chapter 3. When God confronted the guilty couple after the Fall, he addressed the man (3:9-11). After pronouncing the curse, God spoke as if the burden of the guilt rested upon the man (3:22-24). The New Testament traces the universal consequences of the Fall to the man (Rom. 5:12-19; 1 Cor. 15:22).

[49]Scanzoni and Hardesty, *All We're Meant To Be* (1992), p. 28.

[50]Evans, *Woman*, p. 17. Jewett (*Man*, pp. 127-128) and Bilezikian (*Beyond Sex Roles*, pp. 34-35) also press this point.

[51]Van Leeuwen, *Gender*, p. 42.

[52]Mary Hayter, *The New Eve in Christ: The Use and Abuse of the Bible in the Debate About Women in the Church* (Grand Rapids: Eerdmans, 1987), p. 98. This is a misleading use of the term *superiority*. Non-feminists would probably agree with this statement if superiority were distinguished from headship, but feminists have the unfortunate habit of trying to force a choice between two extremes: unqualified equality or superiority/inferiority. Biblical non-feminism's concept of headship is neither.

[53]Hull, *Equal To Serve*, p. 181. See also Bilezikian, *Beyond Sex Roles*, pp. 30, 219.

[54]Mary Stewart Van Leeuwen, "The Recertification of Women: A Review Article," *The Reformed Journal* (August 1986), 36:19.

[55]Jewett, *Man*, pp. 126-127. See also Willard M. Swartley, *Slavery, Sabbath, War, and Women: Case Issues in Biblical Interpretation* (Scottdale, PA: Herald Press, 1983), p. 155; and Richard Kroeger, "A Plea for Restraint," *Priscilla Papers* (August 1987), I:2.

[56]Hull, *Equal To Serve*, p. 181.

[57]Joy Elasky Fleming, "Gender Equality in Genesis 2-3," an unpublished essay (St. Paul, MN: Christians for Biblical Equality, 1991), p. 8.

[58]See Clark, *Man*, pp. 26-27 (footnote).

[59]Fleming, "Gender Equality," is an example of this.

[60]Evans, *Woman*, p. 15; italics added.

[61]From section 3 under "Biblical Truths," in *Priscilla Papers* (Fall 1989), 3:12.

[62]Mickelsen, "An Egalitarian View," p. 183.

[63]Jewett, *Man*, p. 126. See Van Leeuwen, "Recertification," p. 19.

[64]This is not meant to imply that some part of Adam's essence was derived from the divine essence. This is a pagan idea and must be vigorously rejected.

[65]This is not an absolutely one-way dependence, as 1 Cor. 11:12 shows. But it is the *primary* relationship of dependence.

[66]Mollenkott, *The Divine Feminine*, pp. 74-75.

[67]Ibid., p. 75. See Jewett, *Man*, p. 124; Mickelsen, "An Egalitarian View," p. 183.

[68]Mickelsen, "An Egalitarian View," p. 183.

[69]Mollenkott, *The Divine Feminine*, p. 75.

[70]Spencer, *Beyond the Curse*, p. 27.

[71]Ibid., pp. 28-29.

[72]Mollenkott, *The Divine Feminine*, p. 74. To say Adam needed someone "meet" or "suitable" for him was simply to say "he needed an equal," says Anne Atkins in *Split Image: Male and Female After God's Likeness* (Grand Rapids: Eerdmans, 1987), p. 39.

[73]Fleming, "Gender Equality," p. 12.

[74]See James B. Hurley, *Man and Woman in Biblical Perspective* (Grand Rapids: Zondervan, 1981), p. 209.

[75]Clark, *Man*, p. 24 (footnote).

[76]John Piper and Wayne Grudem, "Charity, Clarity and Hope: The Controversy and the Cause of Christ," in *Recovering Biblical Manhood and Womanhood*, ed. John Piper and Wayne Grudem (Wheaton, IL: Crossway Books, 1991), p. 408.

[77]John Mark Hicks and Bruce L. Morton, *Woman's Role in the Church* (Shreveport, LA: Lambert Book House, 1978), p. 19.

[78]Owen Crouch, *Not Guilty: Studies in Romans* (Milligan College, TN: published by author, 1987), p. 169.

[79]Hurley, *Man*, p. 212. He develops this argument on pp. 210-212.

[80]Trible, *God*, p. 92.

[81]Ibid., p. 99.

[82]Ibid., p. 100.

[83]Van Leeuwen, *Gender*, p. 41. See also Evans, *Woman*, p. 16. See Bilezikian, *Beyond Sex Roles*, pp. 220-223; and Fleming, "Gender Equality," p. 17.

[84]See Van Leeuwen, "The Christian Mind and the Challenge of Gender Relations," *The Reformed Journal* (September 1987), 37:18.

[85]Walter L. Liefeld, "A Plural Ministry Response" to Susan Foh, *Women in Ministry: Four Views*, ed. Bonnidell Clouse and Robert G. Clouse (Downers Grove: InterVarsity Press, 1989), p. 114.

[86]H. Wayne House, *The Role of Women in Ministry Today* (Nashville: Thomas Nelson, 1990), p. 27.

[87]Foh, "A Male Leadership View," p. 73. See Kassian, *Women*, p. 19.

[88]Genesis 35:18 is especially significant, because both Rachel and Jacob give a name to their newborn son. Rachel *called* his *name* Benoni, but Jacob *called* him Benjamin. According to the authority-formula theory, this should have been reversed, since the latter is the one that obviously prevailed.

[89]Regarding the Messiah see also Isa. 9:6; Jer. 23:6.

[90]Jewett, *Man*, p. 126.

[91]Clark, *Man*, p. 26.

[92]Mickelsen, "An Egalitarian View," pp. 181-182.

[93]Ibid., p. 184.

[94]Hull, *Equal To Serve*, p. 183.

[95]Ibid., p. 187.

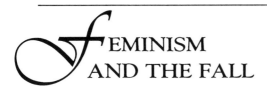EMINISM AND THE FALL

The third chapter of Genesis has generally been viewed as pivotal by feminists of all stripes. Anti-biblical feminists (the secular and goddess types) regard Genesis 3 in a totally negative light, at least as it has been traditionally understood. They hold it responsible for much of the oppression directed toward women in the western world. Carol Christ calls the story of Eve "the fountainhead of a woman-hating tradition within biblical religion."[1] As Adler sums it up, "Feminists and Neo-Pagans naturally feel that the story of Adam and Eve, as commonly interpreted, has probably done more to debase and subjugate women than any other such tale in Western history."[2] These women are referring specifically to the story of the Fall, typical interpretations of which cast Eve in the role of villainess and the cause of the world's ruination.

Biblical feminists of course do not read Genesis 3 in this way. Unlike feminists of all other stripes, they regard the account of the Fall as factual rather than mythical. They accept the details of Eve's role in this tragic event to be true as described in the Bible. But they do not see Eve, and woman by implication, as in some sense the unique downfall of the human race. It may be true, as the others claim, that the story of Adam and Eve is the source of untold grief for women. But, they say, this is not the fault of the story itself, much less the fault of Eve; it is rather the result of centuries of misreading and misinterpreting the text, especially the "curse" pronounced upon Eve in Genesis 3:16.

Thus it is very important for Biblical feminists to set forth what they regard as the correct interpretation of Genesis 3. How they understand the events recorded therein is the subject of this chapter. Here we shall consider three things: the first sin itself (Gen. 3:1-6), the curse pronounced by God after the sin (especially Gen. 3:16), and the effects of the work of Christ as the cancellation of that curse.

I. THE SIN

1 Now the serpent was more crafty than any beast of the field which the Lord God had made. And he said to the woman, "Indeed, has God said, 'You shall not eat from any tree of the garden'?"
2 And the woman said to the serpent, "From the fruit of the trees of the garden we may eat;
3 but from the fruit of the tree which is in the middle of the garden, God has said, 'You shall not eat from it or touch it, lest you die.'"
4 And the serpent said to the woman, "You surely shall not die!
5 For God knows that in the day you eat from it your eyes will be opened, and you will be like God, knowing good and evil."
6 When the woman saw that the tree was good for food, and that it was a delight to the eyes, and that the tree was desirable to make one wise, she took from its fruit and ate; and she gave also to her husband with her, and he ate (Gen. 3:1-6).

This text raises important questions about the nature of Eve's role in the introduction of sin into the world. How does Eve's part compare with that of Adam? Does the narrative contain any indicators concerning God's intention regarding role relationships between men and women? Does the event reveal anything about the inherent nature of woman as such? Does Eve's sin have any necessary implications for the role of women in today's world?

Such questions are especially important in view of two New Testament texts. One is 1 Timothy 2:14, which seems to be giving one reason why women are not permitted to teach men and to have authority over men in the church today (2:12). It says, "And it was not Adam who was deceived, but the woman being quite deceived, fell into transgression." The other is 1 Peter 3:7, which says, "You husbands likewise, live with your wives in an understanding way, as with a weaker vessel, since she is a woman."

Two things are at stake in our consideration of Eve's sin. First, does the fact that Satan chose Eve for this first temptation imply that women as such are spiritually weaker than men? Do they have some kind of inherent weakness that makes them more vulnerable to temptation and sin, as some think 1 Peter 3:7 is suggesting? Second, does Eve's role in the first sin disqualify all women from leadership roles in the church today, as some think 1 Timothy 2:14 says? That is to say, does Eve have some kind of unique responsibility for that first sin that has negative consequences for all women? These two issues will be discussed in turn.

A. Why Did Satan Choose Eve?

The question of why Satan chose Eve as the object of his temptation is made all the more relevant by Paul's remark that "it was not Adam who was deceived, but the woman being quite deceived, fell into transgression" (1 Tim. 2:14). This text, after all, means *something*. Does it mean that Eve was chosen because Satan considered her more deceivable, more vulnerable than Adam? Was Eve truly the "weaker vessel"—emotionally, intellectually, spiritually? Why *was* she singled out for Satan's attack?

1. The Feminist Explanation

In reference to all such questions, feminists deny that Eve (representing womankind in general) was in any way weaker than Adam, or that women as a class are any more inherently vulnerable to temptation and deception than men as a class. In responding to such allegations, they make two main points.

First, feminists assert that as a matter of fact Eve was *not* "singled out" for temptation. Satan did not choose Eve over against Adam, but rather directed his tempting lies toward both of them at the same time. Two reasons are given for saying this. First, when Satan speaks in Genesis 3, he uses the *plural* "you," indicating that he is addressing both Adam and Eve. Richard Kroeger remarks, "Adam was standing at Eve's side while the serpent orchestrated the temptation scenario. . . . The serpent addressed the women [*sic*] with the plural 'you' (Gen. 3:1-7)."[3] Spencer also calls attention to this fact: "It may also be possible that the serpent employs the plural 'you' because it addresses Adam as well as Eve. Adam may have been present although not speaking."[4]

The second reason for saying that Satan did not focus solely on Eve is the interpretation of verse six as saying that Adam was *with Eve* when she was tempted: "And she gave also to her husband with her, and he ate." Spencer calls attention to this point in language that leaves behind the uncertainty shown in the quotation in the previous paragraph: "The possibility that Adam is present during the dialogue is confirmed in verse 6. After Eve eats the fruit, she gives it to her husband 'with her.'" Thus "both Eve *and* Adam appear to have been present during the dialogue."[5] Richard Kroeger agrees: "The Hebrew and Septuagint texts of Gen. 3:6 state that Adam was standing at Eve's side."[6]

If we accept the idea that Adam was standing at Eve's side during the temptation, this becomes all the more significant when we realize that he never said a word during the whole episode. Only Eve had the conviction to speak up in God's defense, misguided though she was. Bilezikian says, "Eve put up a good fight whereas Adam fell instantly, without saying a word." Also, "While Eve was getting inveigled by the tempter, Adam refrained from interfering. His silence was one of assent."[7] Why is this

significant? Because it shows that Eve, rather than representing the weaker sex, is actually the stronger of the two!
Satan knew, says Bilezikian, that "the greatest amount of
resistance would come from the woman"; and in fact "Eve
faced the tempter's challenge with a greater degree of
authority than Adam."[8] Scanzoni and Hardesty reply to the
idea that Satan chose Eve because she was weaker by
making this same point: "Both Adam and Eve were there
(3:6), but Eve alone leaped to God's defense when Satan
sought to discredit the Deity."[9] Thus Adam shows himself
to be the weaker of the two.

The second point made by feminists in response to the
charge that Satan concentrated on Eve is that he knew
that there *was* a sense in which she was more vulnerable
than Adam. But her vulnerability was not due to some
inherent female weakness; it was rather the result of the
circumstances of her education concerning the requirements of God's will. She was at a disadvantage because in
some sense she was less taught than Adam.

One version of this view is that only Adam was taught
directly by God (Gen. 2:16-17), while Eve was taught by
Adam and thus knew of God's prohibition only indirectly or
at second hand. This view is defended with vigor by
Bilezikian. He says,

> The most obvious reason for the tempter's attack being
> focused on Eve was her vulnerability. This vulnerability
> was not the result of a weaker character, as is often sug-
> gested. It had to do with the circumstances surrounding the
> moment when God gave Adam the prohibition to eat from
> the tree.
> . . . She had not been part of the living experience of
> God's putting the tree off limits. For her, the prohibition
> was a matter of theoretical knowledge. She was a victim of
> the second-generation-believer-fadeout syndrome.
> Having received the instruction secondhand, Eve was ill-
> prepared to discern the tempter's lies. . . .[10]

Thus Eve was "less qualified" because she was "less knowledgeable." She was "less informed" because "she had mis-

sed some significant learning experiences about God that had been available to Adam." "She did not have access to the revelational opportunities that had enriched Adam's life prior to her existence." She had access to revealed information only through Adam.[11] "There is no evidence of God's having revealed Himself to Eve in person before the fall. She had a relatively limited knowledge of Him." Thus "she was vulnerable to error because her information regarding the tree was obtained by transmission and not directly from God."[12]

Scott McClelland gives a slightly different version of Eve's "inadequate education." He agrees that Adam most likely taught the prohibition to Eve, since this "would be most natural as a fitting interchange between the supposed cosovereigns of the creation . . . . In any event, it appears *just as likely* that Adam hedged the prohibition to Eve," adding the part about not touching the tree. Thus it is "*just as likely* for the serpent to attack Eve because he knew that her inadequate education regarding the prohibition" would make her vulnerable to doubt concerning God's intentions. Thus the root of the problem was that Adam "improperly taught God's word to Eve."[13]

Another version of the "vulnerable because improperly educated" view is that of Walter Kaiser, which he bases on his interpretation of 1 Timothy 2:13. Most versions translate this according to the sense of the NASB, "For it was Adam who was first created, and then Eve." Some translations (e.g., KJV, NIV) use the word *formed* instead of *created*, giving a more precise rendering of the original verb, *plassō*. Kaiser, however, declares that the sense of it should be that "Adam was first *educated*, then Eve." He says,

> But how could Eve so easily have been duped unless she previously had been untaught? Adam had walked and talked with God in the Garden during that sixth "day," thus he had had the educational and spiritual advantage of being "formed first" (v. 13). The verb is *plasso*, "to form, mold, shape" (presumably in spiritual education) not, "created

first" (which in Greek is *ktizo*). Paul's argument, then, is based on the "orders of education," not the "orders of creation."[14]

This is why Eve could be so readily "tricked, deceived, and easily entrapped."[15] Kenneth Kantzer agrees that Eve was "uninstructed"; and "because Eve was uninformed, she was easily led astray."[16]

This, according to feminists, is why Satan focused his attention upon Eve. He did not "single her out," since Adam was at her side the whole time; but if he did concentrate more upon her, it was because he knew that she was inadequately taught and thus more vulnerable. It has nothing to do with a supposedly inherent female weakness of some kind.

2. Critique of the Feminist Explanation

The first impression anyone will receive from reading Genesis 3:1-6, especially in light of 1 Timothy 2:14, is that Satan was indeed singling out Eve for the first temptation, and that Eve knew the content of God's original prohibition concerning eating from the tree. Feminists' attempts to make the facts seem other than they are simply do not do justice to the relevant data and are completely unconvincing.

First, feminists say that Satan could not be singling out Eve because he uses the plural "you." Thus he must have been addressing both Eve *and* Adam. But this conclusion does not follow from the use of the plural "you," and it is inconsistent with the clear language of the text. The plural "you" appears first not as Satan's word of address to his audience, but in his quotation of God's prohibition (3:1), which referred both to Adam and to Eve.[17] They are discussing the prohibition, which is in the plural form. Every other plural in the exchange between Satan and Eve stems from this fact. The use of the plural is not indicative of who is present at the time, but of who is the *subject* of the conversation. Whatever is said *refers* to both, whether both are present or not.

The fact that the plural "you" is not indicative of who is being addressed is abundantly clear from the text itself, which says that the serpent specifically spoke "to the woman" (3:1 and 3:4). This simple statement is the reason why interpreters through the ages have concluded that Satan was singling out Eve for this first temptation. Though it is indeed determinative for whom the serpent is addressing, it is ignored by feminists who want to deny this fact.

Second, feminists say that verse 6 shows that Adam was *with* Eve when she was being tempted, and this shows Satan was not singling her out. But this assertion is based on several assumptions that are not supported by the text. For one thing, it assumes that the phrase "with her" refers to physical presence alongside Eve. It also assumes that this description of physical presence applies to the whole sequence of events and not just to the time of eating itself. This rests on the further assumption that no time elapsed between the actual temptation (3:1-5) and the eating (3:6b).

Such assumptions, however, are not warranted by the normal reading of the text. The indication from the first part of verse 6 is that some time elapsed between the actual temptation and the sin itself. It suggests that after Satan planted the seeds of doubt in Eve's mind in 3:1-5, he departed and left her to think it over. The language suggests not an instant decision but a process of contemplation: "When the woman saw that the tree was good for food, and that it was a delight to the eyes, and that the tree was desirable to make one wise, she took from its fruit and ate." The text itself gives no indication that Adam was with Eve while Satan was tempting her or while she was allowing his temptation to work its effect upon her mind.

Even if the words "with her" refer to physical presence, then the only time Adam is described as being "with her" in this process is when she gave him the fruit and he himself ate. It does not say he was "with her" during the temptation itself. In fact, this would seem to be ruled out by the fact that when Satan spoke, he spoke "to the woman."

An even more questionable assumption, however, is the idea that "with her" means physical presence alongside Eve. As noted above, Richard Kroeger says that "the Hebrew and Septuagint texts of Gen. 3:6 state that Adam was *standing at Eve's side*."[18] But such terminology is far from precise. The text simply says "with her," and neither the Hebrew nor the Greek term necessarily connotes "physically adjacent to her." It may mean simply that Adam was "with her" in the sense that he was her husband and companion and co-resident of the Garden. He was "with her" in the Garden, somewhere; and once she had picked the fruit and eaten it herself, she sought him out and enticed him to eat also. Such a meaning of "with" is quite common in the Old Testament.[19]

Thus we must conclude that the phrase "with her" in 3:6 by no means warrants the conclusion that Eve was not singled out by Satan and was not alone when the initial temptation occurred.

Third, feminists say that Eve was more vulnerable to Satan's deception because she was improperly taught concerning the prohibition to eat from the tree. But this idea must also be rejected as having absolutely no Biblical warrant. To say that Eve was "untaught" or "inadequately taught" or only indirectly taught (by Adam) and therefore "less informed" or even misinformed is at best speculation based on silence and at worst contrary to the known facts.

Walter Kaiser's view of 1 Timothy 2:13, for example, is wrong on two counts. First, his interpretation of *plassō* in this verse (as meaning "formed" in the sense of "educated") is completely without warrant. The word usually refers to the work of a potter making something of clay. "It means 'to form or fashion out of a soft mass,'" says Herbert Braun.[20] Most significantly, it is the word used in the Septuagint in Genesis 2:7-8 to describe how God formed Adam from the dust, which is the obvious background of Paul's statement in 1 Timothy 2:13. Its usual parallel is *poieō*, which means "to make, to do," and which is occasionally used in the New Testament to refer to the act of creation (Acts 14:15; 17:24, 26; Heb. 1:2). In the Greek world and in Philo, *plassō* did sometimes have the figurative meaning of "to fashion by education and training," but this meaning occurs "hardly in the LXX [Septuagint] and not at all in the NT," says Braun.[21] In view of these facts, Kaiser's attempt to interpret 1 Timothy 2:13 as referring to the order of education rather than creation appears to be more a matter of dogmatic bias than good exegesis.

Kaiser's second error is to leap from the premise that Adam was "formed first," i.e., taught first (as he misunderstands it), to the conclusion that Eve was not taught at all before the Fall. That he draws this conclusion is seen in his remark, cited above, that Eve could not have been so easily duped "unless she previously had been untaught." But anyone can readily see that this is a *non sequitur*: it simply does not follow that being taught second is the same as being untaught. Thus even if Kaiser's interpretation of *plassō* were correct, his conclusion would not be justified. The fact is that 1 Timothy 2:13 says nothing about Eve's being unformed (however this is understood); it actually affirms just the opposite, namely, that both she and Adam were formed. It says, "For Adam was formed first, *then Eve*" (NIV). So even if *plassō* could be taken to mean "educated" in this verse, it would be affirming the fact that *Eve was educated.*

Actually, one needs to read no further than Genesis 3:2-3 to see that this is the case. In Eve's first reply to Satan's temptation, she shows that she is quite familiar with the content of the prohibition first given in 2:16-17. She says, "From the fruit of the trees of the garden we may eat; but from the fruit of the tree which is in the middle of the garden, God has said, 'You shall not eat from it or touch it, lest you die.'" As Gleason Archer says, "In Genesis 3:3, Eve repeated the same teaching that God gave Adam in the previous chapter (Gen. 2:17); there is no reason to think she was less intelligent or less informed than Adam. Nor did that knowledge have any bearing on the decisions that were made: Adam was persuaded to accept the forbidden fruit the same as Eve was."[22]

The fact that Eve added the words "or touch it" cannot be taken as an indication that she was improperly or inadequately taught. Every essential aspect of the original prohibition is included in Eve's recitation of it; nothing is omitted. Nor can it be assumed that the words "or touch it" were added by Eve's teacher rather than by her own imagination. McClelland's suggestion that Adam "hedged the prohibition to Eve" by adding these words, and thus that "he improperly taught God's word to Eve,"[23] is an unfounded assumption with no basis in known fact. The very idea that the Creator would have permitted Adam to pass along to Eve an inaccurate version of this life-and-death teaching hardly merits consideration.

This raises the question of who actually taught the prohibition to Eve in the first place. As noted above, feminists such as Bilezikian have assumed that Adam was her teacher and have asserted on that basis that her "education" was inferior because it was only secondhand. I.e., Adam had an advantage because he was directly taught by God himself, but Eve received God's word only indirectly and thus was more vulnerable to Satan's attack.

This line of thinking must be challenged on two grounds. First, we must deny that a "secondhand" knowledge of God's word is inferior knowledge that leaves the hearer vulnerable to Satan's temptation. We must remember that this is the way that God has chosen to communicate his word to the vast majority of people upon earth. Very few individuals today would even claim to have been taught anything directly by God; we are all secondhandedly dependent on the word spoken through prophets and apostles, namely, the Bible. Evidently, God thinks this is an adequate method of educating us concerning his word and will.

Second, there is no good reason to assume that Eve was taught the prohibition by Adam rather than by God himself.[24] The text is actually silent on this point; to say that Adam taught her, much less that he taught her improperly, is pure speculation. At the same time, though it is not specifically affirmed that God was her teacher, there are indications in the text that this was more likely the case. It is significant that, after the sin, when "they heard the sound of the Lord God walking in the garden in the cool of the day," Adam and Eve recognized that sound and because of guilt "hid themselves from the presence of the Lord God among the trees of the garden" (3:8).

The significant thing is this: the fact that they recognized the sound means that this was not the first time God had come to be with them. The reasonable conclusion is that he had been in their presence before the Fall, teaching them his will in much more detail than is actually recorded in Genesis.[25] That he had continued to remind them both of the original prohibition is also a reasonable assumption. This would account for the change from the singular "you" in 2:16-17 to the plural "you" in 3:1, 3. When God repeated the prohibition for both of them, he would have used the plural. This may also be the origin of the words "or touch it" in 3:3. It is possible that God himself added them to his original instruction.

Though these points are not specifically stated in the text, they are reasonable inferences in view of the circumstances described in 3:8. On the other hand, there is nothing at all in the text to warrant the idea that Adam was Eve's teacher.

Thus we must reject the feminist argument that Satan concentrated on Eve in his original temptation because her understanding of God's prohibition was somehow inadequate or inferior, making her more vulnerable. It would seem that Eve *was* singled out, even though she was just as clearly informed in the matter as was Adam.

This leaves the question unanswered as yet: *why* did the tempter choose to concentrate his wiles upon Eve? One possibility is that he did so as a deliberate attack on the principle of male headship. He was tempting Eve to assume the role of leader. Raymond Ortlund says, "So Eve was not morally weaker than Adam. But Satan struck at Adam's headship. His words had the effect of inviting Eve to assume primary responsibility at the moment of temptation: '*You* decide, Eve. *You* lead the way. Wouldn't *you* rather be exercising headship?'"[26] Thus her specific sin would be that she "usurped Adam's headship and led the way into sin."[27]

But even if this were in effect the essence of the sin, we really have no way of knowing whether or not this was what Satan had in mind when he decided to tempt Eve. The Bible simply does not reveal his motive. It just records the fact that Eve *was* the first to be tempted and deceived, and the first to sin. Maybe this was part of a deliberate strategy of Satan, or maybe his choice was just random. We are not told. But the fact that we do not know for sure why Satan chose Eve does not negate the force of 1 Timothy 2:14, which says that Eve's being the one who was deceived does have *something* to do with women's being prohibited from teaching men and having authority over men in the New Testament church. This leads us to the next point.

B. Was Eve More
Responsible for the First Sin Than Adam?

The question concerning Eve's role in the first sin, especially as raised by 1 Timothy 2:14, can be asked in another way, namely, was Eve somehow more responsible for that sin than Adam? Or perhaps more to the point, was Eve responsible for that sin in some special way, i.e, in a way that brings special condemnation upon all women? Is this what Paul means when he says that "it was not Adam who was deceived, but the woman being quite deceived, fell into transgression"?

Feminists take great pains to deny that Eve, and womankind with her, bear some special responsibility for the first sin. In fact the usual feminist view is that since

Eve was disadvantaged by her inferior knowledge, she was actually *less* responsible. This is how the word "deceived" is understood in 1 Timothy 2:14. I.e., Eve was deceived, thus she did not really know that she was sinning. Adam, on the other hand, was *not* deceived; he was just an out-and-out willful sinner who thus bears the greater responsibility for the transgression. Bilezikian says,

> For this reason, the Bible lays the blame for the fall at the feet of Adam. He sinned knowingly. He was aware of the meaning of his defiant gesture and yet participated in rebellion against God. The less-experienced Eve is said only to have been "deceived." This means that she did not sin willfully. She was fooled into making a fateful error of judgment.
>
> . . . By virtue of the fact that Eve was less informed than Adam regarding the forbidden tree, her sin is described as one of bad judgment. She was deceived. Because he had been the original recipient of God's prohibition, Adam's participation in the revolt carried greater significance.[28]

Austin Stouffer agrees that Paul's point in 1 Timothy 2:14 "is not that Eve's sin was greater than Adam's. In fact, Adam's was worse because he sinned with his eyes wide open, without being deceived! Eve's fault, on the contrary, was less serious because she was deceived and only acted in ignorance."[29]

As noted above, feminists often declare that Adam was standing at Eve's side when the original temptation occurred, but he wimpishly failed to speak up. He did not try to defend God against Satan's lies, nor did he try to dissuade Eve from eating the fruit. This in itself means that he is more guilty of the sin than Eve. He "made no attempt to correct the serpent's twisting and warping of God's words. Adam could well be said to have been more culpable."[30]

These attempts by feminists to ameliorate Eve's responsibility for the first sin are not a fair reading of the Biblical data. She was fully responsible for her part in the sin, just as Adam was fully responsible for his part. As we have already seen, there is no reason to think that she was any less informed than Adam. Thus even if Adam had been standing by her side during the temptation (which is unfounded speculation), Eve was just as prepared to resist the serpent as Adam was.

But does not Paul say that Eve was deceived, and Adam was not? Yes, but feminists tend to draw conclusions from this that are just the opposite of what Paul intended. They imply that since Eve was *only* deceived, she can be *excused* for what she did. But such an idea does not fit Paul's argument at all. He is commenting on why women are not allowed to teach men and have authority over men in the church. To say that this is the case because Eve was deceived and somehow *less* blameworthy involves a *non sequitur* of the first order. The argument makes sense only if her being deceived causes her to bear a *greater* responsibility than Adam.

What is the nature of this greater responsibility? It does not mean that Eve bears the greater overall blame for the sin. It means rather that with regard to this special kind of responsibility, i.e., responsibility for being *deceived*, Eve is more blameworthy than Adam. Thus her blame is two-fold. She is to blame not only for the transgression itself, but also for allowing herself to be deceived into committing it.

According to the Biblical use of the term, being *deceived* into sinning does not ameliorate blame nor excuse one from the responsibility for the transgression. Any sin resulting from being deceived is still considered to be willful disobedience for which one is responsible and blameworthy. Even though the act of deception in itself is primarily a sin of the deceiver rather than the one deceived, there is still a measure of blame attached to being deceived.[31] Therefore to say that Eve was deceived into sinning makes her no less responsible than if she had sinned without being deceived; in fact, she is now responsible not only for the sin but also for being deceived.

Thus regarding whether Eve is more responsible for the first sin as such, the answer seems to be no. In fact, as we shall see shortly, there is a sense in which the opposite seems to be the case. I.e., it would appear that God holds Adam more responsible than Eve. The really significant point, however, is that (according to 1 Timothy 2:14) it is not the transgression itself but the *deception* that is being held against Eve. The fact that Eve was deceived by the Devil is in some way related to the fact that women are not permitted to teach men and have authority over men in the church. We simply cannot deny this connection. The problem, though, is to *explain* it. Exactly what is the connection? There are two main possibilities.

The first possibility is that there is something inherent in women's nature that somehow makes them more vulnerable to deception concerning spiritual matters and therefore less qualified to teach men and have authority over men in the context of the church. This would be consistent with Peter's description of woman as the "weaker vessel" (1 Peter 3:7). Peter does not explain the nature of this "weakness," nor does he suggest that it constitutes some kind of flaw or fault in women. Whatever it is, it would be consistent with the role for which God created woman in the first place. That is to say, the characteristics that make a woman more strongly suited for her intended role in the family and church make her weaker with reference to what is required for duties of headship and leadership. Such characteristics probably have to do more with her affective than her intellectual nature.

Whatever this "weaker" nature may be, it is possible if not likely that this is what Paul has in mind as underlying the fact that Eve was deceived by Satan whereas Adam was not, and that this is the very same thing that disqualifies women from teaching men and having authority over men. If this is so, then the reason for this disqualification is not Eve's sin at all. Neither is the disqualification some kind of penalty, either for her sin or for allowing herself to be deceived. It is simply some inherent, created female characteristic that manifests itself in susceptibility to this kind of deception.

The main Biblical objection to this explanation is that such vulnerability to deception would seem to make women unfit to teach anyone, even children and other women, contrary to Paul's own praise of Lois and Eunice in 2 Timothy 1:5 (cf. 3:15) and his instructions in Titus 2:4. But such a contradiction would not be the case if the susceptibility to deception is itself in some way related to gender roles. That is, it may be that women are especially vulnerable to deception concerning what their intended role is supposed to be, or that they are especially open to deception of all kinds when they wrongfully project themselves into leadership roles. This calls to mind Ortlund's suggestion that Eve's own sin was her attempt to assume headship in the place of Adam. Thus in 1 Timothy 2:12-14 Paul would be warning us that when women try to teach or exercise authority over men, their own nature becomes distorted and defenseless against Satanic deceit. This does not happen, though, when women are teaching other women, especially when they are teaching them to be faithful to their God-intended roles (see Titus 2:4-5).

A second possible explanation of the connection between 1 Timothy 2:12 and 2:14 is that Eve's responsibility for being deceived into sin entails this prohibition as a penalty for all her daughters. Thus the reason for the disqualification of women from teaching and having authority over men is Eve's historical act of participating in the first sin in a particular way, not some inherent predisposition toward anything as such. In this case the prohibition in 2:12 would seem to have the character of a penalty, indeed, a gender-specific penalty similar to the multiplied pain in childbirth (Gen. 3:16) alluded to in 2:15.

This second possibility is not in itself objectionable, since gender-specific penalties are indeed applied to both males in general and females in general as the result of Adam's and Eve's respective roles in the Fall (Gen. 3:16-19). There is no reason why the Holy Spirit could not be disclosing another such penalty through Paul in 1 Timothy 2:14. The main problem with this explanation, though, is that it seems to put 2:14 in conflict with 2:13, whereas the first explanation leaves these verses in perfect agreement with one another. That is, 2:13 gives as the primary reason for the prohibition the fact that Adam was first created, then Eve. In other words, the prohibition is grounded in creation, not in some aspect of the Fall. To say that what is true because of creation is also a part of the penalty for the Fall seems inconsistent. But if the prohibition is related to some inherent female characteristic which itself is related to vulnerability to deception, as the first explanation suggests, then 2:14 is also basing the prohibition on human nature as created, and not on the Fall as such.

In the final analysis we may acknowledge that the exact connection between 1 Timothy 2:12 and 2:14 is not completely clear. Ortlund simply notes that "Paul in 1 Timothy 2:14 cites the woman's deception as warrant for male headship to be translated from the home into the church." Then he makes this insightful comment: "I am not interpreting the logic of the apostle in his making this connection, which logic I am not satisfied that I clearly understand. I merely observe the fact that Paul makes the connection, confident that his logic in doing so was compelling."[32] In other words, we do not have to understand the logic to get the point, if we believe that Paul was inspired by the Holy Spirit when he made the connection between Eve's role in the Fall and the prohibition concerning women teaching and having authority over men. If we can accept the former, then we should accept the latter also.

C. Adam's Responsibility and Male Headship

One other point must be noted concerning the sin itself, namely, the connection between Adam's responsibility for that sin and the fact of the male headship that was already established in Genesis 2. Both the Genesis context and Biblical teaching as a whole seem to point to the fact that

Adam the male bears a greater responsibility for the first sin than Eve. This is exactly what we would expect if Adam was already the appointed head of that two-member family.

Following the sin, when God came to confront his human creatures in their guilt, he specifically addressed the male: "Then the Lord God called to the man, and said to him, 'Where are you?'" (3:9). Why does God first of all specifically call Adam into account for the sin? Because, as Foh says "he is the appointed head."[33] As the head of the human family he had the greater initial responsibility for righteousness and thus received the greater blame for the sin. As Ortlund asks, "Why doesn't God summon both Adam and Eve to account together? Because, as the God-appointed head, Adam bore the primary responsibility to lead their partnership in a God-glorifying direction." Thus we can recognize almost intuitively "that Adam bears the final responsibility for what happened."[34]

The New Testament certainly confirms this understanding. In its theological teaching concerning this event, Adam is the one who is singled out and held responsible for the racial consequences of the Fall. Romans 5:12 says that "through one man sin entered into the world, and death through sin." This "one man" is specifically identified in 5:14 as Adam. Further devastating consequences of this one man's one sin are enumerated in 5:15-19; and in 1 Corinthians 15:21-22 Paul again says the primary responsibility for the sin and its results belong to the first man: "In Adam all die."

Why is such cosmic responsibility laid at the feet of Adam? McClelland's by-now familiar feminist answer to this question sounds quite shallow and trivial, and almost comic, in view of the gravity of the New Testament teaching: "Rather than receiving blame for not asserting his supposed 'headship' and, with it, ultimate authority/responsibility for what happens in his 'family,' it is *just as likely* he is responsible because he improperly taught God's word to Eve."[35] On the contrary, the only thing that can explain the clear teaching concerning Adam's greater responsibility is his immediate headship over Eve and his ultimate and representative headship over the entire human race.

II. THE CURSE

After the first sin God pronounced what is usually called a curse, first upon the serpent (Gen. 3:14-15), then upon Eve (3:16), then finally upon Adam (3:17-19). Of specific interest is the pronouncement concerning Eve: "I will greatly multiply your pain in childbirth, in pain you shall bring forth children; yet your desire shall be for your husband, and he shall rule over you."

A. The Feminist
Understanding of the Curse on the Woman

How do feminists explain God's curse on Eve? As far as its content is concerned, they focus on the last two lines, which refer to desiring and ruling. The more important of these is the one that says, "He shall rule over you." What does this mean? Within feminism the agreement is virtually unanimous that this is the point in human history where hierarchicalism is first introduced into the human race. Up to this time God's original egalitarian intention had prevailed; but now, as a result of the sin, male domination and female submission begin to take root in human hearts. The role equality of Genesis 1 and 2 is replaced by a relationship of headship and subordination.

Feminist affirmations of this understanding are abundant. Mary Hayter says, "In Genesis 3 *female subordination is shown to be . . . a result of sin*. It is Genesis 2, not 3.16, which represents the Creator's intention."[36] DeJong and Wilson say, "The egalitarian structure ordained by creation was changed into a hierarchical structure because of man's sin."[37] "The Bible teaches that the rulership of

Adam over Eve resulted from the Fall and was therefore not a part of the original created order," says a recent feminist doctrinal statement.[38] Van Leeuwen interprets it as man's extension of his original co-dominion over the earth (Gen. 1:26-28) to a sinful dominion over the woman.[39]

How do feminists understand this beginning of male domination to be related to the preceding element of the curse, "Yet your desire shall be for your husband"? There is no unanimity on this point. Some see the desire to be a good and noble longing of the woman's heart. As Bilezikian explains it, "The woman will yearn for the 'one flesh' union that defined the family prior to the fall (2:24). Her desire will be for her husband, so as to perpetuate the intimacy that had characterized their relationship in paradise lost." But her nostalgia for the original mutuality will not be reciprocated by the man. Instead, he will take advantage of this desire and begin to dominate her.[40] Alvera Mickelsen says, "The oneness and equality between Adam and Eve was damaged. Instead of the previous harmony, the male would dominate the female, even though she still desired the old intimacy and harmony."[41]

Other feminists see the woman's desire in Genesis 3:16 as something evil. Some understand it as a desire to rule over the male. Accepting the parallel with Genesis 4:7 as the best clue to its meaning, Mary Evans says that "Genesis 3:16 can be interpreted as indicating that the woman will have a desire to possess or control her husband, but in fact, he will rule over her."[42] Spencer accepts this as a possibility, but suggests that it can also be taken in just the opposite sense, namely, as a perverse desire to be ruled over by her husband. "She would want to be dominated by her husband and he would submit to this desire."[43]

The nature of this desire, whether it be something good or evil, is not the crucial point, since either way the man ends up ruling over the woman. This is the aspect of the curse all feminists agree upon as the main source of all hierarchical evils.

Having briefly explained the feminists' understanding of the *content* of the curse, we now turn to their view of its *character*. The issue here is whether the "curse" upon the woman is something that God is imposing on the sexes as a norm, or whether he is simply announcing what the consequences of the first sin will be. At stake is whether God intends "He shall rule over you" to be *normative* as something women are obligated to endure by divine decree. Some feminists do not hesitate to think of it as such. Spencer, for example, freely calls it a "punishment" and a "curse of God." She speaks of "the curses that the woman has to endure," but only until set free by the work of Christ.[44] Most feminists, however, strongly disagree with the idea that Genesis 3:16 is some kind of new norm instituted by God. They declare that it is in no sense prescriptive of what *must* be the case, but rather is merely descriptive or predictive of what *will* be the case. God is merely informing Eve of the inevitable consequences of her sin, not meting out divine punishment upon her. It is a matter of cause and effect. This perverted man/woman relationship is just the natural result of sin.

A recent statement on Biblical equality says it this way: "Genesis 3:16 is a prediction of the effects of the Fall rather than a prescription of God's ideal order."[45] Ronald Heine says, "The words of the curses are not commands given to men and women to be carried out religiously against one another, but . . . are descriptive statements indicating the nature of life in a fallen world."[46] Scanzoni and Hardesty say, "God speaks not in wrath but in gentle reproof. God speaks of what *will* be, not what *should* be; the words are *descriptive*, not *prescriptive*. God does not institute or condone role stereotypes for the sexes but points to the sinful ways in which men and women would be limited by cultural constructions."[47] Mary Evans agrees that the conditions described in 3:14-19 "are not really punishments" but "the inevitable consequences of Man's sin."[48]

Most feminists believe that it is important to understand the curse in this way. They fear that if 3:16 is taken to be an actual curse imposed by God, then male domination will be considered as the normative and expected relationship. Thus men will use this as an excuse to dominate, and women will feel compelled to submit in order to be in conformity with "God's will."

Whatever their minor differences regarding the content and the character of the curse, feminists are united with regard to its significance. In fact, Genesis 3:16 may well be the most important verse in the Bible for them, next to Galatians 3:28 and possibly Genesis 1:27. It is seen as the initial turning point in history for male/female relationships. Here is where the original egalitarian order was replaced by hierarchicalism. Prior to this point there were no role distinctions; in Genesis 1 and 2 everything was egalitarian. According to Ward Gasque, "It is only the result of the Fall (Genesis 3:16ff) that the woman becomes subordinate to man. There is not even a hint in the narrative of Genesis that woman is in any way subordinate to man prior to the Fall."[49] *All* roles of headship and submission are the result of the Fall and its consequent curse.

B. A Non-Feminist View of the Curse

Regarding Genesis 3:16, the main difference between feminists and non-feminists is that the former see it as introducing hierarchicalism for the very first time, whereas the latter see it as corrupting the hierarchical relationship that already existed, turning male headship into male domination. The fact is that Genesis 3:16 is compatible with either view. Thus how can we decide which is correct?

1. The Pivotal Nature of Genesis 2

Since Genesis 3:16 can go either way, in itself it really decides nothing. The fact is that the meaning of Genesis 3 is actually determined by the meaning of Genesis 2. How one interprets the former is already decided by the meaning given to the latter.

This means that Genesis 1 and 2 continue to be crucial and pivotal for our understanding of gender roles. If these chapters are seen as teaching egalitarianism, as feminists believe, then 3:16 will necessarily be taken as the introduction of hierarchicalism. But if Genesis 2 itself has already established hierarchicalism, then chapter 3 must necessarily be regarded as merely a corruption of it.

As the previous chapter of this book has already shown, Genesis 2 *does* teach that God created the male and the female to exist in a hierarchical relationship. Even before sin and its curse entered the picture, headship and submission existed as God's design for his human creatures. This is indicated by the data of Genesis 2 itself, and confirmed by New Testament commentary. Thus we may conclude, even before looking at the details of Genesis 3:16, that it will necessarily be referring to some sort of corruption of that original hierarchical relationship and not to the beginning of it. This can hardly be called "grasping at preconceptions," as McClelland claims,[50] since it is a conclusion necessitated by the teaching of Genesis 2.

2. The Curse as the Corruption of Created Headship

The content of the curse in 3:16, as well as the context of the entire chapter, confirms this understanding of it. First, we may say again that the nature of the desire (in "your desire shall be for your husband") is not a crucial issue. The most common interpretation, compatible with both feminist and non-feminist approaches, is that the woman's desire is a desire to rule or control her husband. As non-feminists understand it this would be something like a reversal of the intended roles. Whereas God intended woman to be submissive, sin causes her to desire to dominate.

Thus the desire would be a negative and undesirable

thing, which we would expect since it is the consequence of sin. Its negative character is also suggested by a parallel use of the language in Genesis 4:7, where God says to Cain, "Sin is crouching at the door; and its desire is for you, but you must master it." This verse seems to say that sin desires to overcome and control Cain, and it uses the same word for *desire* as 3:16. Thus this part of the woman's curse would be her desire to control her husband, which would turn the original created order upside down. As Kassian says, "The 'desire' of the woman would work against the leadership of the husband, against God's original intent in marriage. Her desire would not contribute to his rule in any way."[51]

Second and more important is the nature of the rule in the last part of 3:16, "He shall rule over you." Since this rule of the man over the woman is a part of the curse itself, it would not be a reference to the original created order of headship and submission,[52] but to a corruption of it. Because of sin the man tends to abuse his leadership role, and loving headship is turned into harsh, domineering rule.

The term for "rule" in 3:16 is *māshal*, which often refers to a conquering and dominating kind of rule. That this is its probable meaning here is made all the more likely by the use of the same word in Genesis 4:7 again, where Cain is told that he must master or conquer sin. This and other considerations, says Clark, "would lead us to think that the curse is referring to a kind of rule that is dominative."[53] As Kassian sums it up, "The curse on woman is that she would desire to conquer/devour/have her husband in the same way sin desired to have Cain. At the same time, the husband would attempt to rule/have dominion/reign over his wife in the same way Cain was to rule over sin." Thus "after the Fall, women would rebel against their designated role and . . . men would abuse their role of leadership."[54]

This understanding of the male rule as a corruption of the already-existing headship is consistent with the other elements of the curse, which are also corruptions or painful distortions of already-existing conditions.[55] The parallel with the curses regarding childbirth (3:16) and work (3:17-19) is especially clear. In these, "a function that is good and that is part of God's plan for the human race even before the Fall becomes painful or at least burdensome through the Fall."[56] In keeping with the nature of these other curses, then, we can say with Hurley that "God's words to the woman concerning her relation to her husband are not pointing to the establishment of a new marital hierarchy, but to the painful distortion of an already existing hierarchical relationship."[57]

Thus we can agree with the feminist sentiment that men's "domination and abuse" of women began with the Fall,[58] but this does not mean that male headship as such began there.

A significant point is the fact that the New Testament never refers to male headship as such in a negative way, and it never appeals to the curse in Genesis 3:16 as the origin of such headship.[59] When prescribing the roles of headship and submission, the Apostle Paul never builds his case on the curse; the only Old Testament basis to which he appeals is the pre-Fall creation order, and he appeals to it as normative.[60] As we saw in the previous section, even the reference to Eve's deception and sin in 1 Timothy 2:14 is best understood as referring to some aspect of the nature of woman as created.

The curse, then, is a corruption of created headship and results in a distortion of the whole male-female relationship. As Kassian says, it brought confrontation instead of complementarity, and sowed the seeds of both male chauvinism and women's liberation.[61]

3. The Curse Is a True Curse

Feminists and non-feminists in general agree that Genesis 3:16 has a negative impact on male-female relationships. Most feminists, however, say that this is merely a description of the negative *results* of sin, and not really a curse. We must sharply disagree with this idea. The elements of Genesis 3:16 are not just a prediction of the consequences that would flow from sin, but are indeed a penalty imposed by God upon the woman, i.e., a true curse.

If the desiring and the ruling are descriptions and not penalties, we would expect the other aspects of the total curse to be merely descriptive also. But this is obviously not the case. No other aspect of the curse is of this nature; each is a negative state brought about by the decision and act of God. That man must fight the ground for his daily bread is God's specific curse upon the man: "Cursed is the ground because of you" (3:17). Increased pain in childbirth is part of the curse upon the woman: "I will greatly multiply your pain in childbirth" (3:16). The fact that the word "cursed" is not used here is irrelevant; what is significant is that God says that he specifically will cause this to happen. (It is difficult to see how increased pain in childbirth could be a *natural consequence* of the first sin anyway.) Bodily death likewise is a penal curse upon both sexes: "For you are dust, and to dust you shall return" (3:19).[62] When Paul describes what Adam's sin brought into the world, including death, he calls it not just a consequence but a *condemnation* (Rom. 5:16, 18).

Thus we cannot escape the fact that the curse upon the woman is a true curse. "Your desire shall be for your husband, and he shall rule over you" is the penalty imposed upon Eve, as the representative of womankind, because of her part in the first sin.

Does this mean, then, that the aberrant male dominance of Genesis 3:16 is now God's intended norm for male-female relationships, something that must simply be suffered by women as a perpetual penance for Eve's sin? In other words, does Genesis 3:16 have the normative force of a moral law? The answer is no. This conclusion, so feared by feminists, does not follow from the understanding that 3:16 is a true curse. The norm for male-female relationships is still that which was established in Genesis 2, namely, hierarchical headship and submission, of which the domineering male rule in 3:16 is a corruption. But even though this corruption occurs as a God-imposed penalty, it does not thereby become a new norm. In other words, to deny that 3:16 is descriptive does not leave just one other choice, i.e., that it is prescriptive in the sense of a moral standard.

The point is that Genesis 3:16 is a *curse*, which means that it is imposed as a judicial punishment and not as a moral norm. While both punishments and moral norms may be thought of as prescriptive, since they are both prescribed by God, they are not prescriptive in the same sense. Genesis 3:16, like every other penalty attached to sin, is indeed imposed upon sinners—*unless and until it is nullified in principle by the work of Christ and then set aside in the life of the individual as a part of his or her experienced fruit of redemption.* In other words it is not a norm that we are obligated to live by, but rather a penalty that must be experienced by those outside of God's redeeming grace. This will be explained further in the next section.

III. THE RESTORATION

The feminist view of Biblical history can be summed up in three points: Genesis 1 and 2 establish egalitarianism as the normative creation order; Genesis 3 introduces hierarchicalism as an alien intruder in human relationships; Jesus Christ restores the original egalitarian order in a "new creation," of which the church is supposed to be the model. We discussed the first of these points in the previous chapter, and we have discussed the second in the first two sections of this chapter. The remainder of this volume, beginning with this section, is a discussion of the third point, thus completing the triad of creation, Fall, and restoration.

A. Feminism and the New Creation

Feminists tend to describe the very purpose of the incarnation of Jesus in terms of reversing the curse and restoring the original order of things in a "new creation." This general theme of the new creation plays a crucial and foundational role in their construction of an egalitarian theology. Heine says, "The question of the role of women in the church is closely related to the three great theological themes of *creation, fall,* and the *new creation in Christ.*"[63] Mollenkott says flatly that "biblical feminism is grounded in the doctrine of the new creation in Christ Jesus."[64] Gretchen Hull takes 2 Corinthians 5:14-21 as the "theme passage" for feminism, especially the idea that "if anyone is in Christ, he is a new creation" (v. 17, NIV).[65] Whenever someone confronts her with some non-feminist interpretation, she says, her first question is "How does that fit with 2 Corinthians 5:17?"[66]

Establishing the new creation involves eliminating the effects of the Fall, which was the specific purpose of the work of Christ. In 1974 Scanzoni and Hardesty wrote, "The redeeming power of Christ makes it possible to go back to the ideals of Paradise, for he came to make the crooked straight. That straightening includes not only our relationship with God but also our twisted, out-of-joint relationships with other people, including male-female relationships."[67] "Christ's redemptive work has a healing effect on the ramifications of the Fall in all areas of our lives," say DeJong and Wilson.[68]

While this includes the eradication of all the effects of sin, feminism's particular focus is on the way Christ reversed the curse of Genesis 3:16 and restored egalitarianism. As DeJong and Wilson continue their thought, "Since one of the consequences of Adam's sin was the development of a dominant-submissive relationship that was foreign to the character of male-female relationships in Creation, the redemptive work of Christ will affect the nature of those relationships. Christ's work will have a restorative or corrective influence in this area."[69] The very title of Spencer's book, *Beyond the Curse*, reflects this emphasis. The Bible shows very clearly, says Van Leeuwen, "that it was Christ's intention, as part of his healing and saving work, to reverse the consequences of Genesis 3:16."[70]

Feminists understand this to mean that Christ overcame all hierarchicalism and restored the complete equality, mutuality, and oneness of the original creation. Aaseng says that Jesus came "to set right all those things that sin has upset, to bring about the completeness God had in mind in creation. And among the benefits he brings is a restoration of the equality of the sexes."[71] Jesus "treated women as equals, looking beyond the Fall and recalling God's original intentions," says Daniel. Thus "in the order of redemption men are called back to the original design of creation," which is the equality of the sexes. "In Christ human distinctions, whatever their basis, are overcome."[72] Christ restores the sex-blind mutuality of Genesis 2, says Hull.[73]

Feminists agree that the one New Testament passage which brings all these ideas together—reversing the curse, restoring the original creation order, establishing the new creation—is Galatians 3:28: "There is neither Jew nor Greek, there is neither slave nor free man, there is neither male nor female; for you are all one in Christ Jesus." Their unanimous testimony is that this verse teaches that Christ eliminated the hierarchicalism of Genesis 3:16 and restored the egalitarianism of Genesis 2. "The egalitarian apologist argues," says Gasque, "that in Christ there is a new creation; the results of the Fall are reversed. Paul makes this very clear in Galatians 3:28." This verse shows that "in the new creation, the church, there is the beginning of the new created order: man and woman are one. They are equal."[74] DeJong and Wilson agree that "the passage most frequently quoted as biblical evidence of the restorative impact of Christ's redemptive work on the male-female relationship is Galatians 3:26-28."[75] "Taken as a point of departure," says McClelland, "Galatians 3:28 stands as an affirmation of the restored oneness of the created order through the work of Christ."[76]

This statement by McClelland succinctly sums up what most feminists believe about the new creation in Christ. A few, however, take a different approach. They say that Jesus did not merely restore the original order of things, but rather *replaced* it with a truly *new* creation order. This allows for the possibility that the first order may have been hierarchical; but it does not matter, since that one has been done away. Don Williams accepts this view of Galatians 3:28: "Here is Paul's radical step beyond the old order. Redemption does not merely restore God's intention in creation. Redemption brings into being a whole new world, a whole new order."[77] This is also Richard Longenecker's basic point. He acknowledges that Genesis 2 may include subordination ideas, but says that redemption is a new order which replaces creation and curse alike. In the order of redemption, all subordination is replaced by freedom, mutuality, and equality.[78]

B. Critique of the Feminist Concept of Restoration

Having briefly explained the feminist concept of restoration through Christ, we now turn our attention to evaluating it. The primary issue is this: exactly how is the curse of Genesis 3:16 affected by the work of Christ? As we saw in the last section, this curse is indeed a true curse, a judicial penalty imposed by God and not just a description of inevitable results of sin. What was God's intention in imposing such a curse? What was his intention regarding this particular curse? Was it intended to last forever? or just until the second coming of Christ? or his first coming? What is its present status, in view of Christ's atonement for sin?

1. Christ and the Curse

There is no disputing the fact that in his propitiatory death Jesus Christ paid the full penalty for human sin. He did indeed "reverse the curse" when he took upon himself every aspect of it and became a curse for us (Gal. 3:13). This was necessary in order to restore his purposes for his creatures and thereby establish the "new creation." The idea of a new creation is a clear and consistent theme of Scripture, as found in Romans 8:18-23; 2 Corinthians 5:17; Galatians 6:15; Ephesians 2:10; 4:24; Colossians 3:10; and 2 Peter 3:13.[79] We accept the framework of creation, Fall, and new creation as a proper understanding of human history.

While the new creation is not just a repetition of Eden, neither does it involve the abolition of the original creation order, especially with respect to male-female relationships. It is not a replacement but a renewal. Those who say that the new creation sets aside not just the curse but the original creation order itself are wrong. If this view were true, then it would be illegitimate for Paul *ever* to appeal to the original creation as the basis for normative conduct in the church, as he does in 1 Corinthians 11:2ff. and 1 Timothy 2:11-14.

Exactly how has Jesus Christ reversed the curse upon sin? He did it specifically through his substitutionary atonement on the cross. He is called "the propitiation for our sins" (1 John 2:2; 4:10), which means that all the wrath due unto us because of our sins was poured out upon him instead. This happened when God "made Him who knew no sin to be sin on our behalf" (2 Cor. 5:21), when "He Himself bore our sins in His body on the cross" (1 Peter 2:24). The reversal of the curse was *not* accomplished by the teaching and example of Christ, however important these are to us for other reasons. It is a serious error to focus on the teaching and example of Jesus as having a causal relation to the new creation, especially with regard to the role of women. Whatever he did toward restoring proper male-female relationships by this means was only incidental to his primary purpose of bearing all the wrath and curses and penalties due unto sin as he hung upon the cross.

Though it is no doubt proper to speak of Christ's work as reversing the curse, and to assume that this includes the curses of Genesis 3, there is actually no specific New Testament reference to Genesis 3:16 in relation to the atonement. To say that Jesus has indeed abolished this curse is really just an inference, though I believe it is a valid one.

2. When Is the Curse Lifted?

Assuming that Christ's atoning work does reverse the curse of Genesis 3:16, we must now ask about the actual time when the curse is lifted from womankind. As theologians have rightly noted, there is a difference between the *accomplishment* of redemption by the historical deeds of Jesus, and the *application* of that redemption to specific historical individuals and circumstances. Thus even though all the elements of the curse are reversed in principle upon the cross, they are not all actually lifted at that precise moment.

In fact, it is fair to say that no element of the curse was actually lifted at the moment of the cross, or at any other time during the earthly sojourn of the Redeemer. There are two main possibilities here, two points of time when the actual application of redemption begins to occur or the elements of the curse begin to be lifted. These are (1) from the very beginning of sin itself, or (2) at the very end of this age with the inauguration of the new heavens and new earth.[80]

Some of the main aspects of the curse will not be removed until the end. This applies especially to those involving the physical universe, including physical death itself (Rom. 8:18-23). Though the basis for their removal has already been accomplished by Christ, the removal itself will not take place until he comes again.

On the other hand, we must realize that other elements of the curse began to be lifted from the shoulders of the repentant from the very beginning. For example, the burden of guilt and condemnation involving separation from God and being sentenced to eternal hell was removed from the very beginning from anyone who depended upon the grace of God. This means that real, true forgiveness of sins (the gift of justification) was being offered and applied to sinners even before the basis for that forgiveness became a historical reality on Calvary. Because of his infallible foreknowledge and the sovereignty of his purposive will (Acts 2:23), God knew that the atonement would be a certainty long before it happened. Indeed, in this sense the Lamb of God was slain from the very foundation of the world (1 Peter 1:20; Rev. 13:8). Thus God was free to begin distributing the benefits of the cross from the time when sin began. A common idea is that the sins of Old Testament saints were "rolled forward" and not actually forgiven until Christ came. This is simply not true. The New Testament's main paradigm of justification (equivalent to forgiveness) is Abraham (Rom. 4; Gal. 3). He and every other Old Testament believer were fully forgiven; the curse of eternal death was already lifted from them.

Thus it is an error to think that the actual possession and enjoyment of restoration, at least in some aspects, must await the second coming or even the incarnation of Christ. Indeed it is fair to say that whatever elements of the new creation do not have to await the second coming were already being bestowed from the beginning (with the exception of the gift of the Spirit). Any element of the curse that does not have to wait until the end for its removal was already being lifted from the beginning in anticipation of the sure work of Christ.

This does not mean that all such penalties and curses were being lifted from everyone universally from the beginning. The judicial or penal results of sin can be dealt with only on an individual basis. With regard to any such penalty, the individual sinner has only two choices: he can continue to defy God and thus continue to suffer sin's curses, or he can acknowledge his sin and turn to God for deliverance from its curses. Those in the former category remain under all the curses of sin for all time. Those in the latter category are delivered from all the curses of sin from the beginning, either in actual experience or in the hope of the second coming of Christ. Thus from the very beginning of post-Edenic times, those who have trusted in the gracious promises of God have been free from the curses of Genesis 3 in one way or the other, either in actuality or in anticipation. Even with regard to those curses whose complete reversal must await the second coming, no believer is under any obligation to simply surrender meekly to them. Since Christ has paid every penalty for sin, the believer is entitled to seek relief from *all* the curses insofar as it is possible in this not-yet-renewed world, and has been so entitled from the beginning.

How does this relate to the specific curses of Genesis 3:14-19? First of all, it does not apply to the curse upon Satan at all, since Christ did not die for the sins of the Devil and his angels. Second, the curse of physical death will not be lifted until the general resurrection, as already noted. Third, the curses concerning increased pain in child-birth and work as toil are both physical in nature and thus probably will not be totally lifted until the new heavens and new earth come into existence. This does not mean, however, that we must accept them passively, any more than we must accept death passively. The atonement of Christ gives us the warrant to fight against these penal effects of sin in whatever ways we can. Unbelievers may take it upon themselves to do the same, but without this warrant.

This leaves the fourth consideration, the curse upon the woman in Genesis 3:16, especially "He shall rule over you." When is this curse to be lifted? For those who never turn to the grace of God, there is no reason to demand or to expect that it should ever be lifted. This is why most women in the world are still the victims of sinful male domination. But what about those who seek the atoning grace of God made possible by Jesus Christ? When is the curse of male domination lifted for them? Since it is a corruption of interpersonal relationships and not a corruption of some physical aspect of the world, there is no reason to think that its removal must await the new heavens and new earth. But neither is there any reason to think that its removal had to await the first coming of Christ. As a corruption of proper male-female relationships, it is similar to the corruption of the relationship between God and human beings. And just as the relationship between God and sinful humanity could be healed and restored from the beginning through the proleptic application of the benefits of the atonement, so also could this penally-corrupted relationship between males and females be set right from the beginning on the same basis.

Thus feminists are right in emphasizing that Jesus Christ has reversed the curse of Genesis 3:16, but they are wrong in thinking that God's people did not or could not actually experience this reversal until the first coming of Christ.

3. Galatians 3:28 and the Reversal of the Curse

The feminist error of thinking that the curse of Genesis 3:16 could not be actually lifted until Jesus came has led to a false understanding of Galatians 3:28. As we have seen, feminists generally see this verse as the ultimate summation of the doctrines of the reversing of the curse and the restoring of the creation order, especially with regard to male-female relationships: "There is neither male nor female; for you are all one in Christ Jesus." But in spite of the feminists' nearly universal tendency to vigorously affirm this connection, exegetically speaking it is no more than an assumption. The fact is that there is no good reason to connect Galatians 3:28 with the reversing of the curse in Genesis 3:16.[81]

As the context of Galatians 3:28 clearly shows, the contrast to which that passage refers is not between the old creation and the new creation, but between existence "in Christ Jesus" and existence under the law, especially the Law of Moses. In this text, the problem that Christ resolves arises not from Genesis 3:16 but from the introduction of the Law (see verses 17ff.). The problem is not with the family of Adam, but the family of Abraham. The unity to which Galatians 3:28 refers is the unity of Abraham's family, not Adam's family (see verses 8, 14).

The three pairs in Galatians 3:28 refer to distinctions that have no common root in the creation order, nor is it possible to trace them to the Fall and the curse of Genesis 3 without reading something into the text that is not there. Most obviously, the Jew-Greek distinction owes its origin to neither. All three pairs do appear in the Law of Moses, however, in a way that puts all three in the same contextually meaningful contrast with existence "in Christ Jesus." This will be explained further in a later chapter.

The main point here is that feminists are very far off base when they try to ground their egalitarian theology on the doctrine of the new creation in Christ, especially in relation to Galatians 3:28. Once the illusion is dispelled that Galatians 3:28 is referring to the replacement of creation-under-the-curse with new-creation-in-Christ-Jesus, there is not one textual basis for linking the new creation with egalitarianism.

4. Conclusion

We grant that the essential structure of the feminist argument is correct, namely, that the work of Christ has reversed the curse of Genesis 3:16 and restored the original creation order. But the crucial question is still this: *what was the original creation order?* The answer to this question is still determined not by Galatians 3:28 nor Genesis

3:16, but by Genesis 2. And as we saw in the previous chapter, Genesis 2 along with its New Testament commentary unequivocally establishes the hierarchical relationship of loving male headship and willing female submission as the intended order of creation. Thus when Christ reverses the curse, *this* is what he restores, not egalitarianism. So even if Galatians 3:28 were talking about "reversing the curse," it would not nullify the roles of headship and submission, but would only remove sinful perversions thereof.

ENDNOTES
CHAPTER THREE

[1]Carol P. Christ, *Laughter of Aphrodite: Reflections on a Journey to the Goddess* (San Francisco: Harper and Row, 1987), pp. 140-141.

[2]Margot Adler, *Drawing Down the Moon: Witches, Druids, Goddess-Worshippers, and Other Pagans in America Today*, revised ed. (Boston: Beacon Press, 1986), p. 200.

[3]Richard Kroeger, "A Plea For Restraint," *Priscilla Papers* (August 1987), I:2.

[4]Aida Besançon Spencer, *Beyond the Curse: Women Called to Ministry* (Nashville: Thomas Nelson, 1985), p. 31.

[5]Ibid.

[6]R. Kroeger, "A Plea for Restraint," p. 2. This point was made by Elizabeth Cady Stanton in her *Woman's Bible*: "And all this time Adam standing beside her interposes no word of objection. 'Her husband with her' are the words of v. 6" (*The Woman's Bible*, Part I [New York: European Publishing Company, 1895], p. 26).

[7]Gilbert Bilezikian, *Beyond Sex Roles: What the Bible Says About a Woman's Place in Church and Family*, 2nd ed. (Grand Rapids: Baker Book House, 1990), pp. 42, 49.

[8]Ibid., p. 42.

[9]Letha Dawson Scanzoni and Nancy A. Hardesty, *All We're Meant To Be: Biblical Feminism for Today*, 3rd ed. (Grand Rapids: Eerdmans, 1992), p. 38. See Stanton, *Woman's Bible*, I:26.

[10]Bilezikian, *Beyond Sex Roles*, pp. 42-43.

[11]Ibid., pp. 43, 44, 45, 47.

[12]Ibid., p. 48.

[13]Scott E. McClelland, "The New Reality in Christ: Perspectives from Biblical Studies," *Gender Matters: Women's Studies for the Christian Community*, ed. June Steffensen Hagen (Grand Rapids: Zondervan, 1990), pp. 57-58.

[14]Walter C. Kaiser, Jr., "Shared Leadership," *Christianity Today* (Oct. 3, 1986), CT Institute supplement, p. 12-I.

[15]Ibid. Such an interpretation is important for feminists because it helps them to support their view of 1 Timothy 2:12, namely, that Paul prohibits the Ephesian women from teaching only because they were not yet adequately educated.

[16]Kenneth S. Kantzer, "Proceed with Care," *Christianity Today* (Oct. 3, 1986), CT Institute supplement, p. 14-I.

[17]The original prohibition, spoken only to Adam, was in the singular (2:16-17). The fact that Satan quotes it in the plural is evidence of the probability that the prohibition was repeated by God to both Adam *and* Eve once Eve had been created. The fact that the conversation in 3:1-5 is based on the quotation which includes the plural is decisive for explaining why the plural is used throughout.

[18]R. Kroeger, "A Plea for Restraint," p. 2; italics added.

[19]The Hebrew preposition is *'im*. For examples of this sort of meaning see Gen. 13:1; 18:23; 21:22; 27:44; 31:3, 5; Josh. 7:24.

[20]Herbert Braun, "*plassō* [etc.]," *Theological Dictionary of the New Testament*, tr. Geoffrey W. Bromiley (Grand Rapids: Eerdmans, 1968), 6:254. This is what it means in its only other use in the New Testament, Romans 9:20.

[21]Ibid.

[22]Gleason Archer, "Ordination Is Not For Women," *Moody Monthly* (February 1987), p. 8.

[23]McClelland, "The New Reality," pp. 57-58.

[24]While admitting that this argument "has a certain natural attraction" for her and other feminists, Mary Stewart Van Leeuwen says that this argument by Bilezikian may be "reading too much into the account of the fall." She suggests that it may be "an example of feminist overkill" ("The Recertification of Women: A Review Article," *The Reformed Journal* [August 1986], pp. 19-20).

[25]There is no reason to think that every word God spoke to Adam and Eve has been recorded for us to read. That he would have made these marvelous creatures in his own image, capable of communication with himself, and then limited his spoken words to two short instructions (Gen. 1:28-30; 2:16-17) would be peculiar indeed.

[26]Raymond C. Ortlund, Jr., "Male-Female Equality and Male Headship: Genesis 1-3," in *Recovering Biblical Manhood and Womanhood: A Response to Evangelical Feminism*, ed. John Piper and Wayne Grudem (Wheaton, IL: Crossway Books, 1991), p. 108.

[27]Ibid., p. 107.

[28]Bilezikian, *Beyond Sex Roles*, pp. 49-50.

[29]Austin H. Stouffer, "The Ordination of Women: Yes," *Christianity Today* (February 20, 1981), p. 13.

[30]R. Kroeger, "A Plea for Restraint," p. 2. See Bilezikian, p. 49.

[31]For example, Ephesians 5:6 says, "Let no one deceive you with empty words, for because of these things the wrath of God comes upon the sons of disobedience." See also Eph. 4:22; Col. 2:8; 2 Thess. 2:10.

[32]Ortlund, "Male-Female Equality," pp. 106; 482, note 38.

[33]Susan Foh, "A Male Leadership View: The Head of the Woman Is the Man," *Women in Ministry: Four Views*, ed. Bonnidell Clouse and Robert G. Clouse (Downers Grove: InterVarsity Press, 1989), p. 74.

[34]Ortlund, "Male-Female Equality," p. 108.

[35]McClelland, "The New Reality," p. 58.

[36]Mary Hayter, *The New Eve in Christ* (Grand Rapids: Eerdmans, 1987), p. 113.

[37]Peter DeJong and Donald R. Wilson, *Husband and Wife: The Sexes in Scripture and Society* (Grand Rapids: Zondervan, 1979), p. 134.

[38]"Men, Women and Biblical Equality," section 5 under "Biblical Truths," in *Priscilla Papers* (Fall 1989), 3:12. See also McClelland, "The New Reality," pp. 58-59.

[39]Mary Stewart Van Leeuwen, *Gender and Grace: Love, Work and Parenting in a Changing World* (Downers Grove: InterVarsity Press, 1990), p. 45.

[40]Bilezikian, *Beyond Sex Roles*, p. 55. See also DeJong and Wilson, *Husband and Wife*, p. 133; and Van Leeuwen, *Gender*, pp. 45-47.

[41]Alvera Mickelsen, "An Egalitarian View: There Is Neither Male nor

Female in Christ," *Women in Ministry: Four Views,* ed. Bonnidell Clouse and Robert G. Clouse (Downers Grove: InterVarsity Press, 1989), p. 184.

[42]Mary J. Evans, *Woman in the Bible* (Downers Grove: InterVarsity Press, 1983), pp. 19-20.

[43]Spencer, *Beyond the Curse,* pp. 36-37.

[44]Ibid., pp. 35-37.

[45]"Men, Women and Biblical Equality," section 5 under "Biblical Truths," in *Priscilla Papers* (Fall 1989), 3:12.

[46]Ronald E. Heine, "The Bible and the Role of Women in the Church," *Christian Standard* (Sept. 24, 1978), p. 6.

[47]Scanzoni and Hardesty, *All We're Meant To Be* (1992), p. 41. See also Bilezikian, *Beyond Sex Roles,* pp. 54, 56.

[48]Evans, *Woman,* p. 19.

[49]W. Ward Gasque, "The Role of Women in the Church, in Society and in the Home," *Priscilla Papers* (Spring 1988), 2:2.

[50]McClelland, "The New Reality," p. 59.

[51]Mary A. Kassian, *Women, Creation, and the Fall* (Westchester, IL: Crossway Books, 1990), p. 26. On the relation to 4:7 see Susan T. Foh, "What Is the Woman's Desire?", *Westminster Theological Journal* (1975), 37:376-383. See also Foh, "A Male Leadership View," p. 75.

[52]Contrary to the view of Foh, "A Male Leadership View," p. 75. See also Ortlund, "Male-Female Equality," p. 109.

[53]Stephen B. Clark, *Man and Woman in Christ: An Examination of the Roles of Men and Women in Light of Scripture and the Social Sciences* (Ann Arbor: Servant Books, 1980), pp. 34-35.

[54]Kassian, *Women,* p. 27.

[55]See James B. Hurley, *Man and Woman in Biblical Perspective* (Grand Rapids: Zondervan, 1981), pp. 217-218.

[56]Clark, *Man,* p. 33.

[57]Hurley, *Man,* p. 219. See also George W. Knight III, "Male and Female Related He Them," *Christianity Today* (April 9, 1976), pp. 14-15.

[58]Fred P. Thompson, Jr., "'Woman: What Manner of Creature?'" *United Evangelical Action* (Spring 1977), p. 34.

[59]See Clark, *Man,* p. 33.

[60]Ibid. Also see Knight, "Male and Female," p. 15.

[61]Kassian, *Women,* pp. 24, 29.

[62]To link death with male dominance, and to say that the origin of both is satanic (as Bilezikian does in *Beyond Sex Roles,* p. 56) is simply to close one's eyes to the truth about God's judgment upon sin.

[63]Heine, "Bible," p. 6.

[64]Virginia Mollenkott, "A Challenge to Male Interpretation: Women and the Bible," *Sojourners* (February 1976), 5:25.

[65]Gretchen Gaebelein Hull, *Equal To Serve: Women and Men in the Church and Home* (Old Tappan, NJ: Revell, 1987), p. 210. For example, see her treatment of this passage in chapter 4 (pp. 64-75). See p. 105.

[66]Ibid., p. 204.

[67]Scanzoni and Hardesty, *All We're Meant To Be: A Biblical Approach to Women's Liberation,* original ed. (Waco: Word Books, 1974), p. 12.

[68]DeJong and Wilson, *Husband and Wife,* p. 136.

[69]Ibid., pp. 136-137.

[70]Van Leeuwen, *Gender*, p. 48.

[71]Rolf E. Aaseng, "Male and Female Created He Them," *Christianity Today* (Nov. 20, 1970), p. 6.

[72]Eleanor Daniel, *What the Bible Says About Sexual Identity* (Joplin, MO: College Press, 1981), pp. 48-49, 204. Daniel allows one exception. Even in the new creation, "there is a structure given to male-female relationships in marriage: he is 'head,' she is follower" (p. 49). This is atypical of feminism, however.

[73]Hull, *Equal To Serve*, p. 80.

[74]Gasque, "The Role of Women," p. 2.

[75]DeJong and Wilson, *Husband and Wife*, p. 137.

[76]McClelland, "The New Reality," p. 66. See Heine, "Bible," p. 6.

[77]Don Williams, *The Apostle Paul and Women in the Church* (Ventura, CA: Regal Books, 1977), p. 82. See also Richard and Joyce Boldrey, *Chauvinist or Feminist? Paul's View of Women* (Grand Rapids: Baker, 1976), p. 33.

[78]Richard N. Longenecker, *New Testament Social Ethics for Today* (Grand Rapids: Eerdmans, 1984), pp. 84-87, 92.

[79]See Ronald Fisher, "Freedom Within God's Appointments," part 2, *The Restoration Herald* (June 1989), p. 3.

[80]The one exception to this is the gift of the Holy Spirit, with his regenerating power and sanctifying presence. This began at Pentecost. The aspects of redemption received from the Spirit, however, are not related to the curses and penalties of sin, which are annulled only by the atoning work of Christ.

[81]Galatians 3:28 will be discussed in detail in chapter 5 below.

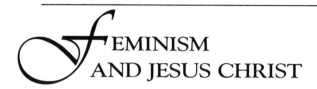EMINISM AND JESUS CHRIST

When studying the Bible feminists encounter basically two kinds of data. First are those texts and teachings which appear to contradict feminist beliefs or which have traditionally been taken to do so. These must somehow be reconciled with egalitarianism. Second are those texts and subjects which appear to support feminist beliefs or at least are compatible with them. These are energetically shaped and tailored as to their content, and extravagantly magnified as to their importance.

When studying Jesus feminists are confronted with both categories. Some things about Jesus just do not seem consistent with their agenda, and thus must somehow be explained away. Included here are the facts that Jesus was incarnated as a male and that he chose no female apostles. Other aspects of christology seem to fortify the egalitarian gospel and thus are greatly emphasized. These include Christ's canceling the curse through his work of redemption (discussed in the previous chapter), his teaching as it relates to women in general, and the nature of his personal relationships with women.

This chapter focuses on the two problem areas for feminism (incarnation as a male; no female apostles) and the last two positive emphases (teaching about women; encounters with women). It will show that the former cannot be adequately explained within the framework of feminism, and that the latter do not require a feminist interpretation and in fact are quite consistent with hierarchicalism.

I. GENDER AND THE INCARNATION

For many feminists the fact that the Logos "became flesh [was incarnated]" (John 1:14) in the form of a human male is a real stumbling block. They wonder *why* the world's prototypical feminist would have made his appearance as a man and not as a woman. This has led some non-Biblical feminists to speculate whether we can expect a counterbalancing female incarnation sometime in the future. As Letty Russell says, "One possibility in approaching this question is to get rid of the scandal by looking for a further incarnation in the form of a woman."[1] Several nineteenth-century sectarians have asserted that at the Second Coming the Messiah will be female.[2] Another possibility is to abandon Christianity altogether and reconstruct a feminism-friendly goddess religion, which many have done.

A. How Feminists Explain the Male Incarnation

Bible-believing feminists are not open to such radical solutions, however. The Messiah came as a male, and that fact has to be accepted and then explained in a way that satisfies the feminist mentality. Most things about the incarnation are a mystery, but "part of the mystery is that Mary brought forth a son. Why did God choose to become flesh in male form?"[3] Several answers are offered.

1. A Concession to the Culture of Patriarchal Judaism

One answer is that it was a necessary concession to the culture into which the Messiah was born. In the culture of patriarchal Judaism, the Messiah could have functioned properly only as a male. Thus it was a purely practical matter. This is how Scanzoni and Hardesty answer the question:

On the practical level, Jewish women were kept in subjection and sometimes even in seclusion. A female Messiah might have had little scriptural knowledge . . . . A female Messiah would not have been allowed to teach publicly in the synagogue, nor would she have been believed if she had, since the testimony of women was not accepted as veracious.[4]

Mollenkott says, "In patriarchical cultures, no incarnation of God in the flesh of a woman would have received a moment's serious notice!"[5] "Since nobody listened seriously to either women or slaves in first-century society, and since Jesus was coming to teach a whole new lifestyle, it is obvious that God would choose to be incarnated as a free male rather than a female or a slave."[6]

2. Jesus Was Anthrōpos, Not Male

Another feminist explanation of the male incarnation is that Jesus was mostly described with the word *anthrōpos*, the Greek word for "man," which is actually generic or gender-neutral. Thus God does not intend for us to think of him as a male, but simply as a human being. If his gender had been important, he would have been described with those Greek words for "man" which specifically mean "male," i.e., *anēr* and *arsēn*.

Some feminists state or imply that Jesus was never called anything but *anthrōpos*. Mollenkott has said, "The New Testament authors refer to Jesus as *anthrōpos*, human, rather than as *anēr*, male."[7] Also, "When New Testament writers refer to the incarnation of Jesus, they do not speak of his becoming *anēr*, 'male,' but rather of his being *anthrōpos*, 'human.'"[8] English versions usually obscure the difference, she says.

Fortunately, even English translations of John 1:14 capture the fact that Jesus is God incarnate as a *human being* rather than as a *male*: "So the Word became flesh; [it] came to dwell among us, and we saw its glory, such glory as

befits the Father's [or Mother's] only [Child], full of grace
and truth" (NEB). The use of the Greek word for "flesh,"
sarx, made it absolutely impossible for the translators to
say that "the Word became man," which promptly would
have become confused with "the Word became male." The
glorious truth is that "the Word became a human being," an
embodying or tabernacling of the glory of God within the
limitations of human nature, with its "male" and "female"
components.[9]

Spencer repeats this idea: "Even the New Testament
writers are always careful to describe Jesus with the
generic Greek term 'human' or *anthropos* rather than the
term 'male' or *aner*. Although God became a male, God
primarily became a human; otherwise, in some way males
would be more saved than females."[10]

In their first edition Scanzoni and Hardesty said, "Jesus
was a man, but he was also Man. English obscures the
distinction, but New Testament writers are careful to
distinguish between *anēr* (male) and *anthropos* (human).
When speaking of the Incarnation, they invariably choose
anthropos." Thus "Jesus came to earth not primarily as a
male but as a person."[11] (In the later editions they change
the word "invariably" to "almost without exception,"[12]
which is certainly more accurate, as we shall see shortly.)

3. Jesus Was both Male and Female

Still another feminist response to the apparent fact that
Jesus was incarnated as a male is to assert that he was
actually both male *and* female in some significant way. One
rather bizarre suggestion is that this may have been true
physically,[13] but more common is the idea that Jesus was
both masculine and feminine psychologically. To show that
he is creating a "new gender-inclusive humanity," say the
Torjesens, "in his work and ministry Christ demonstrates
so many traditionally female characteristics—nurture,
compassion, suffering, tenderness."[14] Atkins says, "Both
feminine and masculine characteristics have their origin in

Him, so we would expect Jesus to exemplify both." On the feminine side Jesus was meek and mild; he was "the epitome of patience and humility"; he "delighted in little children"; he cooked breakfast; he wept.[15] A frequently-cited example of this female imagery is Matthew 23:37, where Jesus said to wayward Jerusalem, "How often I wanted to gather your children together, the way a hen gathers her chicks under her wings." This shows that "Jesus did not hesitate to speak of himself in female terms," says Mollenkott.[16]

Another attempt to find female elements in the incarnation is the equation of the crucifixion with childbirth. Through the pain and the blood of the cross Christ gave birth to his new creation, and even nurses us at his bleeding side. Rebecca Pentz says,

> Childbirth is gory. And so is the cross. Our birth into a new relationship with God was gory just as was our birth into this world. I sometimes think we women have an advantage over men when we come to the cross: we can experience, albeit on the creature's level, what it is like to give birth. So what kind of savior is Jesus? He is a mother who gives us birth and who nurtures us in love. Certainly this is a savior for women as well as for men.[17]

Other attempts to identify Jesus as female focus on his divine nature. Since (it is assumed) the divine nature as such is gender-inclusive, i.e., just as much feminine as masculine, then Jesus' divine nature necessarily includes both. For example, the Torjesens assert that "what Christ assumed in the incarnation was not a particular individual male but our *common human nature* in all its aspects. Christian orthodoxy has always affirmed that the *person* of Christ is the individuality of the Logos and not that of a man." Though physically male, "the identity of Christ is *not* that of a male individual. It is that of the Logos, the second person of the Trinity. Christ is not male, for there is no male identity in Christ only the gender-inclusive individuality of the Logos." I.e., "the human existence of Christ *is* that of the divine Logos." Thus "the humanity of Christ transcends the humanity of a male person." This is important "since what is not assumed cannot be redeemed." The Torjesens call this "high Christology" and declare that it was endorsed by the Council of Chalcedon.[18]

Another version of the idea that Christ's divine nature was feminine is the so-called Sophia Christology, popular among liberal feminists[19] but also being adopted in conservative feminist circles as well.[20] This view starts with the idea that Sophia is the female personification of God's wisdom. (*Sophia* is the Greek word for wisdom and is feminine in gender.) "In the Old Testament," says Mollenkott, "Wisdom is always pictured as a woman"; she is "invariably personified as female."[21] The next step is to recognize that the New Testament identifies Jesus as "the wisdom of God" (1 Cor. 1:24, 30). Thus Jesus is identified with "Sophia herself," in the view endorsed by Pentz. "Jesus is Sophia herself incarnate," she says.[22] Thus even though she became incarnate as a male, her femaleness shows through very clearly in the feminine characteristics exhibited by Jesus, e.g., his weeping, his love for children, and his special way with women. "A Sophia Christology makes sense of these facts. Jesus incarnated the feminine characteristics of the divine." A common idea is that "if Jesus had lived in the 20th century he would have been a feminist." Now, says Pentz, with this understanding of Sophia, "Jesus' feminism has an explicit theological explanation— Jesus is Sophia incarnate."[23]

These are the various ways in which feminists try to deal with the fact that the Messiah was incarnated as a male. First, it was a cultural necessity; second, he is described as *anthrōpos*, which means "human being" and not "male"; third, he embodies both maleness and femaleness, in either his human nature or his divine nature or both.

B. Critique of Feminism's
Approach to the Gender of Christ

Our concern here is to examine each of the three points in the feminists' approach to the gender of Christ and to evaluate them in the light of solid facts. In this process we shall call attention to the weakness of their arguments, their inattention to detail, their magnification of minutiae, and in general their refusal to acknowledge the obvious Biblical emphasis on the maleness of Christ.

1. A Concession to Culture?

Feminists say the Messiah had to come as a male because the patriarchical culture of rabbinic Judaism would have ignored or rejected a female in that role. In order to succeed in that particular culture, Christ had to be male. It was a purely practical matter.

We may say several things in response to this idea. First, it is a mistake to assume that the culture into which the Messiah was born was totally dominated by the patriarchical ethos of rabbinic Judaism. The teaching of some rabbis was without question misogynistic; but, as Stephen Clark has pointed out, the culture of first century Judaism was quite pluralistic, and there is no evidence that the narrow rabbinic view was the prevailing one.[24]

Second, if the maleness of Christ was a concession to culture, in order to make sure that he would receive a proper hearing, then in many ways the strategy was a failure, since even the *male* Christ was scorned and rejected by the rabbinic circle anyway. Would a female Christ have been treated with any more hostility and hatred than the male Jesus?

Third, it is clear from Jesus' own teaching that the mistaken elements of the prevailing culture and the prevailing human traditions were no barrier to the carrying out of his purpose. He met them head-on and slew them like dragons: "You have heard that it was said . . . but I say unto you." Such iconoclasm alienated the rabbinic circles, to be sure; but it increased his acceptance with ordinary people (cf. Matt. 7:28-29; Mark 12:37).

Finally, to say that the culture into which the Messiah was born presented logistical problems for God certainly ignores the fact that God himself is the one who *chose* that particular culture as the time and place for the incarnation. As Susan Foh says, "God chose the culture and time in which his Son was to be born."[25] He not only chose it, but he also to a large degree shaped it through the contents of the Law of Moses, which is unquestionably hierarchical. If he had wanted a female Messiah, he could have chosen or prepared a matriarchal culture.

For these reasons we conclude that the idea that Christ's maleness was a concession to culture is an extremely weak argument. It simply does not take account of the relevant facts.

2. The Meaning and Use of Anthrōpos

Feminists claim that Jesus is not described with the Greek words for "male" but rather is called *anthrōpos*, which means "human being" rather than "male." They conclude that we are therefore not intended to think of Jesus as a male but rather simply as a generic human being.

This argument, however, is faulty from the beginning because it is based on incorrect data and an incorrect understanding of the term in question. The following points will make this clear.

First, the claim or implication that Jesus is described in Scripture *only* as *anthrōpos* and never with the words meaning "male" is simply false. It is true that *anthrōpos* is applied to Jesus more often, about 32 times. But in fact two words that mean specifically "male," i.e., *anēr* and *arsēn*, are also applied to him in the Biblical text. *Anēr* is used six times in unequivocal references to Jesus: John 1:30; Luke 24:19; Acts 2:22; Acts 17:31; 2 Corinthians 11:2; and Revelation 21:2. The word *arsēn* is used in three texts. Luke 2:23 cites an Old Testament requirement and refers it to Christ: "Every first-born *male* that opens the womb shall be called holy to the Lord." Revelation 12, in a symbolic scene that can be referring only to the incarnation of Jesus, uses this word twice. Verse 5 says that the "woman clothed with the sun" (v. 1) "gave birth to a son, a *male* child, who is to rule all the nations with a rod of iron." Verse 13 refers again to "the woman who gave birth to the *male* child." This is a total of nine references to Jesus with terms that emphasize his maleness.

Someone may still say that *anthrōpos* is used more frequently than the terms for "male" (32 vs. 9). Is this not significant? No, it is not. For one thing, some of the 32 uses of *anthrōpos* are parallel passages in the gospels. More importantly, all but six of these 32 references are quotations of statements by uninspired people. These include the people in general,[26] Peter denying Christ,[27] people friendly or not unfriendly toward Christ,[28] and people hostile toward him.[29] In only six places is Jesus called *anthrōpos* with divine authority: in John 8:40 (by Jesus himself), and in Romans 5:15; 1 Corinthians 15:21, 47; Philippians 2:8; 1 Timothy 2:5 (by Paul). Of the nine references to Jesus as "male," we may exclude the rather indirect references in Luke 2:23 and Revelation 21:2. Luke 24:19 may also be excluded since it is a quotation from uninspired persons. But that still leaves six uses of these terms by divinely-inspired persons: John the Baptist (John 1:30), Peter on Pentecost (Acts 2:22), Paul at Mars' Hill (Acts 17:31) and in 2 Corinthians 11:2; and the Apostle John (Rev. 12:5, 13). This means that of statements spoken with divine authority, the number is exactly even: six use *anthrōpos*, and six use the terms for "male."

Scanzoni and Hardesty attempt to qualify the data by saying that the New Testament writers "invariably" (first edition) or "almost without exception" (second edition) used *anthrōpos* "when speaking of the Incarnation." They imply that *anthrōpos* is the word of choice in serious theological contexts such as the Incarnation. (For examples they cite Philippians 2:7 and Romans 5:12, 15.[30] However, Romans 5:12 does not even refer to Jesus.)

We do not dispute the fact that the six inspired references to Jesus as *anthrōpos* make significant theological points. But does this mean that this term is deliberately chosen in order to emphasize Christ's humanness rather than his maleness? This can hardly be the case, especially in view of the heavy theological concepts and soteriological events associated with Christ as male in the six passages where *anēr* and *arsēn* are used. In John 1:30 the Baptist says, "After me comes a Man [*anēr*] who has a higher rank than I, for He existed before me." Here pre-existence is attributed to Jesus in his maleness. In Acts 2:22 Peter refers to "Jesus the Nazarene, a man [*anēr*] attested to you by God with miracles and wonders and signs," a man nailed to a cross but raised up again by God (verses 23-24). Here the male Jesus is approved by God and is crucified and raised up again for our salvation. In Acts 17:31 Paul says that God "has fixed a day in which He will judge the world in righteousness through a Man [*anēr*] whom He has appointed, having furnished proof to all men by raising Him from the dead." Here Jesus is raised from the dead as a male, and he will judge the world as a male. In 2 Corinthians 11:2 Paul says, "I betrothed you to one husband [*anēr*], that to Christ I might present you as a pure virgin." Here our present relationship to Christ is as a male, and it will be so at the Second Coming. Finally, Revelation 12:5, 13 refers to the birth of "a son, a male [*arsēn*]" who will "rule all the nations with a rod of iron." There could be no clearer reference to Christ's maleness as a significant aspect of his incarnation and his kingly rule.

The data cited here should put to rest the myth that Jesus is just a generic *anthrōpos* and not a male. They show that this particular attempt to neutralize the fact that the Messiah was incarnated as a male is completely unsuccessful.

A second point showing the same thing has to do with the meaning of *anthrōpos* itself. This is indeed one of the terms used to describe the incarnate Christ. But is it true, as feminists assert or imply, that *anthrōpos* always means "human being" and is therefore gender-neutral when it refers to Christ? The facts concerning the word *anthrōpos* show otherwise. In general this term is used in the Bible in two distinct ways. First, it often refers to mankind or humanity or human beings *collectively*; second, it often refers to specific and particular *individuals*, in which case it always refers to males.

When used in the first way *anthrōpos* may be in the plural form; or it may be singular, referring to a representative person or individual but not to a specific person. When used in this sense the term is generic or gender-neutral; it refers to human beings as a class, whether male or female. The reference may be to human beings as distinct from animals, or from angels, or from God himself.

This last use is very common in the New Testament, e.g., "With men it is impossible, but not with God" (Mark 10:27), and "We must obey God rather than men" (Acts 5:29). The term may be used in this sense for mankind collectively or for particular individuals. This is probably the significance of several of the references to Jesus as *anthrōpos*, namely, Matthew 9:8; John 10:33; Philippians 2:8; and 1 Timothy 2:5, which says, "There is one God, and one mediator also between God and men, the man Christ Jesus." Thus it is certainly true that Jesus is called *anthrōpos* to emphasize the fact that he is human, and not just divine. But when this is the point, *anthrōpos* calls attention not to his genderlessness as distinct from his maleness, but to his humanness as distinct from his divinity.

The really important point here relates to the second meaning of *anthrōpos*, namely, its reference to male individuals. The fact is this: in the New Testament, when this term is used for specific individuals, it *always* refers to *males*. There are no exceptions. Thus when it refers to specific individuals, it is a practical synonym for *anēr* or *arsēn*. It is never used of a woman when a specific woman or group of women is in view. The term commonly used in such a case is *gunē*, which means "woman" or "wife."

The list of specific men for which *anthrōpos* is used is quite long and need not be recited here.[31] It includes some with names and some who are unnamed. It includes many specific fictional men in parables or illustrations, as distinct from the three times Christ refers to a woman (*gunē*) in a parable (Matt. 13:33; Luke 13:21; 15:8).

That the term *anthrōpos* may have this distinct connotation of maleness is seen from other data about its use in the New Testament. For one thing, on several occasions it is used interchangeably with *anēr*.[32] For another thing, it is sometimes used for males as contrasted with females, as in Matthew 10:35; 19:5, 10; Luke 22:57-60; 1 Corinthians 7:1; and Ephesians 5:31.

The point is that *anthrōpos* can mean "male"; and when used of specific individuals, it is always intended to identify them as males. There is absolutely no reason to think that its use for the specific individual Jesus should deviate from this pattern. That Jesus is an *anthrōpos* means first of all that he is a human being; but it also *means* that he is a *male* human being.

We conclude that there is nothing in the term *anthrōpos* to give any support whatsoever to feminists' attempt to neutralize the fact that Christ was incarnated as a male. In fact the application of this term to Jesus, as well as the little-noticed use of *anēr* and *arsēn*, actually points in the opposite direction and magnifies his maleness.

3. Is Christ both Male and Female?

As we have seen, feminists have tried several ways to introduce a feminine element into the nature of Christ. This is especially true of Jesus' *psychological* nature, which is said to include both male and female characteristics in perfect harmony. In this connection it is very difficult to avoid the impression that the identification of so-called "feminine" characteristics in Jesus is extremely arbitrary. Many men as well as women will find it surprising to learn that such things as compassion, patience, humility, weeping, and love for children—all exhibited by Jesus—are not natural to men.

The most over-worked and over-valued example of femaleness in Jesus is his comparison of his desire to save Jerusalem with a hen's instinct for protecting her chicks under her wings (Matt. 23:37; Luke 13:34). Feminists see this as an indication that Jesus freely spoke about himself "in female terms," as Mollenkott puts it. It is true that the hen is a female animal. But the serious question that must be answered here is this: does Jesus' comparison of one particular desire of his heart with this one example of a hen's behavior reveal some *female* side of his nature any more than it reveals some *animal* side of it? The hen is an animal; thus Jesus compares himself with an animal. But no one feels compelled to say, "Jesus did not hesitate to speak of himself in animal terms." Why not? Because the very idea is ludicrous. Everyone knows that such a limited comparison is only an analogy relating to behavior, and does not imply any essential identity between the nature of Jesus and the nature of a chicken. We do not draw such a conclusion even when Jesus is actually *called* "the Lamb of God" (John 1:29) and "the Lion . . . of Judah" (Rev. 5:5).

Thus it is even more odd to think that Jesus' comparing himself with one instinctive act of one *female* animal is intended to reveal some essential identity between his nature and *femaleness* as such. If anything should strike us as significant about the simile, it is the fact that he compares himself with an *animal* at all; but we rightly draw no conclusions from this about some possible *animalness* of Jesus. Thus the incidental fact that this animal happens to be female gives us even less warrant to speculate about an alleged female side to Jesus' nature.[33]

The idea that the cross is a female act comparable to

childbirth is another desperate attempt to identify some female aspect in Jesus' nature. The fact that pain and blood are involved in any given event does not make it comparable to childbirth. The Bible itself never draws a parallel between the crucifixion and childbirth. Rather, the analogy of birth is applied to Christ's resurrection: Colossians 1:18; Romans 8:29; Acts 13:33. But in this case Jesus is the one being born (or begotten), not the one giving birth. In New Testament soteriology the Holy Spirit, not Jesus, is the agent of birth (John 3:5-8; see Titus 3:5), along with the word of God (1 Cor. 4:15; 1 Pet. 1:23). The events at which a kind of birth occurs are Pentecost (for the church as a whole) and baptism (for individuals, John 3:5; Titus 3:5). Interpreting the cross in such terms is pure poetic imagination.

The same can be said for the so-called Sophia Christology. In the New Testament there is no suggestion that Jesus is the incarnation of some divine female person called Sophia. Jesus is described as "the wisdom of God" in only two related texts, 1 Corinthians 1:24 and 1:30.[34] Verse 24 says, "To those who are the called, both Jews and Greeks, Christ the power of God and the wisdom of God." Verse 30 says that Jesus became to us "wisdom from God, and righteousness and sanctification, and redemption." That these verses are not concerned at all about incarnation is shown from the fact that Jesus is described in other terms also. He is "the power of God," as well as righteousness, sanctification, and redemption. In whatever sense he is "the wisdom of God," he is these things also. Obviously these are not divine persons of whom Jesus is the incarnation. In verse 24 power and wisdom are *attributes* of God; Jesus is called by these "names" because in his work of salvation he is the ultimate display of these attributes. In verse 30 wisdom, righteousness, sanctification, and redemption are *gifts* God bestows upon us; Jesus is called by these "names" because they come to us through him.

But surely there must be other texts that identify Jesus with wisdom. After all, Susan Cady and her co-authors state, "According to a whole series of New Testament texts, Jesus is Sophia." In John's gospel "text after text is proclaiming, 'Jesus is Sophia,'" they say.[35] But where are these other texts? One suggestion is Matthew 11:19, which concludes a lecture on John the Baptist with these words: "Yet wisdom is vindicated by her deeds" (cf. Luke 7:35). Feminists sometimes see this as a statement about Jesus personally: Wisdom/Jesus is vindicated by her/his deeds.[36] But this completely ignores the context (verses 7-19), which is a lesson mainly on the character and work of John the Baptist. Jesus brings himself into the lesson only at the end, and only to show the inconsistency of John's opponents in that they rejected both John and Jesus but on contradictory grounds. The statement about wisdom is added as a sarcastic indictment of these opponents, whose behavior exhibits the very opposite of it. The statement is a general principle, similar in content to "You will know them by their fruits" (Matt. 7:20), and similar in rhetorical function to "Wherever the corpse is, there the vultures will gather" (Matt. 24:28).

Besides Matthew 11:19 and its parallel, there is no other New Testament passage which even comes close to identifying Jesus with *sophia*. He is said to *have* wisdom as a characteristic (Matt. 13:54; Mark 6:2; Luke 2:40, 52; Rev. 5:12), but so are other people, e.g., Solomon (Matt. 12:42) and the church's first seven "deacons" (Acts 6:3). Every other connection between Jesus and some kind of pre-existing divine female person named Sophia is pure speculation and fallacious inference, often involving extra-biblical sources. For example, because "ben Sirach speaks extensively of Sophia's yoke," and because Jesus speaks of *his* yoke in Matthew 11:28-30, Jesus must be equating himself with Sophia. Pentz uses this as evidence that "the case is fairly good that there is a full Sophia Christology in Matthew."[37] For another example, Cady and her co-authors say that John 1:1-3 is clearly referring to Sophia, even though it appears that John has given her a new name— Logos.[38] Such is the nature of the "evidence" for this point.

It is difficult to see how anyone can take this so-called Sophia Christology seriously, since the textual basis for it could hardly be more flimsy. How then can feminists such as Pentz state so dogmatically, "Jesus is Lady Sophia incarnate"?[39] Certainly not as the result of sound, objective hermeneutics.

The Sophia Christology is one example of the attempt to locate Jesus' alleged femaleness in his divine nature rather than his human nature. Any such attempt assumes that God as such is gender-inclusive, or that femaleness is included in the divine nature in the first place. This in itself is a tenuous idea. But even if it were so, the question would still remain whether such a gender-inclusive, male/female divine nature would nullify or neutralize the obvious fact of the maleness of Christ's human nature.

Throughout the history of orthodox Christian thought the point of affirming the divine nature of Jesus has been just that, i.e., to affirm the *divinity* of the Redeemer, not some sort of unique "gender." To switch the emphasis to the latter is to trivialize the whole point of the incarnation. At the same time, orthodox Christian thought has always affirmed the full human nature of Jesus; and this human nature has always been recognized as male. The gender of Jesus comes from his human nature, not his divine nature.

In their attempt to degenderize Jesus, the Torjesens (as cited above) claim that, in accordance with the Council of Chalcedon, Jesus' identity or personhood is not that of a male individual but that of the divine Logos. "The human existence of Christ *is* that of the divine Logos," they say. In other words, the gender of Jesus' human nature is totally irrelevant; his maleness is only "nominal." His true gender comes from his divine nature, which includes both male and female.[40]

Such an approach to the gender of Jesus, however, results in a conclusion that is far afield from anything intended by Chalcedon. In fact, it is hardly distinguishable from the Apollinarian heresy, one of the very doctrines that Chalcedon set out to refute. It is true (and quite Chal-

FEMINISM AND JESUS CHRIST

cedonian), as the Torjesens assert, that the Logos did not *assume* a particular individual male in the incarnation, as if somehow the Logos took possession of an existing male person named Jesus. This would have resulted in a being with two centers of personality; i.e., it would actually be two persons, one divine and one human.

But here is an important distinction overlooked by the Torjesens: though the Logos did not *assume* a particular male individual, he did *become* a particular human male individual, namely, Jesus of Nazareth. The personal (psychological, rational) center of Jesus was just as much human as it was divine; exactly how this could be so is the mystery of the incarnation. But to say, as do the Torjesens, "that the *person* of Christ is the individuality of the Logos and not that of a man," or that "the human existence of Christ was, is, and continues to be that of the gender-inclusive Logos,"[41] is to deny that Jesus has a complete human nature. If "the human existence of Christ *is* that of the divine Logos," then it is no longer a *human* existence. Some essential aspect of the latter has been *replaced* by the divine Logos. This eliminates the human element from the aspects of Jesus and his work that matter most, namely, those involving his personhood.

The Torjesens' view is no different in principle from Apollinarius' heretical view that the Logos replaced the rational soul in Jesus.[42] The criticism of the Torjesens and of Apollinarius must be the same: their Jesus has only a partial human nature. This is the error that led Gregory of Nazianzus to declare in criticism of Apollinarius, "That which he has not assumed he has not healed."[43] That is, if Christ is not fully human, then he has not redeemed the full human nature.

The Torjesens are concerned to affirm that Christ assumed the human nature that is common to everyone, males and females alike. This is commendable. Their error, however, is to assume that someone who is fully male (and presumably, someone who is fully female) would not possess this common human nature. This is simply not true. A fully male (or female) individual possesses the common human nature, but also possesses something *in addition to it*: maleness (or femaleness). Being male, as was Jesus, in no way subtracts from the fullness of the humanity shared by males and females alike. Eliminating his maleness does not make him *more* human; it makes him *less* than human.

This means that there is no basis for the claim or the fear that if the identity of Christ is that of a male, then in the incarnation he represents males only and is able to redeem males only. The common human nature of both sexes is fully represented by either sex. This is proved by the fact that the one man Adam, a male, acted for the whole race of human beings when he sinned in Eden. To say that a male Messiah could not redeem the whole race denies the validity of the parallel Paul draws between Adam and Christ (Rom. 5:12-19; 1 Cor. 15:22).

We conclude that all attempts to combine maleness and femaleness in the person of Christ are unsuccessful. The fact is that they *cannot* succeed, because there is no Biblical basis for saying that Jesus is anything but male.

C. Scripture and the Maleness of Christ

The Logos was incarnated as a male. This is a fact affirmed from the beginning of the Bible to its end, from the masculine seed of woman in Genesis 3:15 to the bridegroom in Revelation 21. This fact cannot be denied, and its significance cannot be obscured by the sincere but misguided feminist attempts to explain it away.

In his human nature Jesus was not just generic but was male. This is the consistent testimony of Scripture. He is called *anthrōpos*, which when applied to a specific human being identifies that person as a male. He is also called *anēr* and *arsēn*, words that specifically mean "male." From prophecy to promise to reality, Mary's child was called a *son*, not a daughter. "Behold, a virgin will be with child and

bear a son" (Isa. 7:14). "And she will bear a Son" (Matt.
1:21). "She gave birth to a Son" (Matt. 1:25; see Luke 2:7).
"And she gave birth to a son, a male child" (Rev. 12:5). He is
the son of David and the son of Abraham (Matt. 1:1). He is
the second and last Adam (1 Cor. 15:45).

In his divine nature, especially in his relation to God the
Father, Jesus is represented by titles and descriptions that
are unequivocally male. He is the *Son* of God (Matt. 16:16;
26:63-64). The Father addresses him thus: "Thou art My
Son, today I have begotten Thee" (Ps. 2:7; quoted in Acts
13:33 and Heb. 1:5). He also says, "I will be a Father to
Him, and He shall be a Son to Me" (Heb. 1:5). The Father
twice declared from heaven, "This is My beloved Son"
(Matt. 3:17; 17:5). Jesus is not only the Son of God; he is
also called the Son of Man, a title which is also best understood as reflecting Jesus' transcendent, divine nature.
Isaiah 9:6 calls the Son the Eternal *Father.*

Jesus accomplished his messianic work in specifically
male roles. He came to earth as a Prince (Isa. 9:6; Acts
3:15) and as a King (Matt. 21:5; John 18:37). He came as
the high priest to offer the true and final sacrifice for sins
(Heb. 2:17), a role which in the Old Testament was always
male. He was not only the high priest but the sacrifice as
well, and the sacrifices of which he is the fulfillment had to
be male. These include the Passover lamb (Exod. 12:5; 1
Cor. 5:7), and the bull and goats offered on the Day of
Atonement (Lev. 16:3, 5; Heb. 10:1-10). Jesus the male was
crucified and raised again (Acts 2:22-24; 17:31). The Father
has appointed his Son as "the heir of all things" (Heb. 1:2),
according to the principle, "If a Son, then an heir" (Gal.
4:7).

The Messiah's maleness was a factor not just during the
course of his earthly ministry; it continues to be prominent
even now in his heavenly ministry toward us who are his
people. He is the bridegroom to whom we are betrothed (2
Cor. 11:2). He is the "Son over His house whose house we
are" (Heb. 3:6). As the Son and heir he shares his inheritance with us (Rom. 8:17). His ministry as our "great high

priest" continues uninterruptedly in heaven for us (Heb. 4:14-16). He reigns from heaven even now as "King of kings and Lord of lords" (1 Tim. 6:17). Every role in which Christ relates to us now is a male role.

In the eschaton his maleness will be magnified. To his people he will come as the bridegroom to receive us as his bride (Rev. 19:7; 21:2, 9). To those who oppose him he will come as a triumphant and destroying warrior under the name "KING OF KINGS, AND LORD OF LORDS" (Rev. 19:11-16). In the final judgment God "will judge the world in righteousness through a Man [anēr] whom He has appointed" (Acts 17:31).

The Bible's overwhelming emphasis on the maleness of Christ, as it assigns to him exclusively male titles and roles, shows unequivocally that it was God's intentional plan to redeem the world not just through a human being but through a human being who is male. It shows that the Messiah's maleness is not arbitrary or accidental. That he continues to relate to us in male roles shows that his gender was not just a cultural accommodation. In view of the abundant and weighty testimony to this maleness, the attempt to continue to push into the foreground the simile of the mother hen becomes a rather pitiful gesture.

We agree that the main point of the incarnation is that God became a *human being*, but this does not nullify or contradict the fact that he became a *male* human being. This is obviously the divine choice; and even if we do not understand all the reasons why God chose to do it this way, it cannot be denied that his choice was deliberate and purposeful. As Thomas Howard has declared in a very perceptive article, "the imagery matters"! To say that the imagery (i.e., of maleness) does *not* matter ignores the acknowledged fact that Jesus' *modus operandi* included the breaking of any cultural icons that stood in the way of the gospel. An ideal way for God to abolish patriarchy would have been to become incarnate as a female, but he came as a *male*. "In the Incarnation, God broke up all the *other* entrenched, established prejudices of antiquity. He missed his cues on this point alone. The Incarnate was a revolutionary, an icon-smasher, a rebel, a liberator. But he came, O rue the day, as a *man*. He missed his main chance."[44]

II. CHRIST'S ENCOUNTERS WITH WOMEN

Both feminists and non-feminists agree that the way Jesus actually treated women in his encounters with them varied from the prevailing norms of that day to a greater or lesser degree. Both also agree that Jesus' treatment of women is a very important consideration in formulating what is normative for today. Along with these general points of agreement, however, serious differences exist in the ways feminists and non-feminists interpret the gospel records on this subject. How to interpret these records is the subject of this section.

A. The Feminist View

How Jesus treated women is a major point for Christian feminists of both liberal and conservative types. Here is a typical remark:

> One of the main thrusts of Jesus' ministry and of the New Testament is the affirmation of the worth of women and their equality with men. Not once is there recorded an incident in Jesus' ministry nor any words of his which indicate that women are second to men in any way. To the contrary, his every relationship with women affirmed their dignity as persons equal with men in the sight of God. Of course, in order to do so Jesus had to break severely with the status quo which denied women such worth.[45]

The way Jesus related to women is seen as all the more striking in view of the negative roles assigned to women in the rabbinic teaching of the time. Women were clearly regarded as inferior. They were not expected to study the Torah, but were expected instead to attend to the affairs of the home. They were seen as intellectually inferior, having little to offer in the way of stimulating thought or conversation. The rabbinic traditions "banned man from conversing with a woman, . . . proclaimed blessings to those whose children were male and woe to those whose offspring were female, . . . described women as greedy eaters, indolent, jealous, and frivolous." As a result "many first century women were downtrodden, persons with little worth beyond satisfying a man's sexual appetites and bearing his children."[46]

In view of this kind of teaching it seems that Jesus strongly challenged the cultural mores of his time. As Bartchy says, "Jesus' words and deeds radically called in question the traditional gender-roles and sense of male/female identity of His culture."[47] In general feminists tend to use very extravagant language to describe how Jesus treated women. It was "startlingly new" and "revolutionary," says Evans.[48] In Atkins' words, "the way Jesus behaved towards women was revolutionary and sometimes shocking," even "bizarre in the extreme."[49] "In the light of first-century patriarchal culture, Jesus' behavior in regard to women is so extraordinary," say Scanzoni and Hardesty, that one scholar "cites it as evidence of Scripture's supernatural authenticity."[50] This sentiment is well summed up in the title of Leonard Swidler's article, "Jesus Was a Feminist."[51]

Remarks such as these usually have in view both Jesus' teachings about women and his encounters with them. This section deals with the encounters, which feminists regard as especially important. As Jewett says, "It was not so much in what he said as in how he related to women that Jesus was a revolutionary. In this relationship his life style was so remarkable that one can only call it astonishing. He treated women as fully human, equal to men in every respect."[52] The following are the most-cited examples of this "revolutionary" behavior.

1. Mary and Martha, Luke 10:38-42

A favorite example is Jesus' rebuke of Martha and defense of Mary when Martha complained that Mary should be helping in the kitchen rather than sitting at Jesus' feet listening to him teach (Luke 10:38-42). Here are Jesus words: "Martha, Martha, you are worried and bothered about so many things; but only a few things are necessary, really only one, for Mary has chosen the good part, which shall not be taken away from her" (verses 41-42). As feminists see it, Jesus is here rejecting the stereotype concerning women's roles. He is saying that a woman need not be a homemaker; she is free to study theology with the rabbis, the modern equivalent being to enter seminary and prepare for any ministry role she chooses. While Martha was busy "fulfilling the role traditionally assigned to women," Mary "turned upside down the role traditionally assigned to her as a woman"—and Jesus praised her for it.[53] He "affirmed the right of female persons to study the theology which had traditionally been closed to them." He "refused to order Mary to play the stereotypical female role."[54]

As Pentz sees it, "He tells Martha in so many words that Mary shouldn't be helping Martha serve: she should be doing theology with Jesus." In other words, Jesus "calls women to develop themselves rather than sacrifice themselves. He calls them to do theology rather than being totally preoccupied with their domestic chores."[55] Sitting at someone's feet in first-century Judaism, says Spencer, was indicative of "higher level formal education." Thus "Luke is indirectly telling his readers that Mary was taking a position typical of a rabbinic pupil, a position unusual for a woman and moreover usually disapproved." Thus Jesus was allowing Mary to learn as his male students would learn; in so doing he "completely reversed the priorities and the consequences of those priorities in Jewish ancient life." He shows that "a woman's role as homemaker is *not* primary"; she may choose education over homemaking.

From this we learn "Jesus' new principle of encouraging women to seek religious training."[56]

Gretchen Hull sees this "crucial passage" as "the most significant encounter" as far as the feminist agenda is concerned. The story is "revolutionary, because it taught that women should prefer studying theology over a preoccupation with domestic chores." According to Hull, "If Jesus had wished to teach that studying theology is a male prerogative, this would have been the ideal place to do that. If Jesus had wished to teach role restrictions, this would have been the ideal opportunity. . . . Yet Jesus did exactly the opposite!"[57]

2. The Samaritan Woman, John 4:5-42

Another example is the encounter with the Samaritan woman recorded in John 4. Besides breaking tradition by even talking to a woman in public, Jesus shattered the stereotypes even further by engaging her in "intricate theological conversation"[58] and appointing her to function as a preacher. As Mollenkott says, "not only was he speaking to a woman in the open," but "was discussing advanced theology with her!" Also, "Jesus commissioned her as his special messenger to her own city." In so doing he was "deliberately breaking customs which were degrading to the self-concept of women. He was providing object lessons for his disciples—and for us all."[59]

The fact that the woman returned to the city and told what had just happened to her (verses 28-29) is very important for feminists. They see this as divine approval for women to serve as preachers and evangelists. Mickelsen identifies the Samaritan woman as "the first evangelist listed in the Gospels."[60] This is an example of how Jesus approves of "women functioning as his representatives" as evangelists, says Bartchy.[61] This is the point of Mollenkott's remark above, that Jesus commissioned this woman as his special messenger.

3. Conversation with Martha, John 11:20-27

When Jesus came to raise Lazarus from the dead, Jesus and Martha talked about resurrection (John 11:20-27). Martha said, "Lord, if You had been here, my brother would not have died" (v. 21). Jesus replied, "Your brother shall rise again" (v. 23). Martha said, "I know that he will rise again in the resurrection on the last day" (v. 24). Then Jesus gave her this most reassuring promise: "I am the resurrection and the life; he who believes in Me shall live even if he dies, and everyone who lives and believes in Me shall never die" (verses 25-26).

Feminists point to this as another example of Jesus' great respect for women's intellectual and spiritual abilities, and how he thus "conversed with them on theological topics."[62] This one is supposed to be especially significant, since it is Jesus' first teaching on the resurrection. Along with others Bilezikian stresses the fact that a *woman*, Martha, was the "recipient of the most emphatic, the most explicit, and the most comprehensive teaching on the subject of resurrection." In fact she was "the first person in history" to be given an understanding of this "momentous teaching."[63] Swidler marvels that Jesus would reveal "the central event, the central message, in the Gospel . . . to a woman."[64]

4. The Women with Jesus, Luke 8:1-3 and Mark 15:40-41

Luke 8:1-3 reports that Jesus' traveling company included some women whom he had healed: Mary Magdalene, Joanna, Susanna, and others "which ministered unto him of their substance" (v. 3, KJV). Such women are mentioned again as observers of the cross. Mark 15:40-41 says, "They used to follow Him and minister to Him."

To feminists these women were part of Jesus' "inner circle" and "traveling seminary."[65] As Spencer describes them, "Jesus had a female group of disciples who, along with the men, followed him wherever he went to learn from him." Jesus wanted them to learn his teachings so that they could teach others and take leadership positions among his people.[66] Mollenkott says that this shows how "Jesus flouted the sexual stereotypes of his day, stereotypes which demanded that women must serve rather than learn the word of God. . . . And remembering the customs of his culture, we can recognize how radically shocking to his contemporaries was the fact that Jesus traveled with female as well as male disciples."[67]

Both Mark and Luke say that these women "ministered" unto Jesus; Luke explains that they did this by using their own money to purchase needed supplies. The word for "ministered" is the Greek word *diakoneō*, from which comes the word "deacon." Swidler points out this fact and then draws a connection between these women and church deacons. "Indeed apparently the tasks of the deacons in early Christianity were much the same as these women undertook."[68]

5. The Women at the Tomb, Matthew 28:8-10 and John 20:17-18

The women who followed Jesus and ministered to him in his life were the first to come to the tomb following his death, in order properly to prepare his body for burial. These included Mary Magdalene, another Mary, and Salome (Mark 15:40; 16:1). According to Matthew 28:8-10 and John 20:17-18, Jesus chose to make his first resurrection appearance to these women. When they fell before him and worshiped him, he gave them these instructions: "Go and take word to My brethren to leave for Galilee, and there they shall see Me" (Matt. 28:10). In a separate order to Mary Magdalene he said, "Go to My brethren, and say to them, 'I ascend to My Father and your Father, and My God and your God'" (John 20:17). John says that she came, "announcing to the disciples, 'I have seen the Lord,' and that He had said these things to her" (John 20:18).

Feminists take this episode to be one of the strongest Biblical proofs of the full equality of women in reference to Christian ministry. Especially significant in view of the fact that rabbinic tradition dismissed women as unreliable witnesses, Jesus selects these women to be the first witnesses of his resurrection and the first evangelists of the good news that he is alive. As Scanzoni and Hardesty sum it up, "Women were the first to receive the central fact of the gospel and the first to be instructed to tell it abroad."[69]

For feminists this settles the question of women's ordination to ministry. Mollenkott says that Jesus "very deliberately reserved for Mary the vision of resurrected being and very deliberately entrusted the . . . message to her. Once again, Jesus was creating an object lesson for the disciples concerning the full personhood and ministry of women." Thus he endorsed "female ministry."[70] Spencer agrees that Jesus' strategy was specifically designed to show that he "wanted women to learn and to testify before others about God's actions on earth. He wanted these women whom he had taught to go on to take authoritative leadership positions themselves. That is why they were chosen to be the first witnesses to the resurrection."[71] The Kroegers compare this with the commissioning of the apostles and suggest the possibility that Mary Magdalene was given apostolic authority. "She becomes the first witness of the Resurrection, a primary requisite for an apostle; and the Risen Lord Himself commands her to proclaim Him. A striking similarity has been noted between Paul's commissioning by the Risen Christ to be an Apostle, and the experience of Mary in the Garden."[72]

6. Miscellaneous

The gospels record many other encounters of Jesus with women, each having special significance for feminists.

When Jesus healed the crippled woman in Luke 13:10-17, he called her "Daughter of Abraham" (v. 16), a title of honor.[73] The Canaanite woman who beseeched Jesus on behalf of her daughter (Matt. 15:21-28) is another example of Jesus engaging in "theological conversation" with women. Jesus "talked with her and deliberately sought to bring out her capacity for understanding."[74] In general, Jesus taught both men and women, healed both·men and women, forgave both men and women, and had both men and women as friends. He regarded women as capable of thinking and commended their faith.[75]

For feminists all these encounters of Jesus with women constitute a complete break with patriarchal culture and hierarchical gender relationships, thus setting women free from centuries of male dominion. He is, as Judy Norris says, "Jesus, My Lord, Emancipator of Women."[76] In his behavior toward women he establishes egalitarianism as the norm for gender roles for all time. "Thus Jesus' life on earth from beginning to end outlines a paradigm for women's place."[77]

B. A Non-Feminist Response

Feminists make some valid and necessary points about Jesus' treatment of women. His example in this area was indeed a good and needed corrective of patriarchal cultures and abuses against women both then and now. We can certainly agree that he treated women as God had intended women to be treated all along. It is obvious that he considered them to have full ontological equality with men, having equal personhood as creatures made in God's image, with the same value and worth in God's eyes. He dealt with them as individuals, as persons, as intellectually and spiritually competent to participate fully in a life of discipleship before God. The rabbinic teaching and all teaching about the inferiority of women are overthrown by Christ's own actions. Insofar as such negative cultural views were a result of the Fall or the curse, we can say that Jesus was in a sense "reversing the curse" by his own example.

Nevertheless there are some aspects of the feminist interpretation of Jesus' encounters with women with which we must strongly disagree. These are as follows.

1. Exaggerated Radicalness

The first point of disagreement relates to the degree to which Jesus' treatment of women was in opposition to the practices current in his day. It seems that it was not as drastic a break with general Jewish culture as it is usually portrayed to be by feminists. The picture commonly drawn is that Jewish women were treated as property or as animals or worse. As Hull puts it, "female life was a throwaway," and women were "considered beneath contempt."[78] The worse it can be made to sound, the more radical Jesus' example will seem to be.

The facts suggest, however, that such grim language is more indicative of a martyr syndrome than of the actual state of affairs in first-century Judaism. Such descriptions seem to be overly narrow and one-sided, because they assume that the most negative rabbinic teaching about women was the norm for that culture. This cannot be established with certainty, however; and there are indications that it was indeed not the case.

Stephen Clark points out that there are extremes in both directions on this issue. That Jesus was a revolutionary is an extreme, as is the view that Jesus' approach to women differed little if at all from contemporary Jewish customs. Clark defends a moderate view which sees Jesus' approach as new in some ways but not totally revolutionary. "The view that Jesus was not revolutionary in regard to social roles and customs for men-women relations, but that he accorded them a higher spiritual status than Jews who were his contemporaries, accords best with the available evidence."[79]

It is true that rabbinic writings such as the Talmud and the Midrash contain some very misogynistic sayings about women, and they relegate women to the very lowest of social roles. But this fact must be qualified in three ways. First, the exact date of the origin of such views is not certain, since they appear in written form only in the second century and afterwards. It is possible but not certain that they existed in oral form in the first century. Second, the "woman-hating" sayings appear to be only one strand of rabbinic teaching. Clark says it would be "much too strong to say that misogyny was characteristic of the rabbis. Their writings also provide numerous instances of praise and honor for women."[80]

Third and most important, the rabbinic writings themselves, and the teachings of the Pharisaic scribes who preceded them, were not necessarily descriptive of normative Jewish practices in the first century. Though this was once assumed, says Clark, the Dead Sea Scrolls have led to a quite different perception. "It is much clearer now that Judaism before 70 A.D. was a variegated phenomenon, and that the Pharisees were only one sect among a number, although they were the strongest."[81]

> In other words, while one can say with some confidence that many of the practices described in the Talmud and Midrash were characteristic of scribe-rabbis in the time of Jesus, one cannot say that all of the practices were characteristic, or even that all scribes held them. Neither can one say that the practices characteristic of the scribes would have been considered normal for most of the Jewish people.[82]

Thus it is an exaggeration to say that Jesus was a revolutionary who broke all categories and went beyond all the accepted norms of his time in the area of gender roles.[83]

The gospel records themselves support this view in both negative and positive ways. On the negative side, if Jesus' treatment of women were as revolutionary as feminists claim, one would expect the gospels to record significant outcries and objections against it from the Pharisees, as is the case with his breaking of their sabbath traditions. But there is an absolute silence in this regard. As Clark says, "The simplest and most striking fact to begin with in examining Jesus' approach to women is the lack of apparent controversy created by it." His enemies objected to his relations with tax collectors and sinners, but not to his relations with women as such. His disciples showed surprise that Jesus was talking with the Samaritan woman in public (John 4:27), but it caused no great stir. In short, says Clark, "the evidence indicates that Jesus' normal behavior with regard to women was not understood to be revolutionary by people in his environment."[84]

The absence of any controversy on this subject in the gospels shows that Scanzoni and Hardesty have absolutely no basis for their extravagant claim that Jesus' actions toward women "upset and appalled his contemporaries, dumbfounded his critics, and flabbergasted his male disciples."[85]

On the positive side, there are indications in the gospels that women were treated with respect and that they enjoyed considerable freedom and equality. For example, the very fact that a number of women traveled with Jesus and supported his work shows "that the cultural status of women was not so low but that such independence was enjoyed to allow this." It also shows that these women controlled enough money to allow them to do this.[86]

For another example, the fact that Jesus conversed with several women on theological topics shows that they were *not* uneducated but already had rather sophisticated understandings of religious matters. The Samaritan woman spoke of the difference between Jewish and Samaritan worship, and she knew about the promised Messiah (John 4:20, 25). Martha already knew about the resurrection on the last day, and she knew about the expected Messiah (John 11:24, 27). When feminists cite Jesus' discussions with these women as evidence "that women were not to be restricted in their quest for faith in God,"[87] they are overlooking the obvious fact that such women were *already* not restricted, as their expressed knowledge shows. This is also seen from the fact that women were in the large crowds that followed Jesus to hear him teach, without objection and without any special invitation or permission from anyone (cf. Matt. 14:21; 15:38; Luke 11:27). They even came into the synagogues to hear him teach (Luke 13:10-11).

There are other indications from the gospel records that women were respected. Joseph's treatment of Mary even before Jesus was born was unselfish and considerate (Matt. 1:19). A woman named Anna was a fixture at the temple (Luke 2:36). The very fact that Jairus begged Jesus to save his dying daughter belies the notion that "female life was a throwaway" (Luke 8:41-42). A large crowd mourned with the widow of Nain at her son's death (Luke 7:12); the same was true for Mary and Martha when Lazarus died (John 11:19). Jesus' mother joined Joseph in participating fully in Jewish religious ceremonies (Luke 2:22ff.; 2:41). At the wedding feast in Cana she spoke with authority (John 2:5). Even the Samaritan woman, supposedly "beneath contempt," was believed by the men of her city when she reported her encounter with Jesus (John 4:39).

There is no reason to think that these circumstances were unusual, or that they were the result of the supposedly "revolutionary" example of Jesus. They show that the rabbis' chauvinistic opinions were not universally held, and that Jesus' behavior was just the way things were in the circles within which he moved. These positive reports about women, along with the absence of any hint of complaint or controversy concerning Jesus' treatment of them, show that feminists have exaggerated the bleak and dismal lot of women in first-century Judaism. They also show that when feminists speak of Jesus' behavior as shocking, bizarre, startling, astonishing, and revolutionary, their language is extravagant and unwarranted. Boucher concludes, "It may be that the contrast between the Jews' subordination of women and the Christians' new interest in their equality has been too sharply drawn, indeed, that such a contrast never existed."[88]

2. Feminist Hyperexegesis

Why are feminists so inclined to see an exaggerated radicalness in Jesus' treatment of women? Giving too much weight to the later rabbinic traditions is only part of the explanation. The other reason is that they read much more into the key encounters discussed earlier than could ever possibly be warranted by the texts themselves—a hermeneutical fallacy which may be called "hyperexegesis."[89] Their desire to enlist Christ's support for the feminist agenda leads them to make inferences that are without basis in the text, and then to make generalizations for all of Christendom based on these unsupported inferences.

For example, it is inferred that the women who followed Jesus and helped to support him were part of his "inner circle" and were being trained for leadership in his "traveling seminary" along with the apostles. But the text is absolutely silent about such a purpose for these women. In fact the text makes a clear distinction between the work of Jesus and the twelve, who were "proclaiming and preaching the kingdom of God" (Luke 8:1); and the activity of the women, who "were contributing to their support out of their private means" (Luke 8:3). The text says absolutely nothing about these women as part of Jesus' inner circle; it says nothing about their studying with Jesus or their preaching along with the disciples.

The only description of the activities of these women is that "they ministered to them," i.e., to the needs of both Jesus and the apostles. The word means "to serve, to minister" (cf. Matt. 27:55; Mark 15:41 also). It is the same word used of Peter's mother-in-law, who "waited on Him" after Jesus had healed her (Matt. 8:15); and of Martha, who "was serving" when Jesus came for supper (John 12:2).

That these women ministered to them "out of their private means" indicates that they were using their own money to provide food and supplies so that Jesus and the apostles could concentrate on preaching and teaching.

The work of these women seems to have been on a volunteer basis, since there is no record of Jesus' calling any women for this purpose. The records also imply that their presence with Jesus' group was sporadic and not constant. Exactly when they began is not indicated. Since they were "women who had been healed of evil spirits and sicknesses" (Luke 8:2), they would not have begun this work at or near the beginning of Christ's ministry. They were not present in John 4 when Jesus' disciples had the responsibility of buying food (v. 8). (The only disciples named to this point were Peter, Andrew, Philip, and Nathanael—John 1:40-45.) That they were not constantly with Jesus and his disciples is seen from the fact that one of the latter—Judas—was the appointed treasurer for the group even near the end of Jesus' life (John 12:6). Mark 15:41 indicates the limitations of the women's service when he says they followed Jesus and ministered to him "when He was in Galilee."

In view of the actual data it is totally irresponsible to use the example of these women to try to prove that Jesus was flouting alleged stereotypes that "demanded that women must serve rather than learn the word of God." To infer that Jesus was training these women "to go on to take authoritative leadership positions" is completely unfounded.

The same applies to the feminists' handling of the accounts of Jesus' encounter with these same women after his resurrection. Jesus' instructions to them are interpreted as a commission to engage in public preaching and evangelism, "to proclaim Him," to announce the fact of the resurrection and "tell it abroad." Generalizations are then drawn from this inference: Jesus thus endorses "female ministry"; Jesus is preparing women for "authoritative leadership positions."

No one can dispute the fact that being the first human beings to see the risen Christ was a tremendous privilege for these women. And no one can dispute the fact that they were entrusted with considerable responsibility when Jesus instructed them to bear a message back to his disciples. But when we look at the text realistically and objectively, we see a picture far different from that which results from feminist hyperexegesis.

In the first place, Jesus did *not* commission the women to "proclaim Him" or to proclaim the message of the reality of the resurrection "abroad." He did not say, "Go and tell the world that I have risen from the dead." The fact is that he gave them a very specific message to pass along to his "brethren": "Go and take word to My brethren to leave for Galilee, and there they shall see Me" (Matt. 28:10). He does not even mention the resurrection itself; and the message was to be passed along to the "inner circle," i.e., the eleven disciples, who were the ones he wanted to meet him in Galilee (Matt. 28:16). The specific message entrusted to Mary Magdalene is of a similar nature: "Go to my brethren, and say to them, 'I ascend to My Father and your Father, and My God and your God'" (John 20:17). Again, the message does not include anything about the resurrection, and it is to be delivered to the "brethren," his disciples (John 20:18).

What is Jesus asking these women to do? He is asking them to serve as messengers and to deliver a specific message to a specific group of people, period. There is nothing about preaching and evangelism that can legitimately be concluded from this incident. There is nothing of the nature of Jesus' instructions to the healed demoniac, "Go home to your people and report to them what great things the Lord has done for you" (Mark 5:19). It is more like his instructions to the two messengers sent by John the Baptist, "Go and report to John what you have seen and heard" (Luke 7:22). It is like the time he "sent messengers on ahead of Him . . . to make arrangements for Him" (Luke 9:52), or when he sent Peter and John to prepare the

Passover (Luke 22:8), or when he sent messengers with a message for Herod (Luke 13:32).

There were occasions during Jesus' ministry when he sent groups out to preach. He specifically chose the twelve apostles "that He might send them out to preach" (Mark 3:14), and he did so: "He sent them out to proclaim the kingdom of God" (Luke 9:2; cf. Matt. 10:5; Mark 6:7). No women were included in this group (a point to be discussed later). Jesus also appointed "seventy others,[90] and sent them two and two ahead of Him" to announce the coming of the kingdom (Luke 10:1, 9). These are not named or specified as males, but the masculine forms used to describe them in verses 1-2 indicate that they were. If Jesus had wanted to make a point about female evangelists or preachers, these were the ideal opportunities. But he did not.

This is not to degrade the role of the women at the tomb by any means. The message they carried was important, and their task was a responsible one; but to equate this with evangelism and preaching and "female ministry" in general goes far beyond the text itself. It is an example of feminist hyperexegesis.

Similar points may be made about the Samaritan woman in John 4. As noted above, feminists call her "the first evangelist" and assert that "Jesus commissioned her as his special messenger." We can agree that what she did was a kind of evangelism, in the sense that she carried good news back to her people (verses 28-29). But the idea that Jesus commissioned her as an evangelist or special messenger is simply not found in the text. The only thing Jesus told her to do was "Go, call your husband, and come here" (v. 16). In fact, she even disobeyed the intent of this order by invoking a technicality (verses 17-18) and then by reporting her conversation with Jesus not to her "husband" but to the men of the city (v. 28). Thus despite her enthusiasm, she could hardly be called a faithful messenger. An independent and knowledgeable woman? Yes. But the prototype for modern women preachers? Hardly.

Probably the passage most misused by feminists, and the most blatant example of hyperexegesis, is Luke 10:38-42, the report of Jesus' encounter with Mary and Martha in their home. To equate what Mary was doing on this isolated occasion with "studying theology," "doing theology," formal religious training, or "higher level formal education" simply boggles the mind. To interpret it like this and then to generalize from this to modern seminary training for ordained ministry can only be called the "hermeneutics of desire."

The feminist approach to this account suffers from two main problems. First, it confuses *lifestyle* with *vocation*. Yes, Jesus defended Mary's choice to sit at his feet and listen to him teach, saying that this is really the only necessary thing in life, the good part of life that cannot be taken away (v. 42). But here he is talking about discipleship as a *lifestyle*, not as a formal vocation. *Every* believer, male and female, is called to "study at Jesus' feet" throughout his or her lifetime, in addition to whatever job or responsibility or bread-winning occupation one may have. What Mary was doing is in general the equivalent to daily Bible study or regular church attendance. More precisely it resembles participation in special seminars or revival meetings or other such programs sponsored by churches today.

These kinds of things do not replace regular responsibilities, either for Mary or for anyone else. After Jesus left her house, Mary would still have to resume her duties in the kitchen or wherever; but her life would be enriched by having heard Jesus teach. In this sense her lifestyle was that of a disciple or learner; what she learned from Jesus would affect everything she did in her everyday life. This one good and necessary thing so well discerned by Mary is thus a *dimension* of life that transcends or underlies everything else we do; indeed, it is the one crucial and enduring dimension. It is the same as Jesus' instruction in Matthew 6:33 to "seek first His kingdom and His righteousness; and all these things shall be added to you." This is not talking directly about one's choice of occupation but rather about a particular lifestyle that will determine how we approach our occupation and everything else we do.

There is no warrant whatsoever for equating Mary's choice in Luke 10 with modern seminary training or vocational ministry. Jesus did issue a number of calls to what was then equivalent to such training and ministry, but they were always to men. "Follow Me, and I will make you fishers of men," he said to Peter and Andrew (Matt. 4:19). "Follow Me," he said to Philip (John 1:43). "Follow Me," he said to Matthew (Matt. 9:9). "Follow Me," he said to the rich young ruler and to another disciple (Matt. 8:22; 19:21). But there is nothing whatsoever of this nature in Jesus' relationship with Mary in Luke 10. She was indeed "following Christ" in her lifestyle, which is quite different from following him in vocational Christian service.

This story is "revolutionary," says Hull, "because it taught that women should prefer studying theology over a preoccupation with domestic chores."[91] Such a statement, though, is a completely false and misleading interpretation of Luke 10. In the first place, Jesus is not talking about "studying theology" in any modern sense of the term. In the second place, it offers a false choice between what Mary was doing on the one hand and "domestic chores" on the other hand. Mary was not choosing one to the exclusion of the other; she was simply putting them in the proper perspective on this particular occasion. In the third place, a "preoccupation" with *any* activity, including studying theology, violates the point Jesus makes here. Nothing must be allowed to detract from our personal discipleship to Jesus and our personal devotion to him, whether it be domestic chores, studying theology, or selling insurance. That is the point Jesus is making, and it has nothing to do with the feminist agenda.

The second main problem with the feminist approach to this story is that it ignores the *uniqueness* of the situation. What was the nature of this occasion? This was not just an ordinary visitor in the house of Mary and Martha; this was the *Son of God himself,* the one whose teaching was the very "words of eternal life" (John 6:68). And Martha was worried and bothered about what to fix him for lunch! That is an understandable concern, and ministering to Jesus' needs in this way was an important service given by a number of women, including Martha (John 12:2). But how often does one have the opportunity to learn from Jesus' very lips? To be sure, Jesus was probably in the home of Mary's family more than any other during the days of his ministry, but that time was still relatively short. How many more occasions like this would there be, before Jesus was no longer with them in person? Mary was simply taking advantage of this unique opportunity while it was available. Indeed, one could rightly say that there was no more important thing on earth that she could have been doing at that moment, given the nature of the circumstances.

To treat this story in Luke as a lesson on the propriety of rabbinical or seminary training for women trivializes the encounter. This was not just some rabbi or some eminent theological professor; this was Jesus himself. This was not just rabbinical training or a doctoral seminar; these were the very words of eternal life. To suggest a rather puny comparison, Mary saw her opportunity the way a devout Catholic in a remote part of the earth would regard a visit from the Pope, i.e., as a once-in-a-lifetime event. There would be plenty of time for cooking and sewing later; but this may well have been an unrepeatable experience, and absolutely nothing was going to take precedence over it.

The error is to think that one can generalize from such an experience by comparing it with particular choices of ordinary life, even choices as important as one's vocation. But there is no such comparison. The uniqueness of the God-man Jesus, and the uniqueness of his mission and purpose on earth, rule out such specific parallels today. The only true comparison, as already noted, is with one's spiritual relationship with Jesus Christ as a dimension that transcends yet permeates all the ordinary choices and relationships of this life.

3. Conclusion

In this section we have seen that Jesus' encounters with women simply do not support the feminist gospel. Once the exaggerations are toned down and the false inferences and generalizations are excluded, we find nothing in the life and example of Jesus that requires or even resembles egalitarianism. Everything in his treatment of women is fully compatible with the hierarchical view in every way. As Clark has well said, "The fact that he did treat women very well, with love and respect, is by no means incompatible with acceptance of role differences between men and women."[92]

What positive conclusions can be drawn from Jesus' behavior toward women? Foh says there are two. "From Jesus' actions, we can conclude that women should be taught about the Bible and women should witness to their Lord. Before any other conclusions can be drawn, it is necessary to consider the rest of the New Testament."[93]

III. CHRIST'S TEACHINGS ABOUT WOMEN

We now turn from Christ's encounters with women to his teachings about women. This is another subject which feminists try to use in a positive way in support of the egalitarian theory. Though Jesus gave very little if any specific teaching that directly relates to the issues at stake, so that the points made by feminists are only of an inferential or general nature, nevertheless they consider these points to be very significant. They believe that Jesus' teaching overthrows the hierarchicalism of the Jewish patriarchal culture, and establishes the feminist view of equality as the norm. Our purpose in this section is to evaluate this claim.

A. The Feminist View of Jesus' Teaching

Whatever difficulty egalitarians may have with Paul, says Gasque, they certainly have none with Jesus. "There is not one hint anywhere in the teaching of Jesus that he ever suggested the idea that women are to be dependent on men, or to be in submission to men, or in any way were to be regarded as inferior."[94] This same argument from silence is used by Mickelsen: "We look in vain for anything in the life or teachings of our Lord that point [sic] to 'differences in function' for men and women in kingdom work."[95]

But are there any positive elements in Jesus' teaching relating to gender roles? Did Jesus teach anything that supports equality in function? Indeed he did, say the feminists. One point that is often made is the fact that in his teaching Jesus used women in his illustrations and parables as much as he did men, something that would not have been expected in that culture and that was a deliberate rebuke to it. "He used both men and women as examples of spiritual truths in his parables," Mickelsen points out.[96] Van Leeuwen insists that he "almost never tells a parable using male images and activities without also using a parallel one involving women."[97]

What are these parables and illustrations? Four parables include women: the kingdom as leaven, Matthew 13:33; the wise and foolish virgins, Matthew 25:1-13; the lost coin, Luke 15:8-10; and the persistent widow, Luke 18:1-8. Six illustrations may be found: the Queen who came to hear Solomon, Matthew 12:42; the widow of Zarephath, Luke 4:25-26; pregnant and nursing mothers, Matthew 24:19; women grinding at the mill, Matthew 24:41; Lot's wife, Luke 17:32; and women in childbirth, John 16:21. On several occasions Jesus also referred to relationships between family members; and he included mothers, sisters, daughters, daughters-in-law, and mothers-in-law (Matt. 12:46-50; Mark 7:10-11; 10:29-30; Luke 12:51-53; 14:26). The following remarks by Mary Evans sum up this point:

Jesus' reference to women in the illustrations which he used in his teaching indicates further his general attitude to them. Rabbinic parables pointedly avoided mentioning women, but Jesus often told stories relating to the life of women. He spoke of using yeast in bread-making, of child-birth, of grinding meal, of wedding attendants, of house-wives and of widows. He used pictures of women to illus-trate themes of vigilance, of perseverance in prayer, of divine mercy and of the joy of God over the salvation of a lost sinner. The impression is gained that women were not, as the Rabbis seemed to imply, necessary but of only secondary significance; but rather that they were an inte-gral part of the creation, both necessary and significant; seen as having worth as persons in their own right and not simply in relation to men.[98]

Another specific element of Jesus' teaching considered to be very important by feminists is the episode in Luke 11:27-28, when an anonymous woman said to Jesus, "Blessed is the womb that bore You, and the breasts at which You nursed." Jesus replied to her, "On the contrary, blessed are those who hear the word of God, and observe it." According to feminists, this means that Jesus consid-ered uniquely female roles such as motherhood to be secondary to roles that can be shared by both men and women. This sets them free from the culturally-imposed domestic prison of bedroom-nursery-kitchen, and even from the biologically-imposed necessity of childbearing. His deliberate intent was to give women this freedom.

As Mollenkott interprets this statement of Jesus, he is rejecting the notion that "Mary is reduced to one womb and two breasts," a biological creature and nothing more. "Jesus will have none of it. He immediately redefines blessedness in a way which transcends either male or female biology." By Jesus' definition, "biology is not destiny. Rather, spiritual commitment is destiny."[99] According to Swidler, the anonymous woman's remark was typical of that sexist culture; "her image of a woman was sexually reductionist in the extreme." And even though it was meant as a compliment, "and although it was even uttered by a woman, Jesus clearly felt it necessary to reject this 'baby-machine' image of women and insist again on the personhood, the intellectual and moral faculties, being primary for all."[100] As Pentz says, Jesus is calling on women "to nurture their relationship to God rather than being defined by their relationships with their husband and children."[101]

Feminists also point out that Jesus' teaching erased the Jews' double standard in matters of divorce, i.e., the practice that allowed men to divorce their wives but not vice versa. The casual treatment and easy dismissal of wives is shown in the apocryphal work Ecclesiasticus 25:26, "If she will not do as you tell her, get rid of her!" By his teaching, however, Jesus not only made divorce more difficult (Matt. 19:9), but applied the same standard to both men and women (Mark 10:11-12). In this way Jesus makes the point that women are responsible persons, "not objects to be dismissed at will."[102]

In a similar way, when Jesus teaches that lusting after a woman is equivalent to committing adultery with her (Matt. 5:27-28), he is condemning the tendency of men to regard women as mere sex objects. He insists instead that "women are to be recognized as subjects in their own right, as fellow human beings, fellow disciples, and not just the objects of men's desire."[103] The real issue, says Mollenkott, is responsible personhood. "To most first-century people, men were persons and women were property to be used or disposed of at the pleasure of men. But to Jesus, women were persons just as fully as men."[104]

A final example of a teaching of Jesus that elevates women to a role of equality with men is Mark 10:29-30. Here Jesus says no matter what one leaves behind for the sake of the gospel, God will make it up to him a hundredfold. He says, "There is no one who has left house or brothers or sisters . . . but that he shall receive a hundred times as much." That Jesus includes *sisters* in the list is important to feminists. As Evans declares, "leaving one's sister" would not have been thought of as a sacrifice by Jews at that time. "However, Jesus valued women enough to assume that leaving a sister would be as much a sacrifice as was leaving parents or children or houses."[105]

Having thus discerned in Jesus' teaching an egalitarian pattern, feminists insist that what Jesus has to say on this subject takes priority over other Biblical teaching, especially that of Paul. This is a "common hermeneutical tendency" among them, says Swartley. "They give priority to Jesus and the Gospels over the Old Testament and Paul."[106] As Judy Norris puts it, "Shouldn't Jesus be heard first on all issues on which we have His recorded statements and example?"[107]

B. Response to the Feminist View of Christ's Teaching

Feminists make some very good points about Jesus' teaching as it relates to women. We agree that he affirms the full personhood of all women, and requires us to treat them as individuals and as persons rather than as property or sex objects. We agree that he abolishes any double standards that might have existed with regard to divorce and sexual morality in general. We agree that he places a very high value on women and their abilities and relationships.

In other words Jesus affirms what has been true of men and women since they were first created, i.e., that they have ontological equality. The fact remains, however, that feminists have uncovered nothing in Christ's teaching that gives any support to their central doctrine, which is egalitarianism regarding roles and functions. In fact, the situation is just the opposite. A detailed look at the way Jesus taught and the content of his teaching shows that it is overwhelmingly male oriented and definitely favors male leadership.

Such conclusions do not come from any teachings of Jesus that specifically deal with this subject, because there are none. This fact in itself is significant, for this reason: if "abolishing patriarchy" was a major purpose of Christ's incarnation and ministry, as feminists assume, why is all his "teaching" on the subject so indirect and inferential? Why are there no direct statements addressed specifically to the subject? As Clark says, "If Jesus wanted to be revolutionary in his approach to the roles of men and women, one could expect something in his teaching that would point in that direction. However, there is no such evidence in his teaching."[108]

Contrary to feminist interpretations and expectations, though, we do find that Jesus' teaching is consistent with hierarchicalism. The following analysis will show how this is the case.

1. The Frequency of Jesus' References to Women

Although frequency of occurrence is not necessarily the decisive factor in judging the importance of any subject, it has been brought into this discussion by feminists themselves and thus may be fairly addressed. Evans says that Jesus "often" told stories with women as their subjects; Van Leeuwen says he "almost never tells a parable using male images and activities without also using a parallel one involving women," as cited above. The impression given is that women appear in Jesus' parables and illustrations almost as often as men do.

This, however, is blatantly false, as any detailed survey of the gospels will readily show. Jesus used male figures in his teaching far more often than female. The following charts concerning both parables and illustrations will help to make this clear.[109] The first chart lists the illustrations Jesus used, with men and women in separate columns. (Parallel passages are not counted.)

Men and Women in Jesus' Illustrations

(MEN)		(WOMEN)
Matt. 5:12	Persecuted prophets	
5:40	Plaintiff in lawsuit	
5:41	Conscriptor	
6:29	Solomon	
7:3f.	Brother with speck in eye	
7:9f.	Needy son, generous father	
9:15	Bridegroom and friends	
12:3f.	David and companions	
12:5	Priests	
12:29	Strong man who was bound	
12:39f.	Jonah	
12:41	Men of Nineveh	12:42 Queen of the South
15:14	Blind men leading others	
16:4	Jonah	
24:17	Man on housetop	
24:18	Man in field	24:19 Pregnant & Nursing Women
24:37f.	Noah	
24:40	Two men in field	24:41 Two women grinding
24:43	Householder	
Mark 12:46	Moses	
Luke 4:25f.	Elijah	4:26 Widow of Zarephath
4:27	Elisha and Naaman	
12:36f.	Slaves and kind master	
13:4	Men killed by falling tower	
14:8f.	Host at wedding feast	
16:19f.	Rich man and Lazarus	
17:28f.	Lot	17:32 Lot's wife
John 3:14	Moses	
6:32	Moses	
8:35	Son and slave	
15:15	Slave and master	16:21 Woman having baby

The next chart shows the parables Jesus told, those with men being listed in the first column and those with women in the second column. (The two marked with asterisks include both men and women. Again, parallel passages are not listed and not counted.)

Men and Women in Jesus' Parables

(MEN)		(WOMEN)
Matt. 7:24f.	Wise and foolish builders	
13:3f.	Sower and seed	
13:24f.	Wheat and tares	
13:31f.	Mustard seed	13:33 Woman and leaven
13:44	Hidden treasure	
13:45f.	Pearl of great price	
18:23f.	Unforgiving servant	
20:1f.	Laborers in vineyard	
21:28f.	Sons working in vineyard	
21:33f.	Vineyard-owner and son	
22:1f.	Wedding feast	
24:45f.	Faithful and evil slaves	
*25:1f.	Bridegroom and virgins	
		*25:1f. Bridegroom and virgins
25:14f.	Stewardship of talents	
Mark 4:26f.	Seed and harvest	
Luke 7:41f.	Lender and debtors	
10:30f.	Good Samaritan	
11:5f.	Friend at midnight	
12:16f.	Rich fool	
13:6f.	Barren fig tree	
13:25f.	Shut door	
14:16f.	Spurned invitations	
14:28f.	Building a tower	
14:31f.	Peace council	
15:4f.	Lost sheep	15:8f. Lost coin
15:11f.	Prodigal son	
16:1f.	Unrighteous steward	
17:7f.	Unprofitable slave	
*18:1f.	Judge & persistent widow	
		*18:1f. Judge & persistent widow
18:10f.	Pharisee and publican	
19:12f.	Nobleman and stewards	
John 10:1f.	Shepherd and sheepfold	

By way of analysis, there are thirty-one illustrations involving men and six involving women, for a five-to-one ratio. Regarding the parables, two have main characters of each sex and thus for statistical purposes are counted twice. Of the rest, thirty have main characters who are men, and only two have main characters who are women. This is a total of thirty-two about men and four about women, for an eight-to-one ratio. It is also significant that many of the parables exclusively about men are quite long and involved, and often include several main characters—all men. Of the thirty in this category, twenty involve two or more male roles.[110] The two exclusively about women are very brief (one verse; three verses) and involve only one woman each.

With the hard data before us, we can only wonder what possible justification feminists can give for continuing to claim that Jesus "often" included women in his illustrative teaching. Van Leeuwen's exaggerated statement that Jesus "almost never tells a parable using male images and activities without also using a parallel one involving women" is shown to be not just false but embarrassingly so. The most that one can honestly say is that Jesus sometimes or occasionally used illustrations and parables about women, but not nearly as often as he did about men. All in all, the data on this subject are totally inconsistent with any alleged revolutionary intent on the part of Jesus with regard to gender roles.

2. Comparison of the Male
and Female Roles in Jesus' Teaching

The frequency—or rather infrequency—of Jesus' references to female *roles* is not the only bad news for feminists with respect to Jesus' teaching. An even worse blow to the egalitarian cause is the nature of the roles assigned to women, especially as compared with those in which men are depicted. Mickelsen has said, "We look in vain for anything in the life or teachings of our Lord that point [sic] to 'differences in function' for men and women in kingdom work."[111] Unless she wants to quibble about the qualification "in kingdom work" (which is hardly possible in view of the fact that so many parables are specifically about the kingdom), this is simply not so. The fact is that the roles Jesus selects for women in his parables and illustrations are quite different from those assigned to men.[112]

Since there are so many more passages about men than women, we would expect more kinds of male roles to be represented, even when actual historical figures are excluded. Indeed, there is a wide range of such roles, from servants to kings. On the lower end of the spectrum the role of servant or slave occurs often, and in several cases the role of laborer or field hand appears. Though sometimes it is clear that the latter is working in someone else's field as a servant (e.g., Luke 17:7-10), at other times the impression is that he is working on his own farm (e.g., Matt. 13:3-9; Mark 4:26-29). Some of the roles for men carried considerable responsibility but were unpopular, such as tax collector or money lender or Pharisee.

The roles named in the previous paragraph may be considered on the lower end of the scale either in terms of social achievement or social acceptability. At the same time, however, many if not most of the male roles are on the other end of the spectrum of respectability and responsibility. These include roles of religious leadership, i.e., a priest and a Levite (even the role of Pharisee would not have been totally unpopular). The role of householder or head of the household seems to occur more often than any other (e.g., Matt. 24:43, 45; Luke 11:5; 13:25). This term is applied to the owner of a vineyard, too (Matt. 20:1; 21:33), which is another role that occurs several times (see also Luke 13:6), along with that of owner of a field (Matt. 13:24; 22:5). Men are also pictured as owners of sheep, owners of farms, owners of houses, owners of businesses and property of various kinds, and rich noblemen with large estates. They are presented to us as builders of houses and of towers. One is a judge; and several times the role of king appears (Matt. 18:23; 22:2; Luke 14:31). Even those pictured in the role of slave or servant are often depicted as responsible stewards of their masters' property, as in the parable of the talents and the parable of the unrighteous steward.

Thus in Jesus' teaching most of the roles in which men appear are roles of leadership and responsibility in the home, in religious life, and in society in general.

What, then, of the female roles chosen by Jesus when he introduced female characters into his teaching? Again excluding the Old Testament historical individuals, we may list the few that do occur: *attending a bridegroom* (parable of the bridegroom and the virgins, Matt. 25:1-13), *preparing food* (grinding at the mill, Matt. 24:41; mixing leaven in the meal, Matt. 13:33), *doing housework* (sweeping, Luke 15:8-10), and *motherhood* (pregnancy, childbirth, and nursing infants; Matt. 24:19; John 16:21). The fact is that every role chosen by Jesus for the female characters he created for his parables and illustrations is a domestic role. There are no exceptions. Does this sound like a feminist revolution? The answer is obvious.

The role of motherhood requires special attention here in view of the feminist interpretation of Luke 11:27-28. This is the passage in which a woman blessed Mary for her role as Jesus' mother, and Jesus replied, "On the contrary, blessed are those who hear the word of God, and observe it." Feminists take this as an indication that Jesus wants women to pursue roles of spiritual and religious leadership alongside of men, and that motherhood is quite secondary to such roles.

This interpretation of the Lukan passage simply is not consistent with what we have just seen about female roles in Jesus' teaching, which includes *no* examples of women as leaders and focuses exclusively on domestic roles, especially motherhood. The two passages that depict women in the role of mothers are Matthew 24:19 (with parallels in Mark 13:17 and Luke 21:23) and John 16:21. The former is illustrating the horrible conditions that would exist in the days preceding the destruction of Jerusalem in A.D. 70: "Woe to those who are with child and to those who nurse babes in those days!" The latter passage presents a brighter picture: "Whenever a woman is in travail she has sorrow, because her hour has come; but when she gives birth to the child, she remembers the anguish no more, for joy that a child has been born into the world." A more positive view of childbearing could hardly be imagined.

In two other places in the gospels Jesus explicitly refers to the woman's role as bearer of children. Of John the Baptist he says, "Among those born of women there has not arisen anyone greater" (Matt. 11:11; parallel, Luke 7:28). "Those born of women" is a way of describing the entire human race, and it is a natural and positive reflection on the role of motherhood as such. It is not a way of speaking that we would expect from someone who regarded this role as overrated in his own culture.

The other passage is Luke 23:28-29. Here Jesus is on his way to Calvary, and a large group of women are mourning and weeping for him. He says to them, "Daughters of Jerusalem, stop weeping for Me, but weep for yourselves and for your children. For behold, the days are coming when they will say, 'Blessed are the barren, and the wombs that never bore, and the breasts that never nursed.'" Here he is again referring to future persecutions and tribulations such as would befall the Jews preceding the destruction of Jerusalem in A.D. 70 (see verses 30-31).

What does this passage say about motherhood? Quite the opposite of the meaning feminists give to Luke 11:27-28. It says that motherhood is so natural and desirable for women that *any* situation that makes childlessness seem like a blessing is a cause for weeping. Only in an upside-down, tragic world could anyone possibly bless "the wombs that never bore, and the breasts that never nursed." In the ideal world—the world of Genesis 1 and 2, and the world of the new creation—we should say, "Blessed are the wombs that bear, and the breasts that nurse."

But the woman in Luke 11:27 said almost this very thing, and Jesus corrected her. "On the contrary," he said, "blessed are those who hear the word of God, and observe it." What did he mean? There are two emphases here. First, the woman did not say the same thing as Luke 23:29, "Blessed are the wombs that bear, and the breasts that nurse." She said, "Blessed is the womb that bore *You*, and the breasts at which *You* nursed." Lurking in her statement was the potential for singling out Mary for special treatment or special veneration, just because she was the mother of Jesus. Jesus' reply was designed to preclude this. It is true that Mary was uniquely favored and blessed among women (Luke 1:30, 42), in that she alone was the mother of God the Son incarnate. But what we should especially remember about Mary is not this unique role which no one else can share, but her submissiveness to the word of God, an attribute which all can imitate, male and female alike. If we want to bless Mary, we should bless her for hearing and observing the word of God (Luke 1:38). If we want to be blessed, we must do the same.

This episode is quite parallel to Matthew 12:46-50, where someone told Jesus, "Your mother and Your brothers are standing outside seeking to speak to You." Jesus replied, "Who is My mother and who are My brothers? . . . Whoever does the will of My Father who is in heaven, he is My brother and sister and mother." Here Jesus is in no way degrading family relationships, nor is he disowning his own human family. He is again issuing a caution not to put his relatives on a pedestal or to think of them as being better than anyone else just because of their physical relationship to him. What is more important is a spiritual relationship with him, something that comes from doing the will of the heavenly Father and thus is available to everyone.

The second element in Jesus' reply in Luke 11:28 is the same as the point of his reply to Martha in Luke 10:41-42. He is not setting these two courses of action over against one another as if one can or must choose between them:

"Either have children, or hear and do the word of God." These are not equivalent to one another, as if each were a role or vocation to be pursued. To interpret "hear the word of God, and observe it" as referring to "doing theology" in the sense of formal seminary training and vocational ministry is quite irresponsible. "Hearing and observing the word of God" is not a *role* at all, in the sense that motherhood is a role. It is rather an all-permeating *dimension* of life, equivalent to that one good and necessary part chosen by Mary and commended to Martha in Luke 10:42. It is the one aspect of life that makes all the other aspects blessed and acceptable to God. Without a heart that hears and observes the word of God, even a role as highly honored as motherhood gives a person no standing before God.

From this point of view Jesus' response applies equally to *every* role in life. That the initiating comment referred to motherhood is incidental; whatever role might have been named (e.g., elder in Israel, physician, theologian), Jesus' reply would have been the same. That is, the point of his statement is to affirm something about everyone's life, not to deny something about a particular role in life. He is telling us that *nothing* is more important than each individual's hearing and honoring the word of God, not even the significant role of motherhood, and not even Mary's uniquely supreme instance of motherhood.

It is not Jesus' purpose here to make a statement about women as such, either to deny that women should be defined in terms of motherhood or to declare that they should be defined as hearers and doers of the word of God. His comment is not even aimed specifically at women but is meant to include all people in general; his statement "Blessed are those" is even in the masculine plural form. What makes a person's activity or role or work blessed before God? Not that work in itself, no matter how necessary and beneficial it may be. What makes it blessed is when it is performed in the spirit of submission to God's word.

This passage can be understood better by comparing it

with a similar idea in Matthew 7:21-23. Here Jesus says, "Not everyone who says to Me, 'Lord, Lord,' will enter the kingdom of heaven; but he who does the will of My Father who is in heaven." He says that in the Last Day many will declare, "Lord, Lord, did we not prophesy in Your name, and in Your name cast out demons, and in Your name perform many miracles?" But he will command them to depart from him. Why? What activities could possibly be grander or even holier than prophesying, casting out demons, and performing miracles? The problem is not with these activities themselves, but with the fact that they were not accompanied by the "submission dimension," the one good and necessary part: hearing and doing the will and word of God.

In sum, Jesus' teaching contains some very relevant points concerning gender roles, and they are all favorable to the hierarchical position. Only exegesis that is selective and subjective can make Jesus sound like a feminist.

3. Conclusion

Our conclusion here is the same as with Jesus' encounters with women, namely, there is nothing whatsoever in the teaching of Jesus that suggests that he was deliberately challenging his culture's view of the role of women or that this was one of the purposes of his incarnation and his ministry. If his teaching can be construed as pointing in one way or the other, it very definitely supports hierarchicalism and contradicts the most cherished assumptions of egalitarianism.

Judy Norris has asked, as noted above, "Shouldn't Jesus be heard first on all issues on which we have His recorded statements and example?" We must resist issuing an automatic affirmative answer to this question, since this would suggest that the words of Jesus are more authoritative than the inspired teachings of the apostles and prophets, which they are not.[113] But in light of our study of the teaching of Jesus on the subject of gender roles, it really does not matter whether we start with Jesus or with Genesis 2 or with Paul. They all teach the same thing: male headship and leadership, and female submission.

IV. WHY WERE THERE NO FEMALE APOSTLES?

The final issue to be discussed in this chapter is why Jesus chose no female apostles. This question is especially pertinent in view of the interpretation of Jesus as a feminist reformer. If he were really serious about restoring the alleged ideal of functional equality, this would have been the decisive and conclusive gesture. No further arguments would be necessary, and no objections could be sustained. But he did not choose a woman. At best this leaves the question of female leadership open; at worst it sets a precedent for the church to follow. Feminists know this; and though they are resigned to the fact, they cannot help but think, "If only . . . ." At the same time they feel constrained to give reasons for the absence of a woman among the twelve apostles, and to explain why this absence is not relevant to the issue of leadership in the church today.

A. The Feminist Explanation

According to feminists, the reasons why Jesus did not choose a woman apostle are all circumstantial. It was basically a matter of culture. The cultural attitudes of the people would have made it impossible for Jesus to do what he had to do, with women as a part of the group that traveled with him. It also would have been a very difficult situation for the women themselves.

The basic assumption here once again is that women in Jewish culture had such a low status that they were practically *personae non gratae* or social outcasts and would have been totally rejected by the people if Jesus had put them into such a position. This attitude meant that he had to exercise "divine patience" in his desire to "instill his will about women," says Owen Crouch. "Jewish low-grade views limited Christ's outreach to and use of women. . . . There was no way in which Jesus could have been listened to, much less respected, had he chosen women to be numbered among his apostles. But he did the best he could." Not choosing a woman was just a matter of "practical strategy," since "Jesus had no *moral* objection to women being apostles."[114] Charlene Hopman agrees that the answer to the question of why no women were chosen must lie in the fact that Jesus was "yielding for a time to existing social conditions." She asks, "What chance would a woman have had to function in a society so male oriented?"[115]

Others agree and state this explanation in similar terms. McClelland says, "The logistics of women becoming full-time disciples and traveling with males around Palestine would have been impossible and would have scandalized and obscured Jesus' true mission."[116] The only choices were single women and married women, and Dorothy Pape says both were ruled out by circumstances: "To have called a single woman would obviously have led to unsavory suspicions, while most married women were presumably busy taking care of their families."[117] Hull sums it up: "Isn't it possible that excluding women from the Twelve was another concession to first-century culture—as well as to decorum?"[118]

Another argument is commonly offered, not as an explanation of why Jesus did not choose a woman apostle but as an *ad hoc* argument against those who try to make this a precedent for male leadership in the church. If the absence of a woman among the Twelve means there can be no women leaders in the church, they say, then the absence of Gentiles and slaves (cf. Gal. 3:28) means there can be no church leaders from among Gentiles and slaves, either. This argument is voiced by Spencer: "If Jesus' choice of twelve male disciples signifies that females should not be leaders in the church, then, consistently his choice also signifies that Gentiles should not be leaders in the church."[119] If we try to use the "no female apostles" argument to exclude women from church leadership, says Hull, then "logic demands" that we restrict leadership to Jewish males.[120]

These are the basic feminist responses to the fact that Jesus chose no female apostles. First, the status of women in Jewish culture made it expedient not to do so. Second, this does not set a precedent for exclusively male leadership in the church, or we would logically have to limit such leadership to Jews as well.

B. Analysis of the Feminist Arguments

There are a number of weaknesses in the way feminists handle this aspect of Jesus' ministry. The appeal to cultural accommodation as the explanation of why Jesus chose no women is especially vulnerable. Several points relevant to this issue have already been established in other sections of this chapter. One is the fact that God himself chose the culture in which Christ's ministry would take place. The question is whether he would have chosen one in which it would be so difficult to accomplish what feminists regard as one of the main purposes of the incarnation. Such seems highly unlikely in view of the fact that Jesus came in "the fullness of the time" (Gal. 4:4).

Another relevant point is the fact that Jesus did not have to refrain from choosing a woman apostle just to make sure he was listened to and respected, since he was neither listened to nor respected anyway by those who would have objected to such a choice. If he declined to appoint a woman to the Twelve just for this reason, then the strategy was futile and a golden opportunity wasted.

Another point already mentioned in another connection is that the gap between the popular Jewish culture and Jesus' own ideal was not as wide as feminists assume; thus it is likely that a woman in this position would not have caused as great an uproar as they think. Women's social status was not as low as they depict it, and Christ's teaching and example were not as feministic as they represent it to be. Besides, Israel was no stranger to women leaders, as feminists themselves like to point out. Jesus could have cited Miriam, Huldah, Deborah, Esther, and Anna as precedents. On what basis, then, could the Jewish leaders have complained?

There are several other considerations that completely deflate the "cultural accommodation" argument. Feminists say that Jesus made this concession to his culture so as not to present any unnecessary stumbling block to the acceptance of his message. He was just "yielding for a time to existing social conditions" in order to gain a hearing. We really must wonder, however, if feminists have thought this argument through very carefully in light of the fact that Jesus never seemed to worry about this sort of thing with regard to any other unacceptable cultural practice. He openly challenged one false Jewish tradition after another, such as the man-made Sabbath rules and the rabbis' applications of the clean-unclean distinction. By disregarding such sacrosanct traditions Jesus made enemies right and left, and aroused hostility so intense that it ultimately drove him to the cross. Why, then, should he have felt intimidated by a possible outcry against his choosing a woman apostle? Why should this issue have been any different?[121]

What is most interesting is that feminists are so openly inconsistent on this point. On the one hand they delight in picturing Christ as an iconoclast, especially in this very area of the nature and roles of women. They describe his treatment of and teaching about women as shocking, startling, and revolutionary. As Hopman says, Jesus "treated women as equals even though he broke pertinent social mores," which she proceeds to list one after another. But then, on this matter of no women apostles, she says that Jesus must have been "yielding for a time to existing social conditions."[122] This is clearly a case of trying to have it both ways, and it does not produce a convincing argument.

In view of Jesus' usual defiance of oppressive conven-
tions, it seems clear that if this were the only thing standing in the way of his appointing a woman to the apostleship, and if he had truly wanted to make a strong point in
favor of female leadership, he would not have hesitated to
make the appointment. Wayne House expresses it well:

> If indeed the Lord broke down pseudo-spiritual "fences"
> the rabbinic teachers had built around valid points of the
> Law, and if He did so in order to illustrate spiritual truth as
> well as a correct understanding of Himself, He had a prime
> opportunity to break a social convention *and* teach the
> higher law of female leadership in His new order. The ques-
> tion remains, then: Why didn't He do so?[123]

Another relevant response to the feminist argument
from cultural accommodation is the fact that most of the
cultural problems assumed to apply to women in the apostleship would also have applied to the company of women
who followed Jesus in order to minister to him (Luke 8:1-3),
especially if these women had been disciples in the full
sense assumed by many feminists. Jesus did permit these
women to accompany him, and no record of any problems
or complaints exists. McClelland notes that Jesus allowed
these women "to follow him as disciples"; but then on the
very next page, to explain the lack of women apostles, he
says that "women becoming full-time disciples and traveling with males around Palestine would have been impossible and would have scandalized and obscured Jesus' true
mission."[124] It seems that he does not realize that there is a
contradiction here.

Pape exhibits the same inconsistency. After using this
explanation of no women among the apostles—"To have
called a single woman would obviously have led to unsavory suspicions, while most married women were presumably busy taking care of their families"—she then immediately says, "It is remarkable, therefore, that we later do
find women traveling in his company."[125] She does not
recognize that this "remarkable" fact, and her own admis-

sion of it, invalidate her explanation of the absence of female apostles. Here are women who obviously did travel with Jesus without scandal, and who were not tied down by family responsibilities. Such would have been potential candidates for apostleship, if Jesus had desired to appoint a woman to this office. But he declined to do so.

Sensing his inconsistency, McClelland does say that "women did follow Jesus in groups"[126] (referring to the women of Luke 8:1-3), as if this would somehow be different from a group of six female apostles to go along with six male apostles. The Kroegers try to skirt the problem in a similar way. Jesus could allow these women to accompany him, but could not appoint women apostles, they say, since "to have sent them forth alone on a public preaching and healing ministry would have been impossible."[127] Where they get the idea that apostles were sent out "alone" they do not say. The Bible does not tell us how the apostles traveled. It says the seventy (or seventy-two) went out "two and two" (Luke 10:1), but no similar information is given about the apostles. If there had been women apostles, nothing would have prevented them from going out in "groups" if necessary.

Thus the very existence of the group of women who accompanied Jesus (at least when he was in Galilee) negates the attempt to explain away the absence of female apostles by an appeal to "cultural accommodation."

There is one other point that reveals the inconsistency of feminists' use of this explanation. On the one hand, they say Jesus chose no women apostles because in that culture women would not have been accepted as leaders; on the other hand, they leave no stone unturned in nominating a whole host of women mentioned in the New Testament as leaders in the early church. Are we to assume that the cultural situation had changed so radically that female leaders were acceptable in the church when they were not acceptable during Jesus' ministry just a few years earlier? Speaking of the latter, Hopman asks, "What chance would a woman have had to function in a society so male oriented?"[128] Crouch says Jesus could not expect to be listened to or respected if he had women among his apostles.[129] But social conditions in both the Jewish and the Gentile communities were not radically different by the time the church is supposed to have had so many women leaders. How, then, would *they* have had a chance to function? How could the church be expected to be listened to or respected, with women among its leaders? The point is that if there were women leaders in the church, there is no reason Christ could not have chosen women apostles. But he did not. This raises the question of whether or not there really were so many women "leaders" in the early church, but this is a question that will be dealt with at a later time.

This leads to the final point of response to the way feminists handle this problem, namely, their attempt to negate the significance of the lack of females among the apostles by pointing out that there were no Gentiles among the apostles either. Thus if we use the former as a reason for denying church leadership to females, we should consistently deny church leadership to Gentiles also. There are two reasons why this is a specious argument. First, there is an obvious reason why there were no Gentile apostles, and it has nothing to do with the denial of this role to females. This is the fact that the context of Jesus' ministry was among the Jewish people who had been prepared to receive him by centuries of special revelation and nurture. He did not come to a mixed population of Jews and Gentiles; he came to the Jews. He himself said, "I was sent only to the lost sheep of the house of Israel" (Matt. 15:24; see Matt. 10:6; John 1:31). As a rule the Jews were the only believers in the true God and the only ones expecting the Messiah; they were the only valid candidates for the role of apostle. Bringing the Gentiles into the kingdom was a part of God's plan all along, but it would not begin until after Pentecost.

Thus the idea that there is a parallel between the lack of women and the lack of Gentiles among the apostles is quite faulty. At that time no Gentiles were ready for such a task, but there were countless Jewish women who were theoretically ready by virtue of their devout faith in the true God and their expectation of the Messiah. The reason for not choosing from among the latter must be entirely different from the reason for not choosing from among the former. (Whether there were any slaves among the apostles is a moot point. All their backgrounds are not given.)

There is a second reason why the parallel between Gentiles and women is a specious argument. It lies in the assumption that the composition of the twelve apostles is somehow being used as the normative pattern for church leadership. I.e., it is assumed that the *reason* why hierarchicalists do not allow women in roles of authority in the church is that there were no women among the apostles. But this is a false assumption. We are not saying, "Now let's see. We need leaders for the church. How do we decide who is qualified? Well, let's look at the ones Jesus chose for apostles. Only the kinds of people he chose for that office will be allowed to serve as church leaders. Hmmm. It appears that he chose only men. Therefore only men can be church leaders." Now, if this were the logic being used, then the parallel between women and Gentiles would have some merit, at least from the standpoint of pure logic and apart from the theological reasoning noted above. The fact is, however, that this is *not* the way the apostleship and church leadership are connected. The content of the former is not what determines the content of the latter. Rather, the content of both, in that both are limited to males, is determined by a higher principle that transcends them both and applies equally to each. Why were there no female apostles? For the very same reason there should be no female leaders in authoritative positions in the church, namely, because God created the human race in the beginning with the principle of male leadership in mind (cf. 1 Tim. 2:12-13). This was his original purpose. Jesus did not choose female apostles because this would not have been in accord with that original purpose. That purpose has nothing to do with the later, temporary distinction between Jews and Gentiles; but it has everything to do with the original, permanent distinction between males and females.

In view of the fact that Jesus chose only men as apostles, and in view of the fact that the only valid explanation for this limitation is doctrinal and not cultural, we must again point out how tragically mistaken is this statement by Mickelsen: "We look in vain for anything in the life or teachings of our Lord that point [sic] to 'differences in function' for men and women in kingdom work."[130] Such a statement is clear evidence that feminists see only what they want to see in the life and teachings of Jesus.

V. CONCLUSION

In this chapter we have discussed four aspects of the life, example and teachings of Jesus that relate to the issue of gender roles in the context of feminism. Our purpose has been to evaluate in detail how feminists interpret the gospel records concerning Jesus. We have examined two elements in the gospels which they enthusiastically embrace as proofs of egalitarianism, namely, Jesus' encounters with women, and Jesus' teaching about women. We have also examined how feminists handle two elements in the gospels which appear to contradict the egalitarian thesis, namely, Jesus' incarnation as a male, and Jesus' choice of only men as his twelve apostles.

Our overall conclusion is that the feminist interpretations of these four aspects of Christology are simply not true to the data of the gospel records when those data are laid out in a careful, detailed, comprehensive, objective manner. When compared with the facts, the character of feminist exegesis and the conclusions drawn therefrom can only be described with such terms as misleading, careless, incomplete, selective, subjective, exaggerated, and slanted. The life and teachings of our Lord, and the inspired gospel records from which we learn about them, deserve better.

ENDNOTES
CHAPTER FOUR

[1]Letty M. Russell, *Human Liberation in a Feminist Perspective—A Theology* (Philadelphia: Westminster, 1974), p. 138. She cites Mary Daly's book, *Beyond God the Father*, for this idea (2nd ed., Boston: Beacon Press, 1985; pp. 79, 96).

[2]Carol P. Christ, *Laughter of Aphrodite: Reflections on a Journey to the Goddess* (San Francisco: Harper and Row, 1987), p. 147. These include Mother Ann Lee, founder of the Shakers; and Mary Baker Eddy, founder of Christian Science.

[3]Letha Dawson Scanzoni and Nancy A. Hardesty, *All We're Meant To Be: Biblical Feminism for Today*, 3rd ed. (Grand Rapids: Eerdmans, 1992), p. 73.

[4]Ibid., p. 74.

[5]Virginia Ramey Mollenkott, *Women, Men, and the Bible*, revised ed. (New York: Crossroad, 1988), p. 54.

[6]Mollenkott, "The Biblical Basis for Male-Female Equality," a brochure (Albuquerque: Galatians 3:28 Press, n. d.), column 2.

[7]Ibid.

[8]Mollenkott, *Women*, p. 48.

[9]Ibid., p. 49.

[10]Aida Besançon Spencer, *Beyond the Curse: Women Called to Ministry* (Nashville: Thomas Nelson, 1985), p. 22.

[11]Scanzoni and Hardesty, *All We're Meant To Be: A Biblical Approach to Women's Liberation* (Waco: Word Books, 1974), p. 56.

[12]Scanzoni and Hardesty, *All We're Meant To Be* (1992), p. 75.

[13]Ibid., pp. 74-75, citing Edward L. Kessel, "A Proposed Biological Interpretation of the Virgin Birth," *Journal of the American Scientific Affiliation* (September 1983), pp. 129-136.

[14]Karen and Leif Torjesen, "Inclusive Orthodoxy: Recovering a Suppressed Tradition," *The Other Side* (December 1986), p. 17.

[15]Anne Atkins, *Split Image: Male and Female After God's Likeness* (Grand Rapids: Eerdmans, 1987), p. 67.

[16]Mollenkott, *Women*, p. 47. See chapter 16, "God as Mother Hen," in her book, *The Divine Feminine: The Biblical Imagery of God as Female* (New York: Crossroad, 1983), pp. 92-96.

[17]Rebecca D. Pentz, "And When the Hour of Birth Came . . . ," *The Reformed Journal* (March 1988), 38:4.

[18]Torjesen, "Inclusive Orthodoxy," p. 17.

[19]See Susan Cady, Marian Ronan, and Hal Taussig, *Wisdom's Feast: Sophia in Study and Celebration* (San Francisco: Harper and Row, 1989). This is a revised version of their 1986 work, *Sophia: The Future of Feminist Spirituality*.

[20]See Pentz, "Jesus as Sophia," *The Reformed Journal* (December 1988), 38:17-22.

[21]Mollenkott, *Women*, pp. 49-50. See her book, *The Divine Feminine*, chapter 17, "God as Dame Wisdom" (pp. 97-105).

[22]Pentz, "Jesus as Sophia," pp. 17-19.

[23]Ibid., p. 21.

[24]Stephen B. Clark, *Man and Woman in Christ: An Examination of the Roles of Men and Women in Light of Scripture and the Social Sciences* (Ann Arbor: Servant Books, 1980), pp. 239-245.

[25]Susan T. Foh, *Women and The Word of God: A Response to Biblical Feminism* (Phillipsburg, NJ: Presbyterian and Reformed, 1980), p. 93.

[26]Matt. 9:8; 11:19; Luke 7:34.

[27]Matt. 26:72, 74; Mark 14:71.

[28]The centurion at the cross (Mark 15:39; Luke 23:47); the Samaritan woman (John 4:29); the temple guards (John 7:46); the man born blind (John 9:11); and the girl who questioned Peter (John 18:17).

[29]Pilate (Luke 23:4, 6, 14; John 18:29; 19:5); miscellaneous Jewish leaders (John 9:16, 24; 10:33; 11:47, 50; 18:14; Acts 5:28).

[30]Scanzoni and Hardesty, *All We're Meant To Be* (1992), p. 75.

[31]A few examples are Matthew (Matt. 9:9), John the Baptist (Matt. 11:8), Judas (Matt. 26:24), Simeon (Luke 2:25), Nicodemus (John 3:1), Stephen (Acts 6:13), Adam (Rom. 5:12, 19), and Elijah (James 5:17).

[32]For example, Matt. 7:24, 26 has *anēr*; Luke 6:48, a parallel passage, has *anthrōpos*. Similar comparisons may be made between Luke 8:29, 33, 35 and Luke 8:27, 38; also Matt. 17:14 and Luke 9:38; also Matt. 27:57 and Luke 23:50; also Acts 3:2 and 4:9, 14, 22; also Acts 15:25 and 15:26; also Acts 25:17 and 25:22; also Eph. 4:13 and 4:24; also James 1:7 and 1:8.

[33]We have no more warrant for this than for concluding that Jesus' nature embodies "plantness" since he compares himself with a vine (John 15:1); or that there is an inorganic side to his nature since he is compared with a rock (Matt. 21:42; 1 Cor. 10:4; 1 Pet. 2:6-8).

[34]The fact that the Greek word *sophia* is feminine in gender and that this noun is applied to Jesus does not warrant the conclusion that Jesus must be somehow feminine. The grammatical gender of nouns is essentially unrelated to the gender of the realities to which they correspond.

[35]Cady et al., *Wisdom's Feast*, p. 33.

[36]See Mollenkott, *The Divine Feminine*, p. 101; "Jesus as Sophia," p. 18.

[37]Pentz, "Jesus as Sophia," p. 18.

[38]Cady et al., *Wisdom's Feast*, p. 37.

[39]Pentz, "Jesus as Sophia," p. 22.

[40]Torjesen, "Inclusive Orthodoxy," p. 17.

[41]Ibid.

[42]For an explanation of Apollinarianism see Aloys Grillmeier, *Christ in Christian Tradition: From the Apostolic Age to Chalcedon (451)*, tr. J. S. Bowden (New York: Sheed and Ward, 1965), pp. 220-233.

[43]Gregory of Nazianzus, "Letter to Cledonius Against Apollinaris (Epistle 101)," in *Christology of the Later Fathers*, ed. Edward R. Hardy, "Library of Christian Classics," vol. III (Philadelphia: Westminster, n. d.), p. 218.

[44]Thomas Howard, "God Before Birth: The Imagery Matters," *Christianity Today* (Dec. 17, 1976), pp. 12-13.

[45]Sharon Neufer Emswiler and Thomas Neufer Emswiler, *Women and Worship: A Guide to Non-Sexist Hymns, Prayers, and Liturgies*

(New York: Harper and Row, 1974), p. 15.

[46]Eleanor Daniel, *What the Bible Says About Sexual Identity* (Joplin, MO: College Press, 1981), pp. 48, 210-211. For documentation from the rabbinic writings see Spencer, *Beyond the Curse*, pp. 46-57.

[47]S. Scott Bartchy, "Human Sexuality and Our Identity," *Mission Journal* (November 1983), 17:11.

[48]Mary J. Evans, *Woman in the Bible* (Downers Grove: InterVarsity Press, 1983), p. 45.

[49]Atkins, *Split Image*, p. 57.

[50]Scanzoni and Hardesty, *All We're Meant To Be* (1992), p. 72. They are citing C. F. D. Moule, *The Phenomenon of the New Testament* (Naperville, IL: Alec R. Allenson, 1967), p. 65.

[51]Leonard Swidler, "Jesus Was a Feminist," *Catholic World* (January 1971), pp. 177-183.

[52]Paul K. Jewett, *Man as Male and Female: A Study in Sexual Relationships from a Theological Point of View* (Grand Rapids: Eerdmans, 1975), p. 94. These sentences were italicized in the original.

[53]Gilbert Bilezikian, *Beyond Sex Roles: What the Bible Says About a Woman's Place in Church and Family*, 2nd ed. (Grand Rapids: Baker, 1990, p. 95.

[54]Mollenkott, *Women*, p. 9.

[55]Pentz, "Hour of Birth," p. 4.

[56]Spencer, *Beyond the Curse*, pp. 58, 60-61.

[57]Gretchen Gaebelein Hull, *Equal To Serve: Women and Men in the Church and Home* (Old Tappan, NJ: Revell, 1987), pp. 116-117.

[58]Ibid., p. 114.

[59]Mollenkott, *Women*, pp. 4-5, See Pentz, "Hour of Birth," p. 4.

[60]Alvera Mickelsen, "An Egalitarian View: There is Neither Male nor Female in Christ," *Women in Ministry: Four Views*, ed. Bonnidell Clouse and Robert G. Clouse (Downers Grove: InterVarsity Press, 1989), p. 187.

[61]S. Scott Bartchy, "Jesus, Power, and Gender Roles," *TSF Bulletin* (January-February 1981), 7:2; and "Human Sexuality and Our Identity," *Mission Journal* (November 1983), p.11.

[62]Scott E. McClelland, "The New Reality in Christ: Perspectives from Biblical Studies," *Gender Matters: Women's Studies for the Christian Community*, ed. June Steffensen Hagen (Grand Rapids: Zondervan, 1990), p. 62.

[63]Bilezikian, *Beyond Sex Roles*, p. 101.

[64]Swidler, "Jesus Was A Feminist," p. 181.

[65]Hull, *Equal To Serve*, p. 114.

[66]Spencer, *Beyond the Curse*, pp. 61-62.

[67]Mollenkott, *Women*, pp. 9-10.

[68]Swidler, "Jesus Was A Feminist," pp. 180-181.

[69]Scanzoni and Hardesty, *All We're Meant To Be* (1992), p. 81.

[70]Mollenkott, *Women*, p. 10.

[71]Spencer, *Beyond the Curse*, p. 62.

[72]Richard and Catherine Kroeger, "Why Were There No Women Apostles?", *Equity* [no date given], p. 11. (This article is distributed in duplicated form without the date by Christians for Biblical Equality.)

[73]Evans, *Woman*, p. 46.

[74]Ibid., pp. 51-52.

[75]Daniel, *Sexual Identity*, p. 211.

[76]Judy Norris, "Jesus, My Lord, Emancipator of Women," *Christian Standard* (Aug. 31, 1980), pp. 9-10.

[77]Scanzoni and Hardesty, *All We're Meant To Be* (1992), p. 81.

[78]Hull, *Equal To Serve*, pp. 114-115.

[79]Clark, *Man*, pp. 242-243; and p. 698, footnote 13.

[80]Ibid., pp. 239-241, 244. Madeleine Boucher has also challenged the notion that "the idea of woman's religious equality was unknown to Judaism." She cites a number of sayings from rabbinic writings which she believes are parallel in content to Galatians 3:28 ("Some Unexplored Parallels to 1 Cor 11,11-12 and Gal 3,28: The NT on the Role of Women," *The Catholic Biblical Quarterly* [1969], 31:50-58).

[81]Clark, *Man*, p. 243.

[82]Ibid., p. 245.

[83]Ibid., p. 251.

[84]Ibid., p. 245. See also H. Wayne House, *The Role of Women in Ministry Today* (Nashville: Thomas Nelson, 1990), pp. 71-73.

[85]Scanzoni and Hardesty, *All We're Meant To Be* (1992), p. 81.

[86]Lewis Foster, "Woman—Where's She Going Today?", part 2 *Christian Standard* (Dec. 18, 1988), p. 9.

[87]McClelland, "The New Reality," p. 62.

[88]Boucher, "Some Unexplored Parallels," p. 55.

[89]This is from the Greek word *huper*, which means "over, above." In compound English words it connotes excess or exaggeration.

[90]Some manuscripts say seventy-two.

[91]Hull, *Equal To Serve*, p. 115.

[92]Clark, *Man*, p. 248.

[93]Foh, *Women*, p. 94.

[94]W. Ward Gasque, "The Role of Women in the Church, in Society and in the Home," *Priscilla Papers* (Spring 1988), 2:2.

[95]Mickelsen, "An Egalitarian View," p. 187.

[96]Ibid. Hull makes exactly the same point: "In His illustrations He used both men and women as examples" (*Equal To Serve*, p. 114).

[97]Mary Stewart Van Leeuwen, *Gender and Grace: Love, Work and Parenting in a Changing World* (Downers Grove: InterVarsity Press, 1990), p. 48.

[98]Evans, *Woman*, p. 48.

[99]Mollenkott, *Women*, p. 8.

[100]Swidler, "Jesus Was A Feminist," p. 182.

[101]Pentz, "Hour of Birth," p. 4.

[102]Evans, *Woman*, p. 46.

[103]Ibid., p. 45.

[104]Mollenkott, *Women*, p. 8.

[105]Evans, *Woman*, p. 46.

[106]Willard M. Swartley, *Slavery, Sabbath, War, and Women: Case Issues in Biblical Interpretation* (Scottdale, PA: Herald Press, 1983), p. 201.

[107]Norris, "Jesus, My Lord," p. 9.

[108]Clark, *Man*, pp. 247-248.

[109]There is some subjectivity in deciding what is a parable and what is an illustration. Some possible illustrations have been omitted altogether (all with male figures), and a few could possibly be shifted from one category to the other.

[110]The characters are determined to be male by specific identification as such, by the roles themselves (e.g., king, son, Pharisee), or by the use of masculine Greek forms.

[111]Mickelsen, "An Egalitarian View," p. 187.

[112]In this analysis we are considering only those roles involving fictional or hypothetical figures, not historical ones such as Moses and Elijah.

[113]See my discussion of the "Christological fallacy" in *What the Bible Says About God the Creator* (Joplin, MO: College Press, 1983), pp. 166-191.

[114]Owen Crouch, *Not Guilty: Studies in Romans* (Milligan College, TN: published by author, 1987), p. 170.

[115]Charlene Hopman, "The Role of Women in the Church" (Cincinnati, OH: an unpublished address [given in French Lick, IN], 1976), pp. 5-6.

[116]McClelland, "The New Reality," p. 62.

[117]Dorothy R. Pape, *In Search of God's Ideal Woman* (Downers Grove: InterVarsity Press, 1976), p. 43.

[118]Hull, *Equal To Serve*, p. 286.

[119]Spencer, *Beyond the Curse*, p. 45, footnote 5.

[120]Hull, *Equal To Serve*, p. 286. See also Mickelsen, " An Egalitarian View," p. 188; Emswiler, *Women*, p. 14.

[121]See Clark, *Man*, p. 248. See also Manfred Hauke, *Women in the Priesthood: A Systematic Analysis in the Light of the Order of Creation and Redemption*, tr. David Kipp (San Francisco: Ignatius Press, 1988), p. 328.

[122]Hopman, "The Role of Women," pp. 4-6.

[123]House, *The Role of Women*, p. 73.

[124]McClelland, "The New Reality," pp. 61-62.

[125]Pape, *Search*, p. 43.

[126]McClelland, "The New Reality," p. 62.

[127]Kroeger, "Women Apostles," p. 10.

[128]Hopman, "The Role of Women," p. 6.

[129]Crouch, *Not Guilty*, p. 170.

[130]Mickelsen, "An Egalitarian View," p. 187.

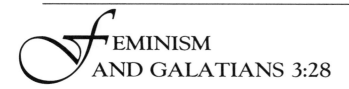

EMINISM
AND GALATIANS 3:28

> There is neither Jew nor Greek, there is neither slave nor
> free man, there is neither male nor female; for you are all
> one in Christ Jesus.

In the feminism debate no passage is more crucial than
Galatians 3:28, primarily because of the immense weight
given to it by feminists themselves. It receives this unique
emphasis, says House, because "it is the only real passage
in the New Testament letters that might appear to prove
their view on women."[1] Although we probably should
amend this to "the only *didactic* passage,"[2] we very much
concur that feminists take this to be the decisive Biblical
passage for their view of the role of women. They also
believe that it has been largely ignored.[3]

In their effort to rehabilitate this "ignored" text, feminists describe it in the most exalted and unrestrained
terminology.[4] They call it the *locus classicus* (main proof
text) for feminism. It is the foundation for the Christian
understanding of women in God's plan. Indeed, it is one of
Paul's foundational statements reflecting his basic theology
as a whole, his central theological conviction. It is a clear
statement of theological principle that provides the theological starting place for discussing the role of women. It is
a revolutionary principle, the great breakthrough, a salva-
tion-historical turning point. In terms of setting women
free from servitude and slavery, it is an emancipation
proclamation for Christian women. It is Paul's great freedom manifesto addressing issues of fundamental human
rights. It is the Magna Charta of humanity, the last word in
Christian liberty. Just as the original Magna Charta guar-

anteed fundamental liberties, so does this Magna Charta of Paul. This liberating vision is the ideal for the church to implement. It is Paul's dazzling vision of a Christian society. It is his basic summary of what it means to be a Christian.

Such lavish descriptions of Galatians 3:28, all from feminists' pens, clearly reflect their view that this verse is a basic doctrinal principle intended to have the broadest possible application. Obviously, then, it must be given very careful attention in our effort to evaluate the hermeneutics of Biblical feminism.

Throughout this discussion of Galatians 3:28 a key issue (if not *the* key issue) is the relationship among the three pairs: Jew/Greek, slave/free, male/female. Why does Paul list these three pairs, and no more? How do they relate to one another? What do they have in common? How do they relate to the context? Is there a specific contextual point that ties them together, or are they intended to be parallel in every way?

Most feminists seem to share two significant assumptions concerning these pairs. First, they affirm that the three pairs are meant to be inclusive of all human relationships, either in themselves or in a representative way. Thus they are universalized or generalized. As Longenecker puts it, they "cover in embryonic fashion all the essential relationships of humanity."[5] Although only the Jew/Greek pair is strictly related to the context, says McClelland, the others are added to "ensure that the newness in Christ should be seen to be an exhaustive and not a limited newness."[6]

In feminist thinking these three pairs represent all the ways human beings make distinctions among themselves in terms of rank, status, power, authority, superiority, or supremacy. They include such things as nationality, race, class, social status, economic status, sex or gender, and age as a basis for discriminating against any individuals or groups. All such distinctions are abolished by Galatians 3:28.

In this way each of the three pairs is taken as standing for a larger category. For instance, the Jew/Greek distinction represents all distinctions made on the basis of race or nationality. The slave/free distinction stands for all others made on the basis of social class or economic status. Likewise the male/female pair includes all kinds of distinctions based on sexual differentiation. Feminists declare that *all* such distinctions are abolished by Galatians 3:28, especially with regard to participation in the life of the church. As Ronald Heine puts it, this text speaks of "an obliteration of human distinctions"; it eliminates all distinctions of race, class, and sex in the new community in Christ.[7]

To emphasize their commitment to the universality of these three pairs, some feminists specifically identify other categories or groups to which Galatians 3:28 applies. The Kroegers add the category of age: "Gender, age, social condition, and racial considerations are all swept away by Galatians 3:28."[8] Twentieth-century terms equivalent to *Gentile* [Greek] and *slave* are "a Black or Latino or a minimum-wage laborer," says Charles Boatman.[9] Gottfried Oosterwal updates the categories in Galatians 3:28 by saying that Christ has healed "the brokenness between men and women, Arabs and Jews, blacks and whites."[10]

The second feminist assumption concerning the three pairs is that they are exactly equivalent. Whatever applies to one pair applies equally to the other two, especially with regard to church practices. As Joseph Webb says, "Whatever the point is concerning Jew and Gentile is to be said about the male-female relationship as well." This applies to "all functions and obligations within the Christian fellowship."[11] Thus if being a Gentile or a slave does not disqualify one from being a preacher or an elder in the church, neither does being a woman. Boatman asks rhetorically, "If (in the light of Galatians 3:28) being a Gentile or a slave . . . is not sufficient reason to keep a man from full participation in the life and leadership of the church, why is being a woman sufficient reason to keep a person from such participation?"[12] This is the standard feminist conclusion from this assumption of complete equivalence of the three pairs.

This leads to the identification of another key issue in the proper interpretation of Galatians 3:28. In addition to the significance of the three pairs, we must ask whether the text is meant to apply to a Christian's religious status only, or to his social status also. Is it limited to one's position *coram deo*—before God? Or does it apply to our relationships within human society as well? Is the oneness in Christ an unlimited oneness, a total equalizing? Most non-feminists believe that only our spiritual status before God is in view, while feminists invariably take it to be inclusive of *all* relationships, especially *social* relationships, and especially *sex roles* within all areas of society, including the home and the church.

This interpretation is vital to the feminist conclusion that no distinction can be made between men and women regarding participation in any role or ministry or function within the life of the church. Because this unlimited oneness eliminates all sex role distinctions in all areas of society, qualified women as well as qualified men must be accepted as preachers, ministers, and elders. Mollenkott calls this "psychological androgyny," i.e., erasing the distinction between males and females and combining them into one group not on the physical level but on the psychological or behavioral level. This means that, according to Galatians 3:28, "in the freedom and psychological wholeness fostered by Christian fellowship, each male and each female would be free to develop his or her gifts and God-given traits without reference to gender-based stereotypes."[13] Hayter agrees. Galatians 3:28, she says, "is the *locus classicus* of biblical texts for those who believe that, ultimately, Scripture does not discriminate between male and female and that it is therefore wrong for the Church to perpetuate such discrimination in its ordination practice."[14] Galatians 3:28 shows, says Ruth Schmidt, that Christ came "to break down every wall separating one human being from another." This includes "the wall between women's and men's participation in the life of the Church." Thus qualified women should be called upon as often as men "to provide leadership in the Church by serving on governing and policy-making boards."[15]

To put it another way, since feminists see in Galatians 3:28 the elimination of male/female role distinctions, they stress the *complete interchangeability* of roles within the church. They "assume that equality between persons requires that roles be interchangeable," says House.[16] As Kassian puts it, feminists are committed to "monolithic, undifferentiated role-interchangeability."[17]

Thus it is quite clear that much is at stake in one's interpretation of Galatians 3:28, especially for feminists, who see in this one text the divine validation of their entire egalitarian agenda. It is crucial, then, that we pursue as careful and as complete and as objective a study of the feminist interpretation of this passage as we possibly can. That is the goal of this chapter.

I. GALATIANS 3:28 AND THE WORK OF CHRIST

We discussed how feminists interpret the accounts of the creation and the Fall in Genesis 1-3. Genesis 1 and 2 are usually understood as teaching that God originally created the man and the woman to exist in a fully egalitarian relationship. Then Genesis 3 is seen as teaching that the corruption of this relationship by the Fall was the beginning of hierarchy and male dominance, which are the result of sin and part of the curse. Finally, most feminists believe that Christ came to nullify the curse and restore women to their original full and unrestricted equality with men. They also believe that Galatians 3:28 is a key passage for linking the work of Christ to this restoration of egalitarianism.

One reason often cited for connecting Galatians 3:28 with this creation-Fall-restoration theme is the specific

Greek terminology used in the expression usually translated "neither male nor female." For one thing, strictly speaking, this is not an accurate translation of the conjunction between "male" and "female." In the first two pairs the conjunction is the Greek negative *oude*, "nor." Thus they are properly translated, "neither Jew nor Greek," and "neither slave nor free man." But in the third pair Paul switches to the positive *kai*, "and." Thus for some reason he abandons what would seem to have been a natural and expected symmetry with the first two pairs and says there is no "male *and* female." For another thing, the terms used for the two genders are the relatively uncommon *arsēn* ("male") and *thēlu* ("female"), instead of the more common words for "man" and "woman."[18]

Why should these characteristics of the Greek terminology be thought to point to an intended connection between Galatians 3:28 and the creation-Fall-redemption framework? Because this very same terminology—*arsēn kai thēlu*—is found in the Septuagint version of Genesis 1:27, "Male and female He created them." Thus it is concluded that Paul must have had this verse, and thus the creation-Fall-redemption theme, specifically in mind when he wrote Galatians 3:28. In the words of Stendahl, "The terminology points directly back to Genesis 1:27."[19] Richard and Joyce Boldrey agree: "Paul quoted the words *male* and *female* (more technical than the usual *man* and *woman*) directly from Genesis 1:27."[20]

In any case it is important for feminists to establish this connection with Genesis 1-3, and with the creation-Fall-restoration theme. As they have constructed the argument, if Galatians 3:28 does relate the work of Christ to this comprehensive historical drama of redemption, then it clearly establishes egalitarianism, because it shows that the work of Christ nullifies the hierarchy of Genesis 1-3.

Though most feminists agree on this general statement of the argument, they disagree as to exactly how the work of Christ sets aside all hierarchical gender relationships. Some say it does this by reversing the curse of Genesis 3;

others say it actually replaces the original creation order of Genesis 1. We shall now examine and evaluate each of these views.

A. Does Galatians 3:28 Reverse the Curse?

Many if not most feminists are firmly committed to the creation-Fall-redemption framework: male-female relationships in the original creation were egalitarian; the Fall introduced hierarchy; the work of Christ eliminates subordinationism and re-establishes egalitarianism, thus abolishing all role restrictions for women. This understanding is quite crucial and is more or less assumed in feminist circles.

Examples of this are numerous. The very title of Aida Spencer's book, *Beyond the Curse*, reflects this theme. Both Genesis 1 and Genesis 2, she says, declare "male and female equality" and "joint rulership." These texts show how "God assigns to females and males tasks without differentiated roles."[21] However, the Fall and the curse of Genesis 3 changed this; the hierarchical relationships of controller versus controlled are "the direct results of the curse of God from which Christ has now freed us."[22] "Jesus by his example and teachings harkened back to God's original intention at creation for women's full participation in the public tasks of life. He also liberated them from the entrenched male domination caused by the fall. . . . Jesus wanted women redeemed from the curse."[23] Thus women are "entitled to go beyond the curse."[24]

This is a major theme of Mary Stewart Van Leeuwen's works as well. In her book *Gender and Grace* she says that all conclusions concerning sex and gender must be "based on the biblical drama of creation, fall, redemption and renewal."[25] After explaining how the Fall corrupted the original egalitarian order, she says that the gospels "show clearly that it was Christ's intention, as part of his healing and saving work, to reverse the consequences of Genesis

3:16."[26] "That is what Christ came to do: to reverse the effects of the fall in both men and women and in their relations with each other."[27]

Peter DeJong and Donald Wilson are very clear in their commitment to this framework. "The egalitarian structure ordained by creation was changed into a hierarchical structure because of man's sin." However, "the redemptive act of Christ was more than sufficient to counteract the results of Adam's sin." The "central message" of Galatians 3:28 is "the restorative impact of Christ's redemptive work on the male-female relationship," along with the other pairs.[28] Such examples could be multiplied.[29]

The point now is this. If Galatians 3:28 is truly the key verse in the Biblical drama of creation, Fall, and redemption, then in some way the three pairs listed there must be *sinful relationships* resulting from the Fall. If the point of this verse is that the work of Christ has reversed the curse, then in some way the distinctions implied in these pairs must be rooted in the curse.

This is indeed how feminists explain them. The point of Galatians 3:28, say DeJong and Wilson, is "that all those distinctions between people that previously were sources of alienation and separation have been superseded by their union in Christ."[30] It shows how Christ has abolished relationships of oppression, elitism, exclusivism, and brokenness among human beings, says Oosterwal.[31] Scholer asserts that the three pairs "represented the oppressive structures of that society, which the gospel was intended to reverse."[32] Schmidt notes that Christ came "to break down every wall separating one human being from another," such as the "prejudices" and "sinful divisions" mentioned in Galatians 3:28.[33] This "Magna Charta of Christian liberty" shows how relationships in Christ are "in stark contrast with the world and its arbitrary divisions in society," says Tucker.[34]

These and other feminists agree that Galatians 3:28 affirms that the work of Christ removes all the effects of the curse and restores the oneness of Genesis 1 and 2, especially the oneness of role equality.

We turn now to an evaluation of this view that Galatians 3:28 is intended to refer to the redeeming work of Christ specifically as it reverses the curse of Genesis 3:16. The most significant point is this: even if we could show that Galatians 3:28 refers to the reversing of the original curse, this would not automatically establish egalitarianism. Such a conclusion would depend on a particular understanding of Genesis 1-3. To be specific, it would establish egalitarianism only on the following conditions: first, that the narratives of Genesis 1 and 2 can be properly understood as teaching that full role equality was the original purpose and result of creation; and second, that such equality actually existed until the Fall and the curse initiated sinful hierarchical role distinctions between men and women, according to Genesis 3:16. As we have seen above, this is in fact how feminists generally interpret these chapters. Indeed, for feminists it is crucial to maintain the view of equal headship, power, dominion, or authority in Genesis 1 and 2, so that Galatians 3:28 can be seen as restoring it.

But as we have already shown above, *this interpretation of Genesis 1-3 is not correct*. Thus this particular feminist understanding of Galatians 3:28, which appeals to the quite valid creation-Fall-redemption schema, is nonetheless invalidated by a false view of how gender roles are related to creation and to the Fall in the first place. If this schema were indeed the intended background for our text, then it should be obvious that *a right view of Galatians 3:28 would require a right view of Genesis 1-3*.

An even more basic problem with the view that Galatians 3:28 restores egalitarianism by reversing the curse is the fact that the restoration of the fallen creation order is not the point of the verse in the first place. Christ has indeed reversed the curse and established the new creation, but that is not the subject of this text. Though the concept of new creation is mentioned in Galatians 6:15, it is certainly not in the foreground of the epistle as a whole and is altogether absent in the context in Galatians 3. In the context, being "in Christ Jesus" replaces being under the rules of the Law of Moses, as will be shown later in this chapter. The creation-Fall-redemption framework is improperly imported into the discussion at this point. Thus there is simply no good reason to connect Galatians 3:28 with the curse of Genesis 3:16.

Another serious problem with this reverse-the-curse view is that it cannot do justice to the symmetry of the three contrasting pairs mentioned in the verse. The assumption is that somehow these pairs have to do with the curse upon sin and are thus the epitome of the fallen order. But just a little reflection shows that these pairs cannot be brought together into a symmetrical relationship under the notion that they somehow have equivalent roots in the curse. In fact, it is not self-evident in this context that they are even intended to represent fallenness at all, much less share a parallel relation to the Fall. In other words, there is really no way to trace the ultimate distinctions within these pairs to the curse upon sin, as if somehow they are the essence of fallenness. To characterize them as "sinful divisions" representing such sinful concepts as alienation, oppression, elitism, exclusivism, and domination is an assumption that has been imported into the context and which will disintegrate when one tries to apply such concepts to all the pairs equally.

Of the three pairs, the distinction between slaves and free men certainly comes closest to the concept of a sinful relationship, but even here this does not seem to be the point Paul is making. Some feminists see these pairs as representing the "oppressive structures" of society, or the "dominant-submissive categories" of human relationships. Such terminology is of course designed to highlight the feminist understanding of the sinful male-female relationships removed by Christ; and at first glance this understanding would seem to be supported by the parallel pair of slave and free man. But a closer look reveals something artificial about this way of describing the relationships. If Paul had had in mind oppression, or domination and submission, would he not have said "neither slave nor *master*" instead of "neither slave nor *free man*"? In other contexts where he specifically has the authority-submission relationship in view, he speaks of slaves and masters (Eph. 6:5; Col. 3:22; see 1 Peter 2:18).

Indeed, to speak of slaves and free men together is not necessarily to speak of a *relationship* at all but rather of a *distinction*. It is important for feminists to represent the two sides of each of these pairs as forming a relationship, and usually a negative one (e.g., elitism, domination, oppression), since this fits best with the idea that the work of Christ heals broken relationships, especially between men and women. But Paul's concern is not with how the two sides of each of these pairs relate to one another (as it would be if he had spoken of slaves and masters), but rather with certain implications of the common distinction between slaves and free men in a particular context, namely, in the Law of Moses. (This will be explained later.)

It must be stressed also that the distinction between slaves and free men is not necessarily a distinction based on sin and the curse. In Biblical teaching the state of slavery is never presented as something inherently evil. The Law of Moses specifies certain valid conditions under which one can become and be a slave (e.g., Lev. 25:39ff.; Deut. 15:12ff.). On the other hand, of course, there are conditions under which the master-slave relationship is sinful (Exod. 21:16), and a slave can certainly be the recipient of sinful treatment from his master (Lev. 25:43). But we cannot assume that every use of the word *slave* implies a sinful condition. Thus in Galatians 3:28 we have no warrant to assume that the slave/free distinction refers to a sinful situation naturally remedied by the work of Christ.

In this same connection it is also worth noting that there is no reference whatsoever to the slave/free distinction in Genesis 3; it is not specifically related to the Fall and the curse in that chapter. In this sense there is no parallel with the male-female distinction and relationship, which are among the points specifically set forth in Genesis 1-3.

These same kinds of things must also be pointed out with reference to the distinction between Jews and Greeks in Galatians 3:28. We must reject the idea that this pair represents some kind of sinful relationship that has been abolished by the redeeming work of Christ. It is a serious misrepresentation of Scripture to declare that the Jew-Gentile distinction is "arbitrary" or that it is in some direct way the result of sin and thus somehow a part of the curse. Indeed, it was God Himself who established this distinction when he called Abraham in Genesis 12; and He did so with a redemptive purpose. It is true that Christ abolished the distinction, not because it was sinful as such but because with His first coming the Jews had fulfilled their purpose as a separate and distinct people.

There is no disputing the fact that this divinely-ordained distinction was often the occasion for perverted relationships between Jews and Gentiles. It was in Bible times and still is today the source of racist attitudes, which to be sure are sinful attitudes of supremacy and superiority. But we must seriously question whether this was in the forefront of Paul's thinking when he wrote Galatians 3:28. If the attitude of racial superiority is his concern, then this pair is clearly out of sync with the other two, since it has no clear-cut villain. This is because each side of the pair was guilty of considering the other to be inferior. Jews certainly placed themselves far above all other peoples, since they were self-consciously "God's chosen people." But at the same time non-Jews looked down upon the Jews as an inferior and rather shabby race.

The same ambiguity is present if we try to view these pairs as examples of "oppressive structures." In this case, who is the oppressor and who is the oppressed? In the context of the apostolic era, who was dominating whom? On the broader scale the Roman government dominated the Jewish nation; but in the context of Galatians the Jews are the trouble-makers. Even then, the way in which they were causing trouble cannot really be thought of in terms of dominance and submission.

In other words, a closer consideration of the Jew/Greek pair shows that the parallel with the other two pairs breaks down when we try to impose on it the interpretation necessary to sustain the feminist view that Galatians 3:28 is speaking of "reversing the curse." This concept does not really describe the effect that the work of Christ had on the Jew/Greek distinction.

What, then, of the male/female distinction itself? Again, there is no parallel between this pair and the other pairs with regard to their relationship to the curse. The male/female distinction of course actually precedes the curse, while the other distinctions follow it.

It is true that the three pairs are alike in that they suggest relationships that can *become* perverted and sinful. But hierarchicalists have always agreed that the Fall and the curse of Genesis 3 resulted in a perversion of the original male-female relationship, and that the redemptive work of Christ removes this perversion. However, even this does not seem to be what Galatians 3:28 is talking about. It does not say that in Christ Jesus there is no longer a perverted relationship between males and females; it says rather that in Christ there is no "male and female." In fact, it is most likely that Paul is not thinking of *any* relationship between males and females, much less a perverted one. As suggested in our discussion of "slave nor free man" above, the point of the passage is not a *relationship* but a *distinction*, and especially a distinction that was made within the context of the Law of Moses. We may also suggest that the choice of the terms *male* and *female* is consistent with this reference to an impersonal distinction, since the terms *man* and *woman* are more personal and relational.

In any case the fact that the male/female distinction precedes the Fall and the curse is seriously inconsistent with the view that Galatians 3:28 is speaking of reversing the curse. This is especially true when we remember that the common feminist explanation of why the expression "male and female" is used is that it reflects Genesis 1:27

and thus calls our attention to the creation-Fall-redemption pattern. If this is indeed the proper focus of Galatians 3:28, then we have the rather ambiguous and irregular circumstance in which Paul uses an expression that originally described the very pristine situation Christ came to restore (Gen. 1:27), to represent the situation he came to nullify (Gal. 3:28).

The fact is this: if we insist on setting Galatians 3:28 within the broad scope of the creation-Fall-redemption theme, then the most consistent interpretation of "neither male nor female" is that the work of Christ set aside *not* the fallen creation of Genesis 3, but the *original creation order itself*. Indeed, this is a view some feminists feel compelled to take, and it will be discussed in the next section.

The main point here is that Galatians 3:28 cannot be understood as affirming that the work of Christ has reversed the results of the Fall and the curse, since the relationship of the curse to the three pairs is quite tenuous and ambiguous and lacks any clear parallel among them. Surely if Galatians 3:28 were speaking of reversing the curse, the three pairs would have to have a clearer, more consistent relationship to the curse itself. If that were the point of the passage, then the very choice of these pairs and not others would be motivated by this consideration. Why then are they not more clearly and consistently reflective of the curse? It seems that we must look for something besides "reversing the curse" as our explanation of Galatians 3:28.

B. Does Galatians 3:28
Replace the First Creation Order?

Another approach to the relation of the work of Christ to the creation-Fall-redemption theme is to say that Christ's work completely *replaces* the original order of creation with a new, redemptive order. A number of feminists interpret "in Christ Jesus" in Galatians 3:28 in this way. The real contrast, they say, is not between the new Christian order and the old creation *as cursed*, but between the new Christian order and the old creation *as such*.

This view is certainly a more consistent approach to the connection most feminists see between Galatians 3:28, "There is neither male nor female," and Genesis 1:27, "Male and female He created them." It avoids the difficulties and ambiguities involved in trying to relate the three pairs in some parallel way to the curse. It recognizes that if there is an intended connection between the two verses, then Paul's thought leaps back beyond the effects of the curse and focuses on the original creation order in and of itself. He would not be saying that there shall no longer be perverted relationships between males and females; he would be saying rather that there shall no longer be "male and female."

Richard and Joyce Boldrey affirm that both the order of creation and the order of transgression are replaced by a third, "new order" in Christ. Paul's terminology, they say, points back "to creation itself." Thus "Paul was saying that, in Christ, relationships between men and women should transcend the male-female division."[35] Longenecker likewise contrasts the category of the original creation with the category of redemption, the gender relationships established in the former being replaced by a different order. In the former, "order, subordination, and submission are generally stressed," while the latter "emphasizes what God has done redemptively, wherein freedom, mutuality, and equality take prominence." Thus "what God has done in Christ transcends what is true simply because of creation."[36] Don Williams agrees: "As the racial and social barriers are broken down, so also are the sexual distinctions due to the creation of 'male and female.' Here is Paul's radical step beyond the old order. Redemption does not merely restore God's intention in creation. Redemption brings into being a whole new world, a whole new order."[37]

One advantage of this view for feminists is that it neutralizes any attempt to argue for the normativeness of male headship based on a hierarchical interpretation of Genesis 1 and 2. Even if God did establish a relationship of authority and subordination between Adam and Eve in their original pre-Fall existence, this would be irrelevant with regard to the norm for gender relationships in the new creation in Christ. At the same time it tends to neutralize Paul's appeal to Genesis 1 and 2 in passages that seem to support female subordination, i.e., 1 Corinthians 11:2ff. and 1 Timothy 2:11-13. These can be viewed as temporary expedients to meet local problems.[38]

How may we evaluate this view that Galatians 3:28 represents the work of Christ as replacing the original creation order? Upon closer analysis we find no more support for this view than for the previous one. The problem is not simply that this is a false understanding of Galatians 3:28. More seriously, the whole concept of the first creation order being replaced by something different is problematic.

The most common understanding of the creation-Fall-redemption framework is reflected in the previous section. Bible students generally see the first creation as being ideal in a qualitative sense; the only improvements that could be made would be quantitative. The Fall and the curse, however, introduced negative qualitative changes in the form of sinfulness, sinful relationships, evil, and suffering. The work of Christ is designed to correct the problems caused by the Fall and to restore the world to its original ideal state. The "new" creation is new in the sense of being renewed.

This second view of Galatians 3:28, however, sees Jesus not just as correcting the problems caused by sin but also as introducing qualitative changes in the created order itself, at least where gender relationships are concerned. Hierarchicalism, even if based on the original creation, is replaced by egalitarianism as one result of the redemptive work of Christ. Now, this view has a most serious implication that cannot be ignored. It is this: if the creation order of Genesis 1 and 2 was hierarchical, and if a work of *redemption* by the incarnate Savior was required to replace it, then this implies that there was a qualitative flaw in the original creation. But Scripture nowhere gives us any warrant for viewing this creation as a qualitatively imperfect version of God's work that would require updating at a certain point. Indeed, God pronounced it "very good" from the beginning (Gen. 1:31). All the flaws and imperfections removed by the work of Christ are traceable to sin alone. Thus the whole concept underlying this view must be rejected.

There are still other significant problems with the view. For one thing, there is a real ambivalence among feminists as to what it would mean to say that the male-female distinction of Genesis 1:27 has been nullified or transcended in Christ. Transcendence seems to be the key concept. The Boldreys say that "in Christ, relationships between men and women should transcend the male-female division."[39] "What God has done in Christ transcends what is true simply because of creation," says Longenecker.[40]

To "transcend the male-female division" would seem to imply unqualified egalitarianism in the sense of a complete ignoring of gender. Some feminists make strong statements to this effect. Our new union in Christ "is a relationship in which differences disappear."[41] Just as "all distinctions between Jews and Greeks are abolished," so also the "plain meaning" of the text is that "in Christ and therefore in the Christian church sex distinctions between man and woman lose their significance. Galatians 3.28 is the first occurrence in antiquity of a doctrine openly propagating the abolition of sex distinctions."[42]

Such statements would not seem to be extreme if they were limited to the status of men and women before God, since no such distinctions apply as far as access to salvation is concerned. But as we have seen, it is crucial to the feminist interpretation of Galatians 3:28 that it not be so limited, but that it be applied to social relationships as well. Thus a consistent replacing-the-first-creation view would actually result in a unisex society. If gender is ignored, then one of these two circumstances must occur: either marriage will be replaced by celibacy, or homosexual unions will be as normal as heterosexual ones. How else could "no male and female" be understood?

Feminists as a rule reject this complete and consistent abolition of gender distinctions. They hasten to deny that the transcending of the male-female distinction is absolutely absolute. They almost always specify certain qualifications, usually in reference to reproduction and marriage. But when these qualifications are made, we have a right to ask, on what *basis* are such to be allowed? The answer will invariably come back, on the basis of other Biblical teaching. In rejecting the unisex conclusion, Longenecker appeals to Paul's other writings thus: "Heterosexuality is presupposed in all of his letters as having been ordained by God, and he has nothing but contempt and condemnation for homosexual practices."[43]

Such an appeal to other Scripture is quite proper, of course, but when feminists employ it in this way they create a dilemma for themselves. Either they must ignore how other texts qualify and limit the extent of "neither male nor female," and embrace consistent unisexuality; or they must use other texts to provide the desired qualifications, thus acknowledging the validity of using other Scripture texts to limit the meaning of Galatians 3:28 as such. The latter is something they are extremely reluctant to do, however, especially in reference to church leadership roles. In fact, as we will see below, it is a feminist axiom that Galatians 3:28 is the starting point for hermeneutics, and all other texts about gender roles must be interpreted in its light. Thus it would seem that they must choose between unisexuality and the hermeneutical primacy of Galatians 3:28.

The fact is that created distinctions between males and females are *not* obliterated by the work of Christ; they are still intact. And it is quite proper to use other Biblical texts to determine what these distinctions are, in a way that certainly qualifies "neither male nor female" in the new creation. In the light of these other texts, it is clear that celibacy is not required nor is homosexuality permitted by this principle. It is therefore appropriate to ask what *other* distinctions may still remain, untouched by the work of Christ. May we not be justified in using other texts about gender roles which speak of headship and submission as qualifications of Galatians 3:28? This will be discussed in detail later.

A final note has to do with the alleged link between Galatians 3:28 and Genesis 1:27 based on the use of the phrase "male and female" in each. The argument is that since this expression is not symmetrical in form to the other pairs and is almost technical, Paul would not have used it unless he was thinking specifically of the Genesis text. This does not necessarily follow, however. One good reason for choosing the terms *male* and *female* (rather than *man* and *woman*) has already been noted above, namely, Paul is here referring to a distinction between genders and not to a relationship between persons. Also, the fact that he changes conjunctions in this phrase, replacing *nor* with *and*, need not in the least mean that he is deliberately switching gears in order to quote the language of Genesis 1:27. In fact, in the parallel statement in Colossians 3:11, Paul uses only the conjunction *and*, with exactly the same negative as in all three pairs in Galatians 3:28 (*ouk eni*); and in Colossians he does not even include the male-female pair. Thus the choice of *nor* or *and* does not seem to be significant.

We must conclude that there is no good reason to see in Galatians 3:28 a reference to the replacing of the old creation order by the work of Christ, and that there are several good reasons against it. Thus this cannot be used as a way of interpreting this verse so as to eliminate all distinctions in gender roles.

C. Does Galatians 3:28
Refer to Distinctions in the Law of Moses?

One other way of understanding "in Christ Jesus" in Galatians 3:28 is that the work of Christ erased certain distinctions that prevailed within the Law of Moses. That is to say, the Christian order initiated by the work of Christ replaced the inadequate status accorded to Gentiles, women, and slaves under the Law in certain specific circumstances. This is the view that will be defended in some detail later in this chapter. When we see how Galatians 3:28 is thus directed against a particular aspect of the Law of Moses, it will be even more clear that it is not directed against either the original order of creation or against the curse as such.

II. THE JEWISH PRAYER

The problem of explaining why Paul should bring the three pairs together in Galatians 3:28—Jew/Greek, slave/free man, male/female—has led to a detailed search of other literature for possible clues. One serious suggestion is that Paul is consciously opposing the low view of women reflected in Jewish culture and embodied in a prayer said to be offered by men.

This widely-quoted Jewish prayer appears in several places. One is from the writing known as the *Tosefta* (or *Tosephta*), which was a kind of supplement to the *Mishnah*. It says, "Rabbi Judah says, 'One ought to say three blessings every day: blessed is he that he did not make me a Gentile; blessed is he that he did not make me a woman; blessed is he that he did not make me a boor'" [brutish, ignorant man].[44] Of course, this was a prayer that only Jewish males would recite. Over and over it is referred to in feminist writings as a likely stimulus for Paul's statement that in Christ "there is neither Jew nor Greek, there is neither slave nor free man, there is neither male nor female." The purpose of this section is to examine this claim.

A. Feminist Claims

Though some feminists suggest only the *possibility* of a connection between the Jewish prayer and Galatians 3:28, others are much more dogmatic and affirm it as if it were an established fact.

Examples are abundant. Scanzoni and Hardesty say, "This verse directly contradicts the prayer of every orthodox Jewish male: 'Blessed are you, Lord our God . . . who has not created me a heathen . . . a slave . . . a woman.'"[45] Paul wrote "with this in mind," says Pape.[46] Bartchy says that the connection among the pairs in Galatians 3:28 "is probably to be found in the Jewish synagogue prayer by which God is blessed by free, male, Jewish worshipers for not having created them either Gentiles, women, or slaves." Paul himself "probably repeated this prayer frequently" as he grew up in the synagogue in Tarsus.[47] "Along with his mother's milk, Saul of Tarsus took in this prayer." Then later he wrote Galatians 3:28 "directly into the teeth of that prayer which he had most probably prayed quite often."[48] Gasque says that Galatians 3:28 "cannot be understood apart from Paul's being brought up to offer the traditional synagogue thanksgiving."[49] "As a rabbi, Paul had given thanks daily . . . that he had not been born as a Gentile, a slave, a woman," avers Brauch.[50]

It is important for feminists to posit such a connection with this Jewish prayer, which is usually taken to be very obnoxious and chauvinistic. It seems to be the essence of elitism, and tends to put all forms of hierarchicalism in a bad light, especially the hierarchical relationship between men and women. Thus if Paul can be pictured as deliberately rejecting the implications of this prayer, then Galatians 3:28 can be assumed to be a repudiation of hierarchicalism and a conscious affirmation of complete role equality.

Another significant reason for making this connection is that it seems to offer a rationale for the linking of the three pairs by Paul, which many find difficult to explain otherwise. Also, if such a prior connection among these pairs can be found, i.e., one that existed before Paul wrote Galatians, then the three-fold formula can more easily be detached from the context of the epistle and represented as a basic theological principle summing up the essence of the gospel.[51]

B. Response

The first thing to be said in response to this feminist tendency to link Galatians 3:28 with the Jewish prayer is that the prayer was not intended to be as obnoxious as it seems in our present context. To the seriously religious Jew, nothing was more important than studying and observing the Torah. Yet to some extent Gentiles, women, and ignorant men were either not able or not required to do these things. Thus, as Bruce says, "the reason for the threefold thanksgiving was not any positive disparagement of Gentiles, slaves or women as persons but the fact that they were disqualified from several religious privileges which were open to free Jewish males."[52] This being the case, the contrast between the prayer and whatever Paul is saying may not be as sharp as frequently thought.

A much more serious question, however, is whether there is a valid parallel between the prayer and Galatians 3:28 in the first place. If the parallel is as clear-cut as often claimed, then we would expect the same three pairs to be named in each list. But this is not the case. The Jewish prayer refers specifically to Gentiles and women, thus reflecting the Jew/Greek and male/female pairs in Galatians. But at least in its early form the prayer does not refer to slaves at all.

This point is very often missed or glossed over in the

feminist literature. By far the greater percentage of those who cite the prayer represent it as referring to Gentiles, women, and slaves. The quotations cited in the preceding section are typical, and almost every one says "Gentile, woman, slave."

This, however, is very misleading. It leaves the false impression that the prayer and Galatians 3:28 are parallel in every way, but they are not. Besides a difference in the order (not significant in itself), the Jewish prayer does not refer to a slave but to a "brutish man" (Hebrew, *bor*), variously translated as "boor, ignorant man, illiterate man, uneducated man," i.e., one who is unable to study the Torah. Apparently some have just mistakenly assumed that the prayer says "slave," when it in fact says something else. Others, however, quote it correctly, then put "slave" in apposition as if it means the same thing as "uneducated man"—which it does not.[53] The purpose seems to be to create or to find a parallel where in fact one does not exist.[54]

The final problem with the view that the three pairs in Galatians 3:28 can be explained as a deliberate negation of the Jewish prayer is the fact that there is no evidence that *any form* of this prayer was being used by Jews in the first century. Most of the feminist references to the prayer just assume it was in existence during Paul's lifetime. Those cited in the preceding section speak of it as a first-century prayer, as contemporary with Paul, as something he grew up with. This is pure speculation, however. The *Tosefta* reference cited above (*Berakoth* 7.18) comes from the late second century, and the rabbi to whom it is attributed, Rabbi Judah b. Elai (or Ilai) is from the mid-second century. No earlier source is cited, even though the teachings of many specific rabbis from much earlier times are known.[55] Spencer says, "We do not have a clear example of this Jewish prayer in the early first century."[56] Her inclusion of the word *early* is misleading, since it implies there may be a clear example from the *late* first century; but this is simply not true. It cannot be traced earlier than the middle of the second century.

We must conclude that the attempt to relate Galatians 3:28 to the Jewish three-fold thanksgiving prayer fails and fails badly. Those who speak of such a connection as if it were an established fact display a lack of familiarity with the facts; and they are guilty of misleading others, even if inadvertently so. The bottom line is that we must look elsewhere for a rationale for the parallel among the three pairs in Galatians 3:28.

III. IS GALATIANS 3:28 A BAPTISMAL FORMULA?

It is sometimes noted that a few other New Testament passages seem to some degree to be parallel either in form or content to the "formula" in Galatians 3:28, especially 1 Corinthians 7:1-40; 1 Corinthians 12:13; and Colossians 3:11. Like Galatians 3:28, these passages speak of various pairs such as Jews and Greeks, and slaves and free men.

Feminists sometimes take this apparent formal parallelism as a warrant for linking the content of these texts together as well. One advantage of this is the possibility of transporting some egalitarian concept into Galatians 3:28 from one of the other passages.

An example is Tucker and Liefeld's view that the clothing image in Galatians 3:27 and Colossians 3:10 is the same, referring to conversion and new life. Thus since the context of the Colossian passage makes practical applications of our new life to social issues, we should interpret Galatians 3:28 in the same way.[57]

This is a very shaky attempt to "compare Scripture with Scripture," however. On closer examination the parallel is purely formal. Each passage speaks of certain pairs, to be sure; but it is very striking and very significant that only Galatians 3:28 includes the male/female pair. Even 1 Corinthians 7 is different, since it refers to the married/unmarried contrast, not to gender as such. Colossians 3:11 mentions neither.

But even if Tucker and Liefeld are right about the parallel between Galatians 3:28 and Colossians 3:11, i.e., that social applications should be made in the former because they are in the context of the latter, the result is counterproductive for egalitarianism. This is true because the only social application regarding gender relationships in Colossians 3 is a hierarchical one: "Wives, be subject to your husbands, as is fitting in the Lord" (verse 18). Thus this attempt to interpret Galatians 3:28 in terms of the content of its so-called parallel passages is not very fruitful.

Feminists see another advantage in pursuing a possible parallel between Galatians 3:28 and these other passages. It is this: if a similar list of pairs can be found in several other passages, then it may be that they represent a formula that was already circulating independently in the Christian community. That would pave the way for detaching these pairs from their immediate literary context in Galatians and viewing them as part of a more general formula or general principle with a very broad application.

A suggestion frequently put forward to this end is that Galatians 3:28 was originally part of a commonly-used baptismal formula. Since Galatians 3:27 mentions baptism, and since it is supposedly a prominent element in the contexts of two of the other passages (1 Cor. 12:13 and Col. 3:11), it is likely that the three pairs were part of such a baptismal formula, and that this is what accounts for their presence in Galatians 3:28 as well as the other two passages.

Though this view is developed most fully by non-evangelical exegetes,[58] a number of Biblical feminists have advocated it as well. Bilezikian notes that "many scholars believe that the actual wording of verse 28 is the transcription of a creed repeated during baptismal ceremonies in Pauline churches."[59] Bartchy declares that "the verse itself seems to be the conclusion of a traditional baptismal confession, which begins in verse 27."[60] "There is much to be said," according to Longenecker, "for the view that Galatians 3:28 was originally part of a baptismal confession of early Christians."[61]

The basic idea seems to be that Paul was moved to use the formula because of its reference to the elimination of a distinction between Jews and Greeks in Christ Jesus. This was relevant to his argument in the context. But since he had already introduced the formula, he just continued to quote the whole thing even though the other two pairs were not really related to his specific argument.

Several lines of evidence are set forth to support this view. Perhaps the most significant is the apparent similarity between Galatians 3:28 and two of the "parallel passages," 1 Corinthians 12:13 and Colossians 3:11. It is pointed out that all three of these passages use the language of baptism, they all refer to certain pairs, and they all emphasize unity in Christ. These similarities "make it quite likely that what we are dealing with is an early, perhaps pre-Pauline, baptismal formula" that Paul simply inserts into his argument in Galatians 3.[62] Langley says the parallel with 1 Corinthians 12:13 and Colossians 3:11 shows that Galatians 3:28 "must have" functioned as part of a baptismal liturgy.[63]

A second argument for the view that Galatians 3:28 is a baptismal formula is the assumption that the male/female and slave/free pairs have no connection with Paul's argument in the context. As Bartchy says, "The opposing pairs, slave/free and male/female, are not immediately relevant to the point regarding Jew/Greek, which Paul strongly emphasizes in this letter. Therefore, it should be asked if the connection between the three pairs might well have existed before Paul wrote the letter."[64] In support of the baptismal formula hypothesis, Bartchy says in another place that "nothing in the Galatian letter can account for the phrase 'no male and female'" in 3:28.[65] Longenecker agrees: "Only the first pair of coordinates in verse 28 ('neither Jew nor Greek') is directly relevant to Paul's argument in Galatians."[66]

Another argument offered by Longenecker is that verses 27 and 28 in their entirety are like a parenthesis in the structure of Paul's argument and have no necessary connection with it. "Structurally, one can go from verse 26 to verse 29, omitting verses 27-28, without noticing any break in Paul's logic or grammar."[67] Langley agrees, averring that New Testament scholarship has "demonstrated conclusively" that verses 26-28 "stand apart in their formality of composition and structure," and "represent an earlier pre-Pauline baptismal formula."[68]

For feminists there are two principal advantages in identifying Galatians 3:28 as part of a baptismal formula. One is that it accounts for the inclusion of all three of the stated pairs, whereas the context alone seems to warrant mention only of the Jew/Greek pair. But more significantly, it allows them to detach this whole verse from the Galatian context and to treat it as a kind of creedal statement that expresses the essence of the gospel and has the broadest possible application. They can call it "pre-Pauline," and treat it as if it "already had a history in the early Christian communities before Paul used it in his argument with the Galatian Christians."[69]

In other words, when seen as a baptismal formula, Galatians 3:28 can more easily be expanded beyond one's faith-status before God and can be applied as well to all cultural and social relationships. The main result for feminists, of course, is egalitarianism with regard to roles in the home and church. As Langley states it, the fact that the parallel pairs in verse 28 are part of a baptismal formula shows that they "define not only the religious, but also the social, cultural and political consequences of being 'one in Christ'." The language of the baptismal initiation "names the old status and by implication claims the new; all barriers of race, class and sex have been eliminated."[70] The very title of her article suggests the connection she is making: "One Baptism, One Ministry: The Ordination of Women and Unity in Christ." As summed up by Longenecker,

> The extremely important point to note here is that on the basis of a form-critical analysis the statement of verse 28 cannot be seen as merely some idiosyncratic notion of Paul's

but probably should be taken as a confession of first-century Christians more generally—a confession included within the baptismal liturgy of the early Church which proclaims both a new status in Christ before God spiritually and new relationships between believers socially.[71]

How may we evaluate this argument? First of all, even if we grant that Galatians 3:28 is derived from a baptismal formula, this in itself would not mean that the expression "neither male nor female" must have the full social implications that feminists read into it. To assume any application broader than *coram deo* actually begs the question as to what the alleged baptismal formula itself meant. As House says, "Whether Paul was quoting or adapting an earlier baptismal formula in no way affects the meaning or impact of his use of it in Galatians 3:28."[72]

The real issue, though, is whether there is any evidence to support the contention that these verses are derived from a baptismal formula in the first place. This idea is based almost entirely on the language of the passages. Though we acknowledge some similarities in this regard, the fact that there are crucial differences in the language of the passages as well. The most significant is the omission of the male/female pair in Colossians 3:11 and 1 Corinthians 12:13. This is particularly striking in view of the fact that Paul seems to make the Colossians statement unusually comprehensive and inclusive. If a baptismal formula is the common source of these texts, and if the male/female pair was included in it, then it is extremely difficult to explain why this pair is not found in all three texts. This is especially true if Paul were really as intent on abolishing gender distinctions as feminists believe he was.

A second difference is the fact that only two of the texts actually refer to baptism, namely Galatians 3 (verse 27) and 1 Corinthians 12:13. That baptism was in Paul's mind when he was writing Colossians 3:11 is only an inference. Though he makes a strong statement about baptism in Colossians 2:12, in chapter 3 he has moved beyond that specific discussion. Without an explicit reference to baptism in the immediate context of Colossians 3:11, its connection with some sort of baptismal formula is just an inference; and the parallelism with Galatians 3:28 is quite diminished.

Another weakness in the contention that these verses reflect a common origin in a primitive baptismal formula is the total lack of evidence that any such formula ever existed, other than the speculation based on these passages themselves. No descriptions of the first-century baptismal ceremony exist outside the New Testament itself; thus there is no evidence from the first century that such language was used in connection with the act of baptism. Several second-century descriptions of baptism exist (e.g., the *Didache* and Justin Martyr), but none of them include any reference to the language of Galatians 3:28. The point is that if there were some pre-existing baptismal formula reflected in these "parallel passages," we would expect to find some continuing use of that formula in the succeeding centuries. That it should have died out completely without a trace makes it highly suspect that it ever existed in the first place.

The final reason for questioning the existence of this formula has to do with the relation between Galatians 3:28 and its context. One of the main arguments for the baptismal-formula view is that it explains why Paul mentions the slave/free and male/female pairs, when there seems to be no contextual reason for including them in the first place. As noted above, some feminists declare that these pairs are not immediately relevant to Paul's argument, and that nothing in Galatians can really account for the reference to male and female especially. Such an idea, however, is totally false, as we shall see shortly. All three pairs specified in Galatians 3:28—Jew/Greek, bond/free, male/female—have a very strong and deliberate connection with the context. Each is intimately related in exactly the same way to the total argument of the chapter. To use the alleged lack of such a connection as a reason for positing some pre-existing baptismal formula is misguided.

Our conclusion is that no valid use of the passages said to be parallel to Galatians 3:28 gives us any basis for interpreting the latter in a way that supports feminist egalitarianism. The passage must be interpreted in the light of its own context; and when this is properly done, the interpretation falls far short of eliminating gender role distinctions.

IV. GALATIANS 3:28 AND OTHER GENDER TEXTS

As pointed out above, Galatians 3:28 is the only didactic passage relating to gender roles that feminists are able to interpret in such a way that it seems to support their egalitarian agenda. There are at least seven other texts with specific teaching about gender roles, but all of them seem to confirm the hierarchical pattern of male headship and female submission. These are 1 Corinthians 11:3; 14:34-35; Ephesians 5:22-23; Colossians 3:18; 1 Timothy 2:11-12; Titus 2:5; and 1 Peter 3:1-7.

This preponderance of hierarchical texts raises a serious question of hermeneutics, namely, exactly how are they to be interpreted in light of Galatians 3:28? If the latter is egalitarian in intent, as feminists claim, then what is to be done with the former? Specifically, which will be used to interpret the other? Which will have hermeneutical priority? Which will be the norm, and which will be adjusted to conform to that norm? What is the proper way to use these texts to allow them to validly interpret one another?

The main emphasis of this section is to explain and evaluate the way feminists answer such questions.

A. The Feminist Approach

As we saw in the introduction to this chapter, feminists regard Galatians 3:28 as the basic principle of Christian doctrine in general, and as the main text for understanding God's will about gender roles in particular. McClelland declares that it is "the point of departure" and "the starting point for our analysis of Paul's view of the role and status of women . . . . The principle enunciated here is at the very center of the entire gospel proclamation of reconciliation in Jesus Christ."[73] It is "the foundation," the "central truth" regarding gender roles.[74] As Gasque says, *"Galatians 3:28 is the necessary theological starting place for any discussion on the role of women in the church."*[75] "Galatians 3:28 remains the most explicit reference to the male-female relation found anywhere in Paul's letters," says Evans.[76] It is "the normative text."[77]

Thus in terms of Biblical interpretation, feminists assign hermeneutical primacy to Galatians 3:28. This is the passage that will determine how all the other gender texts must be understood. But exactly how do feminists see these other texts as relating to Galatians 3:28? Those with a lower view of Biblical authority accept the idea that Paul simply contradicts himself on this issue. For example, Jewett says that Paul sometimes reflects his old Jewish rabbinic training, and sometimes the new Christian gospel. Thus in these texts we have "Paul versus Paul": Paul the Jewish rabbi versus Paul the liberated Christian.[78]

Feminists with a high view of Biblical authority, however, cannot resort to this view of internal inconsistency. Thus another approach must be sought. In the final analysis the most common method of relating these texts is to begin with Galatians 3:28, interpreted as affirming full egalitarianism, as the one immovable hermeneutical rock, and then to interpret all the hierarchical gender texts as somehow being *non-binding exceptions* to it. Only the former has a universal and eternal application; the latter are regarded as being valid only within limited or temporary contexts. As Kassian puts it, "Biblical feminists chose Galatians 3:28 . . . as the crux around which to interpret Scripture."[79]

Feminist affirmations of this methodology are abundant. Roger and Rose Thomas sum it up when they declare that in Galatians 3:28 Paul "laid the foundation for the

Christian understanding of women in God's plan. . . . Every other teaching or dogma concerning women in God's plan must be interpreted in the light of this central truth."[80] Bruce says, "Paul states the basic principle here; if restrictions on it are found elsewhere in the Pauline corpus," as in 1 Corinthians 14:34-35 and 1 Timothy 2:11-12, "they are to be understood in relation to Gal. 3:28, and not *vice versa*."[81] Agreeing with Bruce, Longenecker says that when we come upon the other gender texts we must "first of all take our stand with the gospel proclamation and its principles (i.e., with the confession of Galatians 3:28) and seek to understand these passages from that perspective, and not vice versa."[82] Galatians 3:28, says Gasque, is "an unequivocal statement, a theological statement if there ever was one, of absolute equality in Christ in the church. . . . Everything else that Paul writes must be understood in the light of this clear statement of a fundamental Christian principle."[83]

The rationale for this hermeneutical primacy of Galatians 3:28 is not always stated in exactly the same way, but it always has the same form: only Galatians is regarded as absolute, unqualified theological truth; all the other gender texts are seen as somehow relative or situational.[84] That is to say, the latter were all addressing specific, local, temporary situations; therefore their message was adapted to those situations and was not intended to be universally applied. Only Galatians is stating "unchanging truth."

That the other gender texts are meant to be relative and temporary is seen as an implication of the very nature of epistles as specific and occasional, i.e., as occasioned by specific problems that must be dealt with on an *ad hoc* basis. Johnston warns, "The very nature of 'letters' intended to answer specific questions about particular issues in the life of the churches in Corinth and Ephesus"— i.e., 1 Corinthians and 1 Timothy—"should make the reader extremely cautious in deducing universal principles from their advice." This is in contrast with "Paul's *theologi-*

cal statement of equality in Christ in Galatians 3:28."[85] Likewise, when discussing the passages "where some restrictions seem to be made by Paul," McClelland says that "we want to be careful to note a characteristic of all Pauline literature—it is occasional in nature." For example, 1 Timothy must be regarded as "a response to a contemporary situation and not as a church-order manual." Thus we should expect some of his teaching to be "fit for an emergency situation rather than for an ideal one."[86]

Feminists characterize the alleged distinction between the absolute (Galatians 3:28) and the relative (other gender texts) in a variety of ways. Bartchy says the former is *normative*, while the latter are *problematic*, i.e., dealing with specific local problems in the churches.[87] Anderson sees Galatians 3:28 as "the normative text," and the other gender texts as "specific pastoral injunctions."[88] Scanzoni and Hardesty say the distinction is between a general principle (Galatians 3:28) and passages that deal with particular situations. "Of all the passages concerning women in the New Testament, only Galatians 3:28 is in a doctrinal setting; the remainder are all concerned with practical matters."[89] Since Galatians 3:26-28 "was surely Paul's central theological conviction," says Brauch, then the other texts "must be in response to critical, local situations."[90] In Johnston's words, Galatians 3:28 is "Paul's *theological* statement of equality in Christ," while the other texts are "specific passages of advice" characterized by "particularity and time-relatedness."[91]

Sometimes the distinction is stated in terms of principle versus culture. Langley says that all the texts except Galatians 3:28 "tend to suppress the principle of 'equality' in favour of the expedient approach of cultural sensitivity and the maintenance of social order."[92] Hayter agrees with the view that Galatians 3:28 transcends its cultural setting "so [as] to constitute 'unchanging truth' of eternal relevance for the Church," while the other texts are "so *culturally conditioned* that they may not simply be transferred to present-day issues."[93] Speaking first of the other gender texts, Mollenkott says, "All those passages are addressed to very specific cases. But Galatians 3 . . . is in a fully theological context. So that context tells us that Galatians is normative while the others are cultural."[94]

Another way of saying this is that Galatians 3:28 states the theological principle, while the other texts are *descriptive* of a temporary state of affairs in the church in which the principle had not yet been fully implemented. Jewett is an example of this approach. He says that Galatians 3:28 is Paul's "magnificent affirmation" of basic Christian truth, yet the other texts show that he was "cautious . . . in the implementation of his own Christian insight." He says that we must "distinguish between what the New Testament *says* about the new life in Christ and the actual *degree of implementation* of this vision in the first-century church."[95] Longenecker agrees with Jewett and formalizes what he calls a "developmental hermeneutic" that distinguishes between the normative proclamation and principles of the gospel (especially Galatians 3:28) and descriptions of the imperfect way these were put into practice in the first century (as reflected in the other gender texts).[96]

All these different ways of speaking of the relation between Galatians 3:28 and the other gender texts are just variations on a single theme, namely, that Galatians 3:28 is the normative universal principle, while the other texts are particular and non-binding exceptions to it.

B. Evaluation of the Feminist Approach

The key issue here is hermeneutics, i.e., the proper method for interpreting the Bible. Specifically, it is a matter of the proper application of one of the cardinal principles of hermeneutics, namely, the analogy of faith or the analogy of Scripture. As Demarest explains it, "As a general hermeneutical principle, analogy of faith connotes that an obscure text or passage may be illumined by other texts of Scripture whose meaning is clear. . . . In fact, the meaning of a given text often is established only after a careful consideration of other passages which speak to the issue." The basic assumption is that "Scripture interprets Scripture," which helps to "guard against a one-sided interpretation of the scriptural text." Also, the exegete must remember "that his interpretation must not contravene what is taught elsewhere in Scripture, and that in unfolding the meaning of a text other inspired Scriptures may help clarify the specific intention of the biblical writer."[97]

Feminists will say that this is exactly what they are doing, i.e., interpreting Scripture with Scripture. Specifically, they are using Galatians 3:28 to interpret the other gender texts. The problem, however, is that their application of the principle of analogy is *completely one-sided*; by accepting certain unwarranted (and sometimes implicit) assumptions they totally rule out the possibility that the other gender texts may just as properly be used to interpret Galatians 3:28. Hermeneutically they begin with Galatians 3:28 and interpret it in isolation, as if no other gender texts exist. They conclude that it is a general, timeless and unqualified theological principle that is intended to have the broadest possible application to all social and ecclesiastical relationships. On the basis of this text alone, interpreted in hermeneutical isolation, all distinctions between gender roles are thus condemned as contrary to the gospel of Christ. Only then do feminists look at the other gender texts, in order to find a meaning for them that fits their unilateral interpretation of Galatians 3:28.

Our purpose in this section is to analyze in more detail the faulty hermeneutical methodology that is involved in this procedure. Of particular concern are the numerous unwarranted assumptions used to justify the unilateral use of Galatians 3:28 to interpret the other texts, without allowing the latter in any sense to serve as qualifiers of the former.

1. *Unwarranted Assumptions*

We may identify four specific assumptions underlying feminists' claim that Galatians 3:28 has hermeneutical primacy in the sense that its meaning is clear apart from a consideration of the other gender texts, and that the latter must be interpreted in its predetermined light. None of these assumptions is valid.

The first such unwarranted assumption is the idea that the general always interprets the specific, and not vice versa. Galatians 3:28 is consistently described in the most general terms: the fundamental or basic principle, the central theological conviction, the central truth, the universal ideal. The other gender texts are consistently particularized: they are local, exceptional, specific, occasional, relative, culturally conditioned. Then it is simply assumed that *just because* the former is general, and *just because* the latter are specific, the former must interpret the latter.

Plainly stated, this is simply not a valid hermeneutical principle. Sometimes the general may interpret the specific, but sometimes general statements are interpreted by and even restricted or qualified by specific statements. For example, the general command to obey governmental authorities (Rom. 13:1) is restricted by Acts 5:29. The general command to "make no oath at all" (Matt. 5:34) is qualified by Matthew 26:63-64, Galatians 1:20, and Revelation 10:6. The general truth that God is One (Deut. 6:4; Gal. 3:20) is qualified by specific Trinitarian statements and by specific references to the deity of Jesus and of the Holy Spirit. The general truth that no man can see God (1 Tim. 6:16) is qualified and interpreted by specific texts such as Exodus 24:10, Isaiah 6:1, and Matthew 5:8. The general promise of John 11:26 must be interpreted by such specific facts as Acts 7:60 and Acts 12:2.

In view of such examples, it is certainly fallacious to assume that the so-called general statement of Galatians 3:28 is the normative qualifier of all other gender texts just because it is general and the others are specific. This is simply not a valid application of the principle of analogy.

The second unwarranted assumption underlying feminists' hermeneutical use of Galatians 3:28 is the very designation of this text as a general principle in the first place. Feminists universally assume that this verse is intended to be a general statement of fundamental Christian doctrine or gospel truth, with no specific contextual focus either in the historical circumstances of the Galatian churches or in the epistle itself. While the other gender texts are declared to be situational and limited in application by virtue of the fact that they appear in occasional epistolary literature, Galatians 3:28 is enshrined upon a transcendent altar of heavenly truth that towers above all contingencies, conditioned by none and qualifying them all.

It is time to challenge the inconsistency of such a method. Certainly it is true that 1 Corinthians and 1 Timothy are letters, and that they were occasioned by and deal with specific problems in the life of the church. But how is Galatians any different? It is every bit as occasional and situational as the letters to Corinth and to Timothy, and it is wrong and misleading to pretend that it is not. It was occasioned by a very specific and very serious historical problem, i.e., the false teaching of the Judaizers. It can no more be detached from its historical setting than can 1 Corinthians or 1 Timothy. Galatians 3:28 was directed against just as specific a problem in Galatia as was 1 Timothy 2:12 in Ephesus.

Feminists may grant this point, but will reply that the immediate context of Galatians 3:28 still makes it a general Christian principle. I.e., it describes the universal fruit of redemption, the general result of faith and baptism, or what it means to be "one in Christ Jesus." Thus it seems to transcend the limitations of any specific local problems and of specific contextual connections as well.

In response we can only say that this reflects a false understanding of how Galatians 3:28 relates to its immediate context. Once we perceive the specific and intimate connection of this verse with Paul's overall argument in 3:1

through 4:7, we will see that 3:28 is *not* intended to be a general theological principle with unlimited social implications. It relates to a very specific point he is making in this context, as will be explained below. Thus the crucial feminist assumption that Galatians 3:28 is a general principle and thus has hermeneutical primacy over the "occasional" texts is incorrect.

A third invalid assumption underlying this view of the hermeneutical primacy of Galatians 3:28 is the notion that texts such as 1 Corinthians 14:34-35 and 1 Timothy 2:11-12 are just *descriptive* of local situations and not *prescriptive* in the sense of Galatians 3:28. This idea was presented above especially in the form that Galatians states the new Christian ideal while the other texts are merely descriptive of the actual first-century practice, which was lagging behind the ideal.

One crucial implication of such a view is this: if these other gender texts are understood as descriptive of first-century practice, then they are describing the practice not just of the churches as such but of the Apostle Paul himself. The restrictions concerning the roles of women in these texts are not problem practices being addressed and corrected by Paul; they are rather being *prescribed by* Paul as something that *ought* to be put into practice.

This in itself has two further implications. First, it makes it difficult to avoid the conclusion that Paul is guilty of inconsistency in his practice and teaching. Second, if Galatians states the new ideal and the other texts simply reflect how slow the church (including Paul) was to implement this ideal, it seems strange that in *all* his other instructions on this subject Paul shows no progress or "development" in his thinking *at all*. This is especially true in view of the fact that in practice, according to feminists, Paul is supposed to have endorsed many women in roles of leadership, in the spirit of Galatians 3:28.[98] If this is really what he is doing, then why would practically *all* of his teaching "lag behind" his own practice?

Such considerations reveal the fallacy of calling the

other gender texts merely *descriptive*, in contrast with the prescriptive and normative text in Galatians. To be sure, in studying 1 Corinthians and 1 Timothy one can learn something of the conditions of the church in Corinth and in Ephesus in the first century, and in this sense these texts may be "descriptive." But it is one thing to say that the *situations* being addressed by Paul are descriptive of first-century conditions, and it is altogether a different thing to say that Paul's *instructions* regarding these situations are merely descriptive. These texts are certainly didactic in nature, and in them Paul is without question intending to "prescribe" certain behavior. The only thing they "describe" is the mind of Paul, who was convinced that he was reflecting the mind of Christ (1 Cor. 2:16; 7:40; 14:37).

But even if these other gender texts are didactic or prescriptive in form, if Paul is dealing with specific local *issues* in Corinth and Ephesus, does this not mean that his *instructions* concerning those issues are limited to those times and places as well? This leads us to a consideration of the fourth fallacious assumption that underlies the theory of the hermeneutical primacy of Galatians 3:28, namely, that a specific problem will always be addressed with specific practical advice that applies only to that situation.

Such an idea seems to be universally assumed among feminists in their treatment of the other gender texts, and it is reflected in every characterization of the alleged contrast between these texts and Galatians 3:28. While the latter is the universal and general teaching, the teaching of the former is specific, local, time-related, relative, problematic, occasional, incidental, exceptional, practical, historically or culturally conditioned, and directed to emergency situations. I.e., the fact that these passages deal with specific problems *ipso facto* means that Paul's instructions therein must have a limited, temporary application.

Now, we may grant that the other gender texts are dealing with specific situations. But we must completely reject the notion that specific problems are always addressed with specific teaching that applies only to those problems in those circumstances. Sometimes that may be the case, but we cannot just assume that it is so. In fact, just as often as not, *specific problems are resolved through the application of general principles*. This fact is abundantly illustrated in the first letter to the Corinthians itself, which deals with numerous problems in the church at Corinth. The problem of fornication is addressed through the general truth that the body of every Christian is the temple of the Holy Spirit (6:19). The problem of eating meat offered to idols is addressed through the general truth that God is one and idols are not real (8:4), through the general principle of expediency (10:23), and through the general exhortation to do all things to the glory of God (10:31). Problems with tongue-speaking are addressed through the general principle of the supremacy of love (13:13).

This list could be expanded from practically every book of the Bible. Thus we may reasonably ask how anyone could ever assume that Paul's teaching on gender roles in 1 Corinthians and 1 Timothy and elsewhere must be limited to the circumstances he was specifically addressing. There is simply no basis for such an assumption, and it is contrary to common Biblical practice. We may grant that Paul had a specific problem in the Ephesian church in mind when he wrote 1 Timothy 2:12 (although it is not at all clear what this might have been), but this in no way precludes the understanding that this verse is itself a general principle that was intended to be applied in all churches in all times and places. The same is true of the other gender texts as well.

Our point here is to evaluate the way feminists use the principle of analogy in relating Galatians 3:28 to the other gender texts. Their general approach is to begin with the former as the general norm, and then to use it to interpret and limit the latter as if it were obvious that the hermeneutical flow must move in this one direction only. In this section we have indicated that this method rests on four basic assumptions, all of which are fallacious. When we recognize this, it becomes clear that it is no less appropriate to use the other texts to interpret and limit Galatians 3:28 than vice versa.

2. A Consistent Approach

Even though feminists are very emphatic about the hermeneutical primacy of Galatians 3:28, they are not always consistent in that they do in fact allow certain other texts to interpret or limit it, as long as the egalitarian gospel is not threatened thereby. Galatians 2:11-14, which is not in the immediate context of 3:28, is allowed to qualify the latter because it allegedly reveals that the gospel has a *social* dimension.[99] Romans 1:26-27 is used to show that the general principle of Galatians 3:28 does not imply an endorsement of homosexualism.[100]

In principle we have no quarrel with this use of Galatians 2:11-14 and Romans 1:26-27 to explain and restrict the meaning of Galatians 3:28. We are only asking for consistency: if we can use Romans 1 in this way, why should it be illegitimate to use 1 Corinthians 14 and 1 Timothy 2 and 1 Peter 3 to limit the meaning and application of the Galatians text? To allow the one and then to reject the other on the basis of hermeneutical principle seems arbitrary and ideologically motivated. If we grant that Galatians 3:28 can be true while *some* distinctions remain, we cannot rule out other distinctions *a priori*.

We have questioned whether Galatians 3:28 was meant to be a general principle in the first place, and have affirmed rather that it was meant to have a very specific application in its context. As far as gender roles are concerned, in the final analysis it really does not matter whether it is general or specific, as long as we consistently and fairly apply the principle of analogy. We can take it either way as long as we recognize the validity of using other texts to interpret and qualify it.

The fact is that if we do take it as a general principle, it is so general that we should welcome any other Biblical teaching that shows what limitations might be put upon it (e.g., Romans 1). With regard to its application, it is hardly "explicit" or "crystal clear," as feminists like to characterize it. How it should be applied, especially to role distinctions, is simply not self-evident. Kassian quite correctly points out that Galatians 3 is unclear about this. It is "at best 'fuzzy' in terms of addressing social roles." Yet, she says, "there are other passages in the Bible where the relationship between men and women *is* clearly addressed." These should be used to clarify Galatians 3.[101] This is proper hermeneutical methodology.

The bottom line, however, is that Galatians 3:28 was never intended to be a general principle with broad social application in the first place. This becomes evident when we see how it ties in with its immediate context. It is time now to turn to this most important issue.

V. THE MEANING OF GALATIANS 3:28 IN ITS CONTEXT

The last section discussed how Galatians 3:28 relates to other gender texts; our subject now is how it relates to its own context. How does it fit into the purpose of the epistle as a whole? Especially, how does it fit into the more immediate context of Galatians 3:1-4:7? This is a key issue, since one of the most fundamental rules of hermeneutics is that a text must be interpreted first of all in the light of its own context.

A careful examination of verse 28 in its context is crucial also because it clearly illustrates the subjectivity of feminist hermeneutics. In terms of the feminist tendency to lift texts out of their contexts, says Smith, "no passage has been abused more blatantly than Galatians 3:28."[102] Pawson emphatically agrees: "If ever a text was used out of context as a pretext, this is it!"[103] These are rather harsh judgments, but the following discussion will show that they are accurate.

A. Analysis of Feminist Approaches

How do feminists treat verse 28 within its context? Everyone grants, in theory at least, that the context is important; feminists are no exception.[104] The problem is that the context of Galatians 3:28 is not friendly toward the usual feminist interpretation. This has led to some very interesting and often subtle approaches to this issue on the part of feminists.

One approach is the attempt to formally detach this verse from its context in Galatians as much as possible. An example of this is the view that verse 28 is a baptismal formula, a point that has already been discussed above. If this view could be established, then theoretically the reference to "neither male nor female" would have no contextual limitations. As we have seen, however, this suggestion is mostly speculation.

By far the most common feminist approach to Galatians 3:28 takes the standard rule of hermeneutics and turns it completely upside down. Instead of interpreting the passage in light of its context, feminists generally interpret the context in light of a preconceived understanding of the text. This is done in the following manner. First, the three pairs in Galatians 3:28 are considered and analyzed in and of themselves, in isolation from the context. Then, an egalitarian-friendly conclusion is drawn as to the significance of these pairs. Finally, this conclusion is used by implication as a kind of funnel by which to pour content into the context, content that is actually alien to the context and would never have been "discovered" there without the assignment of an ideologically predetermined meaning to verse 28.

Thus ideas and issues and problems are imported into the context which are not the point of the epistle as a whole or of this specific passage in particular, but which instead reflect the feminist agenda. This will now be explained in more detail.

First of all we frequently find the general affirmation

that Galatians 3:28 is dealing with social problems and not just spiritual issues. This is affirmed without contextual justification, simply because the feminist agenda requires that this verse be seen as addressing sinful social conditions and relationships. As Diehl says, Biblical feminists see Galatians 3:28 as Paul's summary of "the social application of the Gospel," which "leads to egalitarianism in the home, church, and society."[105] Snodgrass, for example, calls this verse "the most socially explosive statement in the New Testament."[106] Likewise Longenecker declares that the reason Galatians 3:28 is so important is because "there the gospel is clearly stated as having revolutionary significance for the cultural, social and sexual areas of life." This verse, he says, is "the most forthright statement on social ethics in all the New Testament."[107]

These are illustrations of how feminists abstract Galatians 3:28 from its context, declare that it refers to the whole spectrum of social relationships, and then proceed as if this were natural to the context. The fact is, however, that nothing in the context points in this direction. Despite the fact that the context contains only salvation terminology—"sons of God," "baptized into Christ," "clothed with Christ" (3:26-27), feminists simply assume that 3:28 extends to social relationships.[108] For example, Longenecker declares that the phrase "neither slave nor free" is "pregnant with societal implications," even if most early Christians understood it in only a spiritual sense. Not only does he fail to provide any contextual justification for the alleged "societal implications" of this verse, he also admits that its last two pairs are not directly relevant to Paul's argument in Galatians at all.[109]

In addition to the general idea that Galatians 3:28 refers to social issues as such, it is common for feminists to import into the text certain specific social themes consistent with their agenda. Even though the context addresses none of these, it is affirmed that Paul's main point is how the Gospel abolishes social ills such as division, attitudes of superiority, domination, and subservience.

The specific theme most commonly attributed to Galatians 3:28 in feminist literature is division. The pairs are understood as the major forms of social schism, segregation, and separation; the message of the verse is thus how this problem of division is solved by the gospel of Christ: "You are all one in Christ Jesus." I.e., unity in Christ overcomes all forms of societal schism.

Numerous examples may be given. DeJong and Wilson cite Galatians 3:26-28 as "biblical evidence of the restorative impact on the male-female relationship." After quoting these verses they assert, "The central message appears to be that all those distinctions between people that previously were sources of alienation and separation have been superseded by their union in Christ."[110] Jewett likewise assumes that the reference to oneness in Christ in 3:28 must mean that the problem being addressed is division. "The thought of the apostle, then, must be that in Christ the basic divisions that have separated Man from his neighbor, divisions which have threatened human fellowship, are done away. . . . Divisions which destroy fellowship by leading to hostility and exploitation . . . have no more place in Christ." The three pairs "are bracketed together because they have been the source of the most bitter hostility and antagonisms; this they have in common, and from this point of view they all stand, in the apostle's mind, over against the new oneness or unity which is in Christ."[111] As Gritz says, Galatians 3:28 "does affirm that the deepest divisions which split the society of the ancient world find unity in Jesus Christ. The new creation in him excludes racial, social, and sexual distinctions." The point is "the unity and equality of these three contrasting pairs."[112]

In response we may grant that societal divisions along the lines of the three pairs do exist, and that they may have existed in Galatia. But the question still remains: is this the point of Galatians 3:28? The answer is no. The context shows that Paul is not addressing the question of division or segregation or social schism within any of these pairs, not even between Jews and Gentiles. To focus on such an idea misses the real issue altogether, which is whether any of these distinctions makes any difference as to how one may *receive* the promised salvation. In other words the point is not how salvation affects divisions, but whether divisions (actually, distinctions) affect salvation. Paul is discussing the *cause*, not the *result* of salvation.

But what about the statement in verse 28 that all are "one in Christ Jesus"? Again, the point of this oneness is not the general healing of all social divisions, a healing that *results* from salvation through Christ. The subject of oneness is not introduced to counter the problem of division as such. Rather, the reality of this oneness in Christ is cited as a guarantee that none of these named distinctions (not divisions) will prevent anyone from *receiving* the gift of salvation. In fact, the point is not so much oneness *in* Christ as oneness *with* Christ, as will be made clear below.

Another specific theme imported into the text as the problem with which Paul is dealing in Galatians 3:28 is the attitude of *superiority*. The three pairs supposedly represent social relationships in which one side of the pair assumes that it is superior to the other side, thus resulting in hostility and animosity and separation. The idea is that Paul is dealing specifically with attitudes of supremacy or superiority, and is emphasizing the leveling and equalizing power of the gospel.

An example of this view is Manfred Brauch, who sees the three pairs in Galatians 3:28 as "distinctions of superior and inferior" that were abolished in the new order of things inaugurated in Christ."[113] "In the new humanity created in Christ, the . . . view that some human beings, on the basis of gender or race or social status, were in some sense inferior could no longer be maintained." Remarkably, Brauch calls this "Paul's central theological conviction."[114]

Joseph Webb takes a similar approach. The issue in Galatians 3:28 is not salvation, he says. Rather, "the problem centered around a deep-seated belief among the Jewish Christians that they were, for various reasons, *superior* to Gentile Christians. They appear to have been treating Gentile Christians as inferiors," as "second-class Christian citizens." This "hierarchical *spirit*," this "centuries-old exclusivity and superiority," was the real problem.[115] The same applies to the male-female relationship. In the Kingdom of God being born a man "no longer gives the male superiority—of any kind—over the female."[116]

Joan Chatfield sums up the point of Galatians 3:28 in the same way. "National, racial, economic, and sexual supremacy are leveled in Christ Jesus. National identities, racial and economic differences, sexual distinctions remain. It is superiority of the one over the other which is named for what it is: a travesty outside the plan of God."[117]

Our reply here is basically the same as in the previous point. We grant that such notions of supremacy exist, and that they are contradicted by Scripture as a whole and by the gospel of Christ. But the question is whether this is really the issue Paul has in mind in Galatians 3:28; i.e., is this view warranted by the context? The fact is that literally nothing in the context suggests that the spirit of superiority is the problem Paul is addressing in this passage, and that this is what links the three pairs together. This concept, and the feminist agenda with it, are actually imported into the context via an analysis of the three pairs in isolation from the context itself.

This same faulty methodology is seen in those who import the theme of *dominance* into the text. The allegation is that in Galatians 3:28 Paul is addressing the problem of domination and submission, and is specifically saying that all forms of the subjugation of one group to another are abolished in Christ Jesus. For example, Stouffer declares that in Galatians 3:26-28 "Paul is speaking of three different dominant-submissive categories, all of which have been nullified by our being baptized into and clothed with Christ."[118] Richard and Joyce Boldrey likewise speak of the Gentile, the slave, and the female as "the subjugated ones," and cite Galatians 3:28 as teaching that Christ "broke down all the rules and regulations, including the Jews' privileged position, the masters' control, and the males' authority over females."[119]

Our response is again the same. Even if this type of relationship does exist and even if it is abolished in Christ, there is no indication in the context itself that this is what Paul has in mind when he links these three pairs together as distinctions that are made irrelevant through oneness in Christ. In fact it is difficult to see how the concepts of domination and subjugation even apply to the first two pairs. In first-century society, who "dominated" whom—Jews or Greeks? Also, it should be noted that Paul does not say "slave nor master," but "slave nor free man." The Boldreys boldly ignore this fact and discuss the three pairs as "Jew and Greek," "*Master* and Slave," "Male and Female."[120] However, the very fact that Paul does *not* say "slave nor master" is a clear indication that he is not concerned here with relationships of domination and submission. Again it is a concept imported into the context because such terminology serves to align Galatians 3:28 with the interests of the feminist agenda.

Another version of this pattern is to interpret Galatians 3:28 in terms of bondage and freedom. Paul is said to be discussing the plight of those who are in some sense not free, and is showing how they have been set free through the work of Christ. Just as the Magna Charta "guaranteed fundamental liberties for the English people," says Tucker, so does salvation in Christ set us free; and "part of that freedom" is enunciated in Galatians 3:28. "This passage speaks not only to women whose freedom has been curtailed on the basis of gender but also to women and men whose freedom has been curtailed on ethnic or legal grounds."[121] In a similar way Langley calls this passage "Paul's great 'freedom manifesto'" in which he is "addressing issues of fundamental human rights."[122]

In Galatians Paul does discuss the question of bondage and freedom (see 5:1). He is speaking, however, of *spiritual* bondage to law, and of how salvation through Christ sets us free from the restrictions and the curse of law. This is not the same, however, as the *social* subservience of one group of people to another group of people, which feminists say is the problem to which Galatians 3:28 is the solution. That this is not the problem Paul is addressing can be seen from the fact that it does not really apply to the Jew/Greek distinction. Jews as a group were in no sense holding Gentiles as a group in any kind of bondage. The only proper sense in which this terminology in Galatians may be applied to this pair as such has to do with the Judaizing controversy, which is indeed the main problem which occasioned the writing of the epistle. But the Judaizer problem involved only *some Christian* Jews who were trying to bind part of the Law of Moses on Gentiles as a condition for their *spiritual* salvation. This is in no way parallel to the notion of the liberation of slaves as a class from their masters or women as a class from submissive role distinctions, which is the notion feminists want to import into Galatians 3:28.

In summary, there may have been good reasons for an apostle such as Paul to have discussed sinful social situations and abuses such as division, attitudes of superiority, domination, and bondage; but none of these is what Paul is actually discussing in Galatians 3:28. In fact, as non-feminists generally agree, in naming these three pairs Paul is asserting that there is no distinction in their spiritual status before God (*coram Deo*), with no intention of going into detail as to how this equality before God applies to any specific practice or function. As Stott puts it, this verse means "that *as regards our standing before God,* because we are 'in Christ' and enjoy a common relationship to him, racial, national, social, and sexual distinctions are irrelevant. People of all races and classes, and of both sexes, are equal before him."[123]

This does not mean that this oneness has no implications with reference to practices and functions in the church and in society; it simply means that these implications are not in view in this text and must be worked out in light of other Biblical teaching. To cite this text alone as being in and of itself a sufficient basis for a completely egalitarian society is a mockery of the hermeneutical rule that a text must be interpreted first of all in light of its own context. And the context very clearly refers to spiritual standing before God.

To be more specific, and to pursue an idea introduced above, this text in its context is not talking about how these three pairs or relationships will unfold *after* salvation has been received or will be affected by the experience of salvation *post facto*. Rather, the text in its context is talking about how these three distinctions disappear or become irrelevant *before* salvation or leading up to salvation or as they relate to the reception of salvation.

This will be discussed in more detail below, but it may be summed up here. The salvation of which Paul speaks in Galatians is described in chapter 3 as an inheritance which technically belongs to only one person, namely, Jesus himself (3:16-18). Thus the only way any individual can share in this inheritance is to become united or identified with Christ Jesus. But the good news of the gospel of grace is that this union with Christ is available to anyone through faith in baptism (3:26-27), whether that person is Jew or Greek, slave or free, man or woman (3:28). Once one assumes the identity of Christ through faith in baptism, the inheritance that belongs by right only to Christ is bestowed upon that person also. The distinctions named in verse 28 thus become irrelevant with regard to who is qualified to inherit the promised salvation (3:29). This is the point of the verse—no more and no less.

In conclusion to this section we say again that feminists do not interpret Galatians 3:28 in light of its context; if anything, they interpret the context in light of the preconceived spin placed on 3:28 in the interests of undergirding the feminist agenda. Peter Davids refers to this problem when he makes these comments on Chatfield's article: "Within the context of this debate we must express some concern about the use of Scripture for relatively free theologizing which obscures its contextual meaning. Gal. 3:27-28, for example, is frequently used, as here [in Chatfield's article], simply as catchword for *our* theology." He refers to this as a kind of "exegetical weakness" in terms of which "Scripture is apparently cited with a desire to find some legitimation there" for one's point of view.[124] S. Lewis Johnson likewise refers to the way in which this process "has, in effect, lifted [Galatians 3:28] from its exegetical underpinnings and set it as a lonely text, a kind of proof text, in the midst of swirling theological debate." The peril involved here is "the human tendency to forget sound hermeneutics and find things that are not really in the text."[125]

The only way to avoid such problems is to be true to the overall context. Davids rightly says of Galatians 3:28, "Paul's meaning will not appear until we struggle with what he meant in the context of all of Galatians and also in that of all his letters."[126] The rest of this main section will be an attempt to do just this, at least in relation to the context of Galatians itself.

B. The Law of Moses

The question of context must be addressed in both general and specific terms. In general terms, it seems quite obvious that the problem being addressed in the epistle as a whole, and in chapter 3 especially, has something to do with the Law of Moses. The question is not how the gospel relates to the original creation, or to the curse in Genesis 3:16, but how it relates to the Law of Moses. As applied to individuals, the issue is not how Christians are to function in society as such, but what the Law has to do with one's relation to God under the New Covenant. How are Christians supposed to relate to the Old Testament Law?

The immediate source of this problem and thus the historical occasion for this epistle was the influence of a number of individuals commonly called the Judaizers. Although their identity is not specifically known, they were probably a group of Jewish Christians who accepted the Messiahship of Jesus but who were not willing to surrender the binding nature of the Mosaic Law. Not only did they cling to the Law themselves; they also tried to bind it upon all Gentiles who wanted to become Christians. Their message is summed up in Acts 15:1, "Unless you are circumcised according to the custom of Moses, you cannot be saved." In writing Galatians Paul's main goal, or at least one of his main goals, was to refute the claims of the Judaizers. This is especially the focus of 3:1-4:7.

Not all who acknowledge this point have a proper understanding of the *specific* context of the verse, however. Thus we must be more specific about the contrast Paul is drawing between the Law and the gospel. Exactly what is the point is he making about the Law of Moses in 3:28?

Here I will call attention to some inadequate answers to this question, given sometimes by feminists and sometimes by non-feminists. First there is the idea that Paul is indeed dealing with the Law of Moses, but only insofar as it perpetuates the curse of Genesis 3:16. This is the view of the Boldreys, who assume that the "law" that says women should be subject to men (cf. 1 Cor. 14:34) is limited to the curse in Genesis 3:16. The Law of Moses codifies this curse, but Galatians 3:28 tells us that this law/curse was abolished by Christ.[127] Thus there is no longer any basis for such subjection.

It is true that Galatians 3 refers to a curse that is abolished by the gospel, but it is not the curse of Genesis 3:16. It is rather the curse connected with all law as such, including the Law of Moses, i.e., that anyone who does not keep all God's commandments must suffer the curse of condemnation (Gal. 3:10). This is the very nature of any kind of law-keeping as a way of salvation, namely, anyone who seeks to be saved by law-keeping must keep all of the Law, not just part of it, or else be damned. But "Christ redeemed us from the curse of the Law" (Gal. 3:13), i.e., from the necessity of perfect law-keeping as a means of salvation, and from the condemnation that will surely come upon anyone who seeks to be saved in this way. This is the only curse Paul has in view in the Galatians context.

Also, we should note that the issue raised by the Judaizers, with which Paul deals in Galatians, is not how Christians relate to the *curse* of the Law at all, but how they should relate to its commandments and regulations, especially circumcision. It is Paul himself who introduces the curse element, as a part of his refutation of the Judaizers. Thus the problem to which Galatians 3:28 is the solution is not the *curse* of the Law, but something *required* by it.

This leads to a second inadequate answer to the question of the contextual relation between Galatians 3:28 and the Law of Moses. This is the idea that the centrality of the issue of circumcision in the Judaizing controversy is why Paul includes "neither male nor female" in the list of pairs in 3:28. This is how Witherington explains it. He rightly notes that in the epistle as a whole "Paul is mainly arguing over the issue of circumcision and the law and how these relate to the Christian community." He opposes the Judaizers' contention that circumcision has a kind of saving significance, that it is "a means of obtaining right standing before God and salvation." Since such a view would naturally lead to the idea that a woman's position in the community was "inferior to that of a man," Paul specifically says that such gender distinctions do not apply in Christ.[128] That this is Paul's point is confirmed by the reference to baptism in verse 27. The Judaizers were linking circumcision to salvation, but "Paul counters this by arguing . . . that the covenant sign for Christians is a universal and all inclusive one—Baptism—which Jew, Gentile, male, female, slave, and free man may participate in equally without requiring them to do more than make a commitment to faith."[129]

In response, we may say first of all that this view does get closer to the truth in that it emphasizes the issues raised by the Judaizers, especially the question of how regulations within the Law of Moses relate to the

Christian's status before God. It also brings into focus the fact that Galatians 3:28 deals with spiritual relationships, not social ones. This view goes off the track, however, when it assumes that the specific issue in this particular section of Galatians (3:1-4:7) is circumcision. This assumption turns the discussion in a completely wrong direction.

It is true that in the Judaizing controversy and in Galatians as a whole, circumcision is a key issue, and Paul is definitely concerned to show that it is not required of Christians (cf. Gal. 5:6; 6:15). But even more important is the fact that circumcision symbolizes the Mosaic Law as a whole, in the sense that anyone accepting the necessity of circumcision commits himself to live by the whole Law (cf. Gal. 5:3). In this section of Galatians (3:1-4:7) Paul is denying not simply the necessity of circumcision, but the whole idea that law as such is capable of providing salvation. This is especially true of the Law of Moses, and Paul makes it very clear that this Law does not apply to Christians. But even in this regard, the specific requirement of Moses' Law which Paul is opposing in 3:28 is not circumcision but something altogether different, as will be explained below.

The fact that circumcision is not the main point in Galatians 3:28 should be obvious from the inclusion of "neither slave nor free man" along with the other two pairs. If the reference were just to Jews and Greeks, and males and females, it would be much easier to accept the idea that circumcision is the issue. But the distinction between slaves and free men has nothing to do with circumcision and is completely out of place if this is specifically what Paul has in mind here.

Our contention in this section is that the proper explanation of Galatians 3:28 in context has something to do with the Law of Moses. Some acknowledge this but miss the point as to the exact nature of the connection. We have looked at two such inadequate views; one other now draws our attention. It is the notion that 3:28 does indeed counter certain conditions that existed under the Law, specifically, the inferior status accorded therein to women, slaves, and

Gentiles. This is Mary Hayter's view. The subject of Galatians 3, she acknowledges, is the relation between the Law and the promise. The main point of Galatians 3:28 is the improvement in status within the community for three specific groups. "The three pairs in verse 28 highlight three fundamental areas of inequality manifested in the law, where Gentiles, slaves and women were at best third-class citizens, at worst 'non-persons.'" In Christ, however, all such distinctions in status are removed.[130]

When we go back to the Law of Moses, however, and read its actual requirements as related to men and women, slaves and free men, Jews and Gentile proselytes, we find that the restrictions placed on women, slaves, and Gentiles are not nearly as severe as many think. Women were to be as fully committed to the covenant as men (Deut. 31:12). Both "sons and daughters" and "male and female servants" were to worship and sacrifice before the Lord (Deut. 12:12, 18; 16:11, 14). Men and women were equally held guilty of sin and required to make restitution and atonement (Num. 5:6).

Some distinctions did exist within the Law of Moses, but they are often exaggerated. Faith Martin makes this point very well in reference to women. She says that the various ways in which the Old Testament supposedly relegates women to an inferior status "were only natural complications of the intricate ritual surrounding the worship of God in the Old Testament. None of them can be considered directed against women or designed specifically to exclude them from worship or leadership."[131]

Martin discusses how this relates to the priesthood, to ritual uncleanness, to attendance at festivals, and to circumcision.[132] For example, exclusion of women from the priesthood was not strictly a male-female thing, since this office was open only to a relatively few men: unblemished specimens of the descendants of Aaron of the tribe of Levi.[133] One reason women were not required to attend certain festivals is that this would often "involve travel and great inconvenience, if not danger, if she were pregnant or nursing. This exception should be considered an acknowledgement of woman's importance and a concern for her welfare rather than a slight." Also, "compulsory attendance at the festivals would be impossible for a woman because of her periodic uncleanness, over which she had no control."[134]

In short, to say, as Hayter does, that the Law makes women "at best third-class citizens, at worst 'non-persons'"[135] is a serious exaggeration.

This is not to deny that the Mosaic Law did make some distinctions between men and women that were abrogated by Christ. In fact, one such distinction is the key to the proper understanding of Galatians 3:28, as we shall see very soon.

This concludes our discussion of various specific ways in which the contextual connection between Galatians 3:28 and the Law of Moses is inadequately explained. They are, first, that verse 28 abrogates the curse of the Law; second, that it abolishes distinctions based on circumcision; and third, that it eliminates the inferior status to which women, slaves, and Gentiles were consigned by the Law.

C. The Metaphor of Inheritance

We turn now to what is perhaps the most important section in this study of Galatians 3:28, namely, our explanation of the true connection between this verse and its context. In the previous section we saw that in a general way the contextual issue is the role of the Law of Moses in the gospel era. Does the Law of Moses in any sense determine our relation to God in the New Covenant age? This is the *general* question Paul is addressing in Galatians, especially in 3:1-4:7.

We have also pointed out that it is necessary to go further and to determine the *specific* connection between Galatians 3:28 and the Law of Moses. Is Galatians 3:28 directed against some specific aspect of the Law? If so, what is it? After looking at three inadequate answers to this question, we will now explain what we believe to be the right answer.

The question raised by the Judaizing controversy is how the Law relates to salvation. There can be no question that the role of the *Law* is central to the discussion in Galatians, nor can anyone doubt that the issue is *salvation*. What is at stake is one's spiritual status or relationship with God, not ecclesiastical and societal roles. As noted above, the question is how one *enters* into a saving relationship with God, not the ongoing implications of that relationship.[136]

In this discussion, as we try to see how Galatians 3:28 relates to all of this, we must remember that a key issue is the significance of the three pairs in this verse. What is there about the context—salvation and the Law of Moses— that leads Paul to mention these three in particular?

We must be very careful not to misunderstand this point. For instance, it is important to see that the issue is not *whether* Gentiles (or slaves or women) can be saved, since these groups were certainly not excluded from salvation under the Law. Rather, the issue is *how* salvation is received.[137] The Judaizers themselves were not trying to exclude Gentiles from salvation; they were just insisting on a certain way of salvation that included submission to the requirements of the Law of Moses. In addressing this situation Paul raises a question that relates not just to Gentiles and slaves and women but to everyone: how can *anyone* be saved? By what means or method is salvation received?

The overall framework of the discussion in Galatians, especially in 3:1-4:7, is that there are two choices or two approaches to this kind of question. In broader Biblical terminology (as in Romans) it is the choice between *law* (as such) and *grace*. Here in Galatians 3, since the issue is so closely related to the Judaizing controversy and thus to the Law of Moses specifically, the two approaches are contrasted as *Law* (of Moses) and *promise*.

In Galatians 3 Paul explains that the first covenant— the Old Covenant—was given in two stages. First came the promise segment, given to Abraham as summed up in

Genesis 12:3 and cited by Paul here in Galatians 3:8, "All the nations shall be blessed in you." This covenant promise was spoken "to Abraham and to his seed" (3:15-16). But then, 430 years later, a law segment was added to the covenant (3:17-19). This refers to the Law of Moses. Paul stresses the fact that adding the law segment did not invalidate or nullify the promise element of the covenant (3:17) or in any way contradict it (3:21). Each had its own purpose and its own function within the covenant.

The crucial question now, under the New Covenant (Luke 22:20; Heb. 8:8), is this: which aspect of the Old Covenant is the New Covenant patterned after, the promise or the law? It should be noted that this is not a question about the *content* of either covenant, since the requirement of circumcision (central in the Judaizing controversy) was present in both segments of the Old Covenant. The issue rather is the *way* of salvation: does the New Covenant way of salvation follow the law track or the promise track? Do sinners today receive "the blessing of Abraham" (3:14) by believing a promise or by obeying a law, specifically the Law of Moses?

This is Paul's main point, as it relates to the Judaizers and their insistence on circumcision as a condition for salvation: if you accept their message, you are committing yourself to the *law* track, and are saying that salvation is by law and therefore by works, rather than by promise and therefore by faith. But the New Covenant is not a covenant of law and works; it is a covenant of promise, like that given to Abraham in the beginning. Salvation does not come by way of law, and especially not in terms set by the Law of Moses.

Paul begins his confirmation of this fact by appealing to the Galatians' own experience: "Did you receive the Spirit by the works of the Law, or by hearing with faith?" (3:2; cf. 3:5). Then he appeals to Abraham himself, who set the example of being justified (counted righteous) by faith (3:6-9). The fact is that no one can be justified by law, since this would require perfect obedience (3:10-12). The addition of

Moses' Law to the Abrahamic promise was not the introduction of a new way of salvation; even under the Old
Covenant salvation came to Jews only if they, like
Abraham, believed God's promises (3:15-17). This always
has been and always will be God's way of saving sinners. If
the blessing of salvation "is based on law, it is no longer
based on a promise; but God has granted it to Abraham by
means of a promise" (3:18). This is preeminently the way of
salvation under the New Covenant, "that the promise by
faith in Jesus Christ might be given to those who believe"
(3:22). The Law may function to lead us to Christ, but
actual justification comes through faith in him (3:23-26).
We inherit the blessing of Abraham "according to promise"
(3:29), not according to the Law.

To get this point across most forcefully, throughout this
section of Galatians Paul uses the metaphor of *inheritance*.
When he refers to "the blessing of Abraham" (3:14), by
which all nations shall be blessed (3:8; cf. Gen. 12:3), he
presents it as an inheritance that will ultimately be
bestowed upon Abraham's *seed* (Gen. 13:15; 17:8; 22:18).
This inheritance, he says, is based on promise, not on law:
"For if the inheritance is based on law, it is no longer based
on a promise; but God has granted it to Abraham by means
of a promise" (3:18). Those who receive this promised
inheritance are spoken of, appropriately enough, as heirs:
"And if you belong to Christ, then you are Abraham's
offspring, *heirs* according to promise" (3:29; cf. 4:1, 7).

The theme of inheritance is not just incidental but is the
backbone of Paul's whole argument in 3:1-4:7. Especially, it
is the key to the right understanding of 3:28, with its reference to "neither male nor female." As we have noted above,
the specific issue here is *how* one may receive the promised
salvation. Since salvation is identified as an *inheritance*,
the issue may be rephrased thus: how may one inherit the
promise? How may one become an heir?[138] This is the key
that unlocks the meaning of Galatians 3:28, especially the
mystery of why Paul lists these three particular pairs
together. The concept of inheritance is the link between

3:28 and the Law of Moses in this context.

What is the flow of Paul's argument in reference to inheritance? First of all, there is an inheritance. This theme is not unique to Galatians but is stressed throughout Scripture. In Galatians 3 the content of this inheritance is quite specific, reflecting the "double cure" of salvation. It includes justification or imputed righteousness, which is received not in terms of law but through faith (3:21-22). This is recognized by everyone as a main theme in Galatians (3:6, 8, 11, 21; see 2:16-17). The inheritance also includes the regenerating and sanctifying presence of the Holy Spirit, a point that is stressed by Paul but relatively overlooked today. This is the Apostle's challenging question in 3:2, "Did you receive the Spirit by the works of the Law, or by hearing with faith?" God "provides you with the Spirit," he says (3:5); we "receive the promise of the Spirit through faith" (3:14). Because we are sons and therefore full heirs, "God has sent forth the Spirit of His Son into our hearts" (4:6).

The second element in Paul's argument is that (in addition to Abraham) there is only *one true heir* of this inheritance, namely, Jesus Christ, who is "heir of all things" (Heb. 1:2). Paul refers to God's promise to Abraham concerning the land: "I will give it to you and to your descendants [seed] forever" (Gen. 13:15; cf. 17:7-8). God also promises Abraham, "In your seed all the nations of the earth shall be blessed" (Gen. 22:18). Paul focuses on the fact that the Hebrew word for "seed" in these texts is singular in number, and he says that ultimately it refers to only one person, one seed: Jesus Christ. "Now the promises were spoken to Abraham and to his seed. He does not say, 'And to seeds,' as referring to many, but rather to one, 'And to your seed,' that is, Christ" (3:16). Jesus is the one seed to whom the promise has been made (3:19).

Paul's point is the singularity of heirship: there is only one heir of the blessing of Abraham. Since Jesus is the one seed, he is the one heir. The point is not that he needs the elements of salvation (the "double cure") for himself.

Rather, as the one rightful heir of this blessing, it is his to do with as he chooses. It is under his control.

The third element in Paul's argument concerning inheritance is this: even though technically there is only one seed and one heir, under the New Covenant *anyone* may still become an heir and inherit the blessing of Abraham. It is available to everyone. We may all become "heirs of God and fellow-heirs with Christ" (Rom. 8:17).

How is this possible? *Not* by the rules of law, especially not in accord with the regulations and limitations of the Mosaic Law. "For the promise to Abraham or to his descendants [seed] that he would be heir of the world was not through the Law, but through the righteousness of faith" (Rom. 4:13). Why is the unrestricted availability of the inheritance impossible in terms of the Law? Because under the provisions of the Mosaic Law—the law portion of the Old Covenant—inheritance was ordinarily restricted to *sons*. It belonged to the sons of the sons of the sons of Abraham (through Jacob), i.e., to free Jewish males. Limiting heirship to sons seems to have been the traditional custom in the ancient Near East in general; it was more or less assumed in the family of Abraham and was codified into the Law of Moses (Num. 27:8), though there was no specific statement to that effect at the beginning.

Of course, Jesus himself qualifies as a rightful heir of the blessing of Abraham, even under the rules of the Law, since he is a *son*. But when New Covenant salvation is described as an inheritance, the Law has no provisions allowing for its general distribution to non-Jews, slaves, and women. Francis Lyall remarks, "One of the most remarkable phrases in the whole New Testament is that the Christian is the 'heir of God,'" even though such an idea has no basis in present law, "nor did it have a basis in the Jewish law of Paul's time."[139]

Specifically, under the Old Covenant only Jews were rightful heirs. This limitation was based on God's choice of the Jews as his unique people, and his gift to them of the land of Canaan. This land was the fundamental inheritance. Lyall points out, "As any concordance will show, the most frequent use of 'inheritance' in the Old Testament is in connection with the Land itself. . . . Indeed, the Land was commonly thought of as the inheritance of the Jewish people."[140] For example, see Genesis 15:7; 28:4; Exodus 32:13; Leviticus 20:24; Deuteronomy 2:31; 16:20; Isaiah 60:21; Hebrews 11:8. Thus, says Lyall,

> The Jew, drawing on the Old Testament imagery, considered that only his people were the heirs of God. It would have been difficult for him to conceive of an outsider becoming one of the heirs, because under the Jewish law of inheritance an outsider could not inherit, could not be brought into the family relationship in this way.[141]

Gentiles (strangers, aliens) simply did not have the status of heirs.

Another limitation on inheritance in the Old Testament was that slaves ordinarily did not qualify as heirs. As with Gentiles, they could receive property as gifts but not as an inheritance. That slaves did not inherit property is the basis of Paul's explanation of the spiritual status of Jews under the Old Covenant in Galatians 4:1-7. Though they were technically sons and heirs, they were still in the childhood stage of God's plan of salvation and thus did not have full possession and control of the inheritance. In this sense they were still like slaves. "Now I say, as long as the heir is a child, he does not differ at all from a slave although he is owner of everything" (4:1). But under the New Covenant God's people have the actual status of sons and heirs rather than slaves: "Therefore you are no longer a slave, but a son; and if a son, then an heir through God" (4:7).[142]

The third and final limitation on inheritance procedures under the Law was that ordinarily only sons, not daughters, could inherit the father's estate. "The seed continued in the male line only," says Lyall.[143] This appears to have been something that was just taken for granted; miscellaneous laws and comments simply seem to assume that the inheritance passes from father to son(s). Proverbs 13:22 is usually translated as in the NASB, "A good man leaves an inheritance to his children's children"; but it literally says "to his sons' sons." Proverbs 19:14 assumes that the heir is a son, and specifically states that the inheritance is received from the father: "House and wealth are an inheritance from fathers, but a prudent wife is from the Lord." Reflecting Hebrew parallelism Jeremiah 49:1 asks, "Does Israel have no sons? Or has he no heirs?" Instructions concerning the double blessing upon the first-born son (Deut. 21:15-17) also assume that heirship belongs to sons, as does the law concerning Levirate marriage (Deut. 25:5-10). One motive for this arrangement, says Lyall, was to get a male heir and thus to prevent the inheritance from passing outside the family.[144]

In early Israelite history and at the beginning of the Mosaic dispensation it was apparently assumed that daughters did not inherit property. "It is not certain that women could own property at all," says Raymond Westbrook.[145] If so, it would be received as a gift and not as an inheritance. When marrying, women received gifts as a dowry, usually in the form of personal and household items. "In richer households, general slaves and livestock might be included; the rarest item was land, which was reserved rather for the male inheritance."[146] A possible example is Joshua 15:16-19; Judges 1:13-15.

The clearest indication that women as a rule were not counted as heirs is the petition of the five daughters of Zelophehad (Num. 27:1-11). Their father had died without any sons and thus without any heirs in accordance with the established norm. But the daughters asked that they be allowed to inherit their father's property. "Why should the name of our father be withdrawn from among his family because he had no son? Give us a possession among our father's brothers" (v. 4). Moses took their request to God, who granted it: "The daughters of Zelophehad are right in their statements. You shall surely give them a hereditary possession among their father's brothers, and you shall transfer the inheritance of their father to them" (v. 7). God also made this a permanent and general rule for Israel: "If a man dies and has no son, then you shall transfer his inheritance to his daughter" (v. 8).

The establishment of such a rule codified into law what had been practiced all along, namely, that when sons were part of a father's progeny, they alone inherited his estate. It was a new provision, though, that in a sonless family the estate must go to any existing daughters rather than to other male relatives of the deceased. But since most families would have at least one son, even after this exception was made women ordinarily could not expect to be among their father's heirs.[147]

In the final analysis, following the terms of the Law, in ordinary circumstances only free Jewish males were heirs. The term *son* covers it all. A *son* of Abraham could not be a Gentile, a slave, or a female. Thus if the blessing of Abraham were distributed today according to the rules of law, it would be limited to sons. In fact, since it was promised to just one seed of Abraham, it would be limited to just *one* son, Jesus Christ. So how is it possible to make this inheritance universally available?

The answer is that the inheritance is given not according to law, but according to *promise*. It is not grounded in the Mosaic Law, but in "the promises . . . spoken to Abraham" (Gal. 3:16). "For if the inheritance is based on law, it is no longer based on a promise; but God has granted it to Abraham by means of a promise" (3:18). The adding of the Law did not nullify the promise aspect of the covenant (3:17), nor was it "contrary to the promises of God" (3:21). The Law only made transgressions more visible (3:19), making it clear that the only effectual way of salvation is "the promise by faith" (3:22). The inheritance is thus given as a promise, not as a legal provision; we are "heirs according to promise" (3:29). This is a basic gospel principle. (See also Rom. 4:13-14; Heb. 6:12, 17; 9:15; 11:9; James 2:5. See Acts 26:18; Titus 3:7.)

When salvation is inherited in accordance with the principle of promise, the restrictions imposed and sanctioned by the Law of Moses do not apply. A promise by its very nature is something to be believed; thus the inheritance comes by faith, not by works and provisions of law. The Law has no provisions restricting who can or cannot believe.

There is still one obstacle to be overcome, however. How can the inheritance be available to everyone through faith, if the promise was made only to *one* seed of Abraham, the *one* true heir, Jesus Christ? The answer is that when anyone accepts the promise through faith in Christ, he becomes *one with* Christ, the true son and heir. When through faith we are baptized into Christ, we become clothed with Christ, we become identified with Christ, we take on *his* identity, and thus we *all* become sons and heirs: "For you are all sons of God through faith in Christ Jesus. For all of you who were baptized into Christ have clothed yourselves with Christ" (Gal. 3:26-27). Thus whatever belongs to Christ belongs to those who are in him. Though technically he is the only seed of Abraham and the only true heir, when we are one with him and a part of him, we are counted as Abraham's seed and thus as heirs: "And if you belong to Christ, then you are Abraham's offspring [seed], heirs according to promise" (3:29). We are fellow-heirs with Christ" (Rom. 8:17).

In the Galatians passage three terms are inseparably linked: seed, son, and heir. Jesus is the one seed, the one son, the one heir. Those who become identified with him are also Abraham's seed (3:29), sons (3:26; 4:5, 7), and heirs (3:29; 4:7), by virtue of this oneness with him. The terminology is not arbitrary but is intimately related to the argument. For example, to treat the term *sons* in 3:26 as incidental or representative misses the whole point. In Romans 8:17 *children* is satisfactory—"if children [*tekna*], heirs also," but the nature of Paul's argument in Galatians requires the term *sons*. We become sons because we become one with Christ, who is a son. Likewise we become seed and heirs because we become one with Christ, who is the seed and heir.

This is contrary to Bilezikian, who translates Galatians
3:26 as "sons [or children] of God," as if it does not
matter.[148] It is contrary to Spencer, who seeks to replace
sons with *descendants,* as if it does not matter.[149] It is
contrary to Clark, who says that "sons and daughters of
God" is a "good translation of 'sons' into modern
English."[150]

All of these alternatives miss the point. Paul says *sons*
because he means *sons.* The idea is that in one sense even
the traditional and technical requirement of the Law still
applies, i.e., that only a son can be an heir. But this applies
literally only to the one seed Jesus, who was *born* as a son,
"born of a woman, born under the Law" (4:4). Thus Jesus is
a rightful heir even according to the terms of the Law. But
through his establishment of the New Covenant Jesus
made it possible for *everyone* to become a son in a spiritual
sense through spiritual rebirth, and thus to have the inheritance privileges of a son. He was "born under the Law, in
order that He might redeem those who were under the
Law, that we might receive the adoption as sons" (4:4-5)—
"and if a son, then an heir through God" (4:7).

Under the New Covenant, then, the inheritance of the
blessing of Abraham is openly available to all, and is freely
given to anyone who chooses to enter into union with
Christ Jesus. Such union is accomplished "through faith in
Christ Jesus" and by being "baptized into Christ" (3:26-27).
Though the gracious conditions for entering this union are
clearly stated here, this is not Paul's main point in this
passage. His main point is the union itself, and he asserts
the reality of this union in several different ways for
emphasis. Baptism, he says, is "into Christ" (3:27), i.e., into
the closest relationship with him. As a result we actually
become "clothed with Christ" (3:27, NIV); his identity
becomes ours. We all become "one with Christ Jesus" (3:28),
and thus the promise to the *one seed* (3:16) is still bestowed
just upon the one but at the same time upon all. Also, we
actually "belong to Christ" (3:29), i.e., we are his own spiritual seed (Isa. 53:10) and thus are also Abraham's seed and

thus heirs (3:29).

How does this speak to the problem raised by the Judaizers? The key point is that salvation—the blessing of Abraham—does not come according to the Law and by following its requirements; it comes by means of promise and by faith in God's promises. The Judaizers' circumcision mandate was in reality a repudiation of the way of promise and a restoration of the way of law. They were distorting and negating the gospel by attempting to place it in the larger framework of the Law, thus subjecting it to all the limitations and restrictions of the Law. That this is contrary to God's purposes is clearly explained through the metaphor of inheritance.

D. The Place of Galatians 3:28 in Paul's Argument

At this point it should be clear how Galatians 3:28 fits into Paul's argument in Galatians, and especially how it relates to the context of 3:1-4:7. The three pairs reflect the limitations placed on inheritance under the Mosaic Law. Under that Law, ordinarily, the rights of heirship were held by sons, or free Jewish males. Gentiles, slaves, and women ordinarily did not inherit property. But the New Covenant has no such restrictions. With regard to inheriting the blessing of Abraham these distinctions are now irrelevant: there is neither Jew nor Greek, there is neither slave nor free man, there is neither male nor female. All baptized believers are one with Christ Jesus and thus qualify as heirs of the blessing.

It is important to realize that this understanding is drawn directly from the context and ties Galatians 3:28 to the context in a logical and substantial way. It is not read into the verse in the interest of some ideology, but is consistent with the ordinary rules and procedures of sound hermeneutics. As such it completely undermines and destroys the feminist approach to this verse, with regard to both method and meaning. It shows the validity of the charges made earlier in this chapter, i.e., that feminist interpretations of 3:28 totally disregard sound hermeneutical method; and it shows that the meaning imposed upon the verse by feminists has no exegetical basis in the text itself.

These conclusions will be reinforced in more than adequate detail as we now examine a number of significant implications that may be drawn from the preceding discussion of the theme of inheritance in Galatians 3:1-4:7. The first is that the inheritance theme is the *only* explanation that makes every part of the verse meaningful; especially, it is the only approach that makes sense of each of the three pairs. Each pair is directly and equally related to the main point of the context; not one of them is incidental.

This is in stark contrast to most feminist approaches to the text, which have great difficulty in explaining how all three pairs fit into the context in any parallel way. Longenecker, for example, being committed to egalitarian presuppositions and speculating that Galatians 3:28 is a detached baptismal confession, declares agnostically, "Just why these three matters, and not others, were incorporated into the confession of early Christians is impossible to say."[151] McClelland says that since Paul's main concern in this whole discussion is Jew-Gentile relations, "he need not have included the other pairs."[152] The following statement by Webb is typical of this inability of feminism to relate the verse to its context: "A careful reading of the entire letter, particularly of chapters 2 and 3, shows us that there is nothing within its content that directly relates to either of the second two statements, the slave-free or to the male and female relationships." The immediate context, he says, deals only with the first pair; the other two "are *excluded* from the letter's discussion."[153]

The centrality of the inheritance theme in the context of Galatians 3:28 shows that statements such as these have obviously missed the point. Each of the pairs is intimately, directly, and equally related to the major point that salvation in Christ considered as an inheritance is not bestowed in terms of the Law. The inclusion of the male-female pair is thus no mystery; indeed, it is actually demanded by the theme of the context.

Even more significant, as Pawson points out, is that "its *only* relevance is in the context of our inheritance in Christ." This is why it makes perfect sense in Galatians 3:28 but *not* in the so-called "parallel texts" such as 1 Corinthians 12:13 and Colossians 3:11.[154]

A second implication from this understanding of the context in terms of inheritance is that the three pairs are not intended to be parallel or equal in every way. They are brought together here because of their common relationship to the issue of heirship; it is irresponsible to try to press the parallelism further, as if *whatever* is true of one pair must be true of all alike.

Feminists make this very mistake, however, when they claim that if we disregard the Jew-Gentile and the slave-free distinctions in reference to church roles and functions, then the parallelism in Galatians 3:28 demands that we make no such distinctions between the genders either. If we do not restrict Gentiles and slaves in this way, then we have no right to put such restrictions on women. An example of this fallacious thinking is the following question by Charles Boatman: "If (in the light of Galatians 3:28) being a Gentile or a slave . . . is not sufficient reason to keep a man from full participation in the life and leadership of the church, why is being a woman sufficient reason to keep a person from such participation?"[155]

This idea falls short in view of the very specific contextual reason for linking these three pairs together. It also does great injustice to the many Biblical texts which *do* make distinctions between men and women with regard to roles and functions in both home and church. One such text that is especially important is 1 Peter 3:1-7, which makes a clear distinction in gender roles while at the same time affirming the principle of equality of heirship. (This text will be discussed further below.)

A third implication of the fact that the inheritance theme

is the key to understanding Galatians 3:28 is that it shows the true relation between this verse and the flow of the argument as a whole. Feminists approach verse 28 as if it were the climactic apex of the gospel, as if it were the main point Paul is making in the context. This verse is treated as if everything else Paul writes in Galatians is meant to point to it and lead up to it as the central and climactic conclusion to his whole argument. Snodgrass, for example, extravagantly refers to "the climactic positioning of . . . Galatians 3:28, as the center or climax of the Epistle," and declares that it is Paul's basic summary of what it means to be a Christian.[156]

But such an approach simply fails to read the text and its context aright. Verse 28 is not the climax or apex of the gospel in general or of the epistle in particular; it is not even the conclusion of the argument in 3:1-4:7. It is simply a subpoint or minor conclusion which then functions as a premise to support what is the main point or general conclusion of the argument, which is that everyone who is in Christ is already by virtue of that very fact the son or seed of Abraham and therefore a full heir of the blessing of Abraham. This conclusion is stated in 3:29, "And if you belong to Christ, then you are Abraham's offspring, heirs according to promise"; and again in 4:7, "Therefore you are no longer a slave, but a son; and if a son, then an heir through God." A major element of this conclusion, which may perhaps be seen as its major supporting argument, is the fact that our status as sons and heirs is achieved "according to promise" (3:29), not according to the Law. Verse 28 functions as a part of this supporting argument; it explains in part how heirship "according to promise" differs from heirship according to the Law. Thus it is not the climax of the argument; it is just a step along the way.

When seen in this light, not only the first part but also the second part of Galatians 3:28—"for you are all one in Christ Jesus"—becomes contextually meaningful. This statement is commonly understood to be an affirmation of the unity and equality that now exist between the members of each of the three pairs. It is taken as a statement about how the various groups of people are meant to relate to each other in a state of unity or oneness which all share in Christ Jesus. It is assumed that "You are all one in Christ Jesus" means "You are all one *with each other*." It is then concluded that this verse says we should no longer make distinctions with regard to roles and functions based on whether one is Jew or Greek, slave or free, male or female.

However, when seen as a part of the argument concerning heirship, it is apparent that this expression has an entirely different meaning in Galatians 3:28. The main emphasis is not relationships among human beings as such, but rather the relationship we all (as baptized believers) have *with Christ Jesus*. "You are all one *with* Christ Jesus." We are suggesting that the phrase *en Christō Iēsou* should be translated "*with* Christ Jesus," not "*in* Christ Jesus." This is grammatically possible, because the Greek preposition *en* often means "with." It is also contextually appropriate, since Paul's whole argument concerning heirship rests upon the fact that through faith in baptism we become identified with Christ, *one with Christ*, who is technically the only true son and seed and thus the only true heir of the blessing. With regard to inheritance, under the Law it made a difference whether one was Jew or Greek, slave or free, male or female. But now, under the New Covenant, with regard to the spiritual inheritance of grace, all that matters is whether a person is "one with Christ Jesus," the one rightful heir. Thus the distinctions of the Law simply have no relevance where inheritance is "according to promise."

When we understand how Galatians 3:28 thus fits into the flow of Paul's argument in this context, we can clearly see how inappropriate and misleading it is to use Galatians 3:28 as the foundation for egalitarianism in human interrelationships.

A fourth implication of the inheritance theme is that Galatians 3:28 was never intended to function as a general principle embracing all human relationships. We are completely unjustified in regarding it as an open-ended principle that applies equally to all groups, divisions, and distinctions in church and society in any way that happens to come to our minds.

Feminists usually treat the three pairs in 3:28 as representative of other pairs or relationships of a similar nature, whether that be understood as conflict, division, superiority, dominance, or something else. McClelland's approach is typical. Paul's main concern, he says, is to show how being in Christ abolishes all differences of attitude and practice between Jews and Gentiles. However, "the other couplets ensure that the newness in Christ should be seen to be an exhaustive and not a limited newness."[157] Assuming this same kind of open-endedness, others arbitrarily add to the list of pairs in the text itself. For example, Bartchy says that all sorts of racial and religious pride are shattered by our "new identity in Christ, in whom there is neither Jew nor Greek, neither slave nor free-born, neither male nor female, black nor white, American nor Russian."[158]

We must reject this approach to Galatians 3:28 as completely unjustified; it can be accepted only by ignoring the context. The attempt to give this verse an unlimited application violates the contextual reason for including the three specific pairs that do appear in it. It ignores the specific function these pairs serve in the context, where they have only one thing in common, namely, they reflect the distinctions ordinarily made in determining heirship under the Mosaic Law.

A fifth implication is perhaps the most important one of all, namely, that Galatians 3:28 is not addressing the question of gender roles as such, either directly or indirectly, explicitly or implicitly. In the final analysis there is *nothing* in this text that helps us to answer the question of whether or not God intends for men and women to have different roles in the home, in the church, and in society. It neither affirms nor denies role distinctions, since this subject is simply not in view.

Perhaps the most often-debated issue in relation to this verse is whether it speaks of our relationship with God or our relationships with one another. I.e., is it concerned with vertical or horizontal relationships, with salvation or service? As a rule feminists have persistently ignored or discounted all explanations of Galatians 3:28 that limit it to the issue of salvation status. My point here is that they have done so only because they have refused to see this verse in its context, in violation of basic hermeneutical rules. When the contextual framework of 3:28 is seen to be the question of *inheritance*, there is absolutely no conscientious way to evade the conclusion that the verse addresses the way of salvation, not the details of service. Feminists simply cannot continue to pretend that the context does not exist.

This conclusion—that Galatians 3:28 is not addressing the question of gender roles—is implicit in or grows out of the other implications already listed above. For example, since inheritance is the specific theme, the pairs cannot be regarded as equal in every way. They were intended to be parallel with regard to only one question: who qualifies as an heir to the blessing of Abraham? Therefore what may be obvious regarding one pair in reference to role relationships may not apply to the other pairs at all. Also, since Galatians 3:28 is not the climactic point but has only a limited part to play in the whole argument, it cannot be regarded as a general, open-ended principle that has all sorts of implications in directions not even hinted at in the context. In a real sense, everything that has been said up to this point forms part of the basis for this one basic conclusion, that 3:28 has very little relevance to the question of gender roles, if any at all.

F. LaGard Smith sums up this point very well by using a sports analogy. If we think of God's people (the church) as a kind of sports team, then we can think of Galatians as discussing the question of who will make the team, not of what positions we are supposed to play. "As individuals, we are all on God's team—equal in importance, equal in access to God. But being a team member with equal team status doesn't mean we all play the same position."[159]

A sixth implication related to the inheritance theme is that Galatians 3:28 itself is not concerned with the *content* of the inheritance but the the *manner* in which it is received. This has been mentioned before but is so important that it must be stressed again as a main idea. It is a conclusion strongly resisted by feminists, of course. For example, Bilezikian, speaking in opposition to James Hurley, says, "Galatians 3:28 does not describe the 'basis of membership in the body of Christ'. . . or the conditions for entering the church. It describes the conditions that should prevail *within* the body of Christ."[160] He is very adamant about this, since his feminist presuppositions depend heavily upon it. But such a statement is simply a dogmatic assertion that takes no account whatsoever of the context. It completely misses the connection between 3:28 and the theme of inheritance. That is, Bilezikian's claim fails to see that 3:28 is part of the argument about *how* the inheritance is received, namely, by promise and not by the rules of the Law.

This point reinforces the preceding one, and further demonstrates that the main issue in Galatians 3:28 is our relationship with God and not role relationships in the church as such. Thus it further shows the fallacy of trying to draw conclusions from this verse about gender roles in relation to such things as church leadership.

This point also negates the attempt by some feminists to expand on the very idea of inheritance itself as implying egalitarianism in church functions. Although they recognize the centrality of the inheritance theme in the context of Galatians 3:28, they attempt to evade the implications thereof by focusing on the *content* of that inheritance, and by attempting to include within it the elimination of all role distinctions between men and women. The argument is basically this: receiving an inheritance involves the right and the necessity of administering or managing what has been inherited; all Christians (Jews and Greeks, slaves and free-born, men and women) have received the *same* inheritance; therefore all have an equal right to the roles of administering and ruling over the inheritance (including ordained ministry and eldership). In other words, equal heirship necessarily entails role equality.[161]

All attempts to expand Paul's use of the inheritance theme in Galatians 3:1-4:7 to include rulership over the inheritance are invalid, however, because they go beyond the way this theme actually functions in the context. Whether or not inheritance involves rulership, and exactly what this might mean for gender roles if it does, are legitimate questions; but they are not questions that can be answered on the basis of what is taught in Galatians 3:28. Here the metaphor is used only to explain *how* salvation is received. It explains the way or manner of salvation, not its content. The content of the inheritance is simply not the point of the metaphor in this verse.

The argument ultimately comes back to the assumption that equal heirship necessarily implies equality of roles. We are not questioning the concept of equal heirship as such. Within the limitations of the Galatians context, we may agree that men and women are equal heirs of the Abrahamic promise. That is, they both have the same salvation and they both receive it in the same way. What must be vigorously questioned and vigorously denied is that equality of roles is a valid implication of equal heirship.[162] It is certainly not part of the teaching of Galatians; and even though it may seem like a logical extension of the concept, it is contrary to reality itself.

For example, 1 Peter 3:1-7 shows that the equal heirship of husband and wife does not affect the very clear distinction between their roles in the home. Even more significantly, we are in a real sense "equal heirs" with Jesus Christ himself. The point of Galatians is that Christ is the only true seed and son of Abraham and thus the only true heir (3:16), but through our oneness with Christ we too become the seed and sons of Abraham and thus heirs with him. Romans 8:17 specifically says we are "fellow-heirs with Christ." Does this imply, then, that we and Christ must have equal roles in the Kingdom of God? The very idea is ridiculous, but it clearly shows that it is likewise invalid to assume that equal heirship in Galatians 3:28 necessarily entails role equality.

In short, this assumption has the same problems as the entire feminist treatment of Galatians 3:28, i.e., it is the product of faulty hermeneutics. Rather than allowing the context to interpret 3:28, it pours preconceived content into this verse and then reads it back into the context. Also, it fails to let Scripture interpret Scripture. That is, it attempts to arrive at a final and dogmatic conclusion as to the basic meaning of 3:28 along with its whole range of applications, without taking into account what is said on the same subject by other passages of Scripture.

The final implication in reference to the connection between Galatians 3:28 and the theme of inheritance is this: all conclusions concerning the practical implications of our common salvation in Christ, including a proper understanding of gender roles, must be drawn from texts other than Galatians 3:28 itself, namely, those which specifically speak to this subject.

As we saw earlier, Galatians 3:28 is not intended to be a general principle concerning the whole spectrum of human relationships; indeed, it is not addressing the question of human social relationships at all. Thus it is inappropriate to generalize from it because of its very nature. But even if 3:28 were addressing issues such as gender roles, it still would be wrong to generalize from it without taking into account all the other texts which have something to say on the subject. Whatever Galatians 3:28 says about men and women and their alleged oneness or equality has to be understood in the light of any qualifications, modifications, applications, and implications found in other texts.

For example, someone might insist that total role equality and the elimination of all role distinctions between men and women, applied consistently, justifies homosexual marriages. Almost all Evangelicals, however, would say that this is not a valid conclusion because other New Testament texts, such as Romans 1:26-27 and 1 Corinthians 6:9-10, clearly forbid homosexual relationships. In other words, in this case other texts are allowed to set the limits on the extent of the role equality assumed to be taught in Galatians 3:28. The fact is that this same procedure must be followed for *any* practical application of Galatians 3:28, since the verse does not contain *any* information on how it is meant to be applied or how it might be appropriate to apply it. The *only* information we have as to application comes from other texts.

We certainly grant that there *are* social implications stemming from the oneness of which Galatians 3:28 speaks. This is not the issue. What is at stake is whether we can learn anything from verse 28 itself as to what these implications are. Some appeal to Galatians 2:11-14 to show that oneness in Christ has social implications,[163] but this passage says very little about what they may be. Especially, it tells us nothing as to gender roles in relation to church leadership and church functions. We can no more generalize from 2:11-14 on this matter than we can from 3:28.

Thus we agree with Pawson, that even if Galatians 3:28 were intending to cancel certain psychological or sociological differences between the genders, we cannot learn what these cancelled differences are supposed to be from Galatians itself. As Pawson says,

> Neither the verse nor its context supplies any guidelines for this exercise (hardly surprising, since Paul was here dealing with a purely spiritual issue and not directly considering any sexual or social outworking of it). So we must look elsewhere in the New Testament to see how the principle of Galatians 3:28 was worked out in practice. To put it simply, do the apostolic writers assume that all differences between male and female (other than the physical) have been abolished "in Christ?"

Pawson's emphatic answer: "Clearly, they do not!"[164]

When we examine other didactic texts that do speak to

the question of gender roles, we see that they uniformly support the continuation of role distinctions even for those who are "in Christ." This is true both in the church and in the home. Regarding the former, both 1 Corinthians 14:34-35 and 1 Timothy 2:11-12 must be understood as qualifying or restricting the "equality of heirship" in Galatians 3:28. Regarding the home, passages such as Ephesians 5:22-24; Colossians 3:18; Titus 2:5; and 1 Peter 3:1-7 must be seen as continuing to mandate the headship-submission relationship between husbands and wives.

As we have noted before, 1 Peter 3:1-7 is especially significant as a qualifier of Galatians 3:28 because it specifically affirms the equality of heirship taught in 3:28, while at the very same time it emphasizes the submission of wives to their husbands. The description of Christian wives as "fellow-heirs of the grace of life" in verse 7 could not be any more clear as an echo of Galatians. What is striking is that this directly follows an extended instruction for wives to "be submissive to your own husbands" (verse 1; see 1-6). This passage all by itself exposes as complete fiction the feminist claim that Galatians 3:28 is a principle of total gender equality. It is no wonder that feminists usually ignore it altogether. Hull, for example, in her major work *Equal To Serve,* barely mentions it and does not discuss it at all.[165]

Our point is that passages such as 1 Peter 3:1-7 are the ones to which we must turn for information about gender roles, since these speak specifically to the subject while Galatians 3:28 speaks to a different point altogether. Pawson's comment sums it up very well: "To enlarge one verse of Scripture into a social or an ecclesiastical manifesto is unwarranted and misleading, particularly in view of Paul's [and Peter's] other teaching on the subject."[166]

ENDNOTES
CHAPTER FIVE

[1]H. Wayne House, *The Role of Women in Ministry Today* (Nashville: Thomas Nelson, 1990), p. 22. See also Mary A. Kassian, *Women, Creation, and the Fall* (Westchester, IL: Crossway Books, 1990), p. 155.

[2]We say this because feminists believe that certain descriptive passages in the epistles support their view, e. g., Rom. 16:1-7.

[3]"The church visible has in its life and ministry ignored to a frightening degree the truth of Galatians 3:28" (Ruth A. Schmidt, "Second-Class Citizenship in the Kingdom of God," *Christianity Today* [January 1, 1971], 15:13). See also Patricia Gundry, *Woman Be Free! The Clear Message of Scripture* (Grand Rapids: Zondervan, 1977), p. 25.

[4]The descriptions in this paragraph are direct quotations from feminist writings. Documentation can be provided.

[5]Richard N. Longenecker, *New Testament Social Ethics for Today* (Grand Rapids: Eerdmans, 1984), p. 34.

[6]Scott McClelland, "The New Reality in Christ: Perspectives from Biblical Studies," in *Gender Matters: Women's Studies for the Christian Community*, ed. June Steffensen Hagen (Grand Rapids: Zondervan, 1990), p. 65.

[7]Ronald E. Heine, "The Bible and the Role of Women in the Church," *Christian Standard* (September 24, 1978), 113:6. See also Catherine Clark Kroeger, "Toward an Egalitarian Hermeneutic of Faith," *Priscilla Papers* (Spring 1990), 4:7; Joan Chatfield, "Women and Men: Colleagues in Mission," *Gospel in Context* (April 1979), 2:8; and Gilbert Bilezikian, *Beyond Sex Roles: What the Bible Says About a Woman's Place in Church and Family*, 2nd ed. (Grand Rapids: Baker, 1990), pp. 127-128.

[8]Richard Clark Kroeger and Catherine Kroeger, *I Suffer Not a Woman: Rethinking 1 Timothy 2:11-15 in Light of Ancient Evidence* (Grand Rapids: Baker, 1992), p. 39.

[9]Charles R. Boatman, "Wondering About Women," *Christian Standard* (January 6, 1991), 126:8.

[10]Gottfried Oosterwal, "Dialogue," *Gospel in Context* (April 1979), 2:22.

[11]Joseph M. Webb, "The Mailbox," *Christian Standard* (October 2, 1988), 123:13; see p. 22.

[12]Boatman, "Wondering," p. 8.

[13]Virginia Ramey Mollenkott, "A Challenge to Male Interpretation: Women and the Bible," *Sojourners* (February 1976), 5:24.

[14]Mary Hayter, *The New Eve in Christ: The Use and Abuse of the Bible in the Debate About Women in the Church* (Grand Rapids: Eerdmans, 1987), p. 134.

[15]Schmidt, "Second-Class Citizenship," pp. 13, 14.

[16]House, *The Role of Women*, p. 23.

[17]Mary Kassian, *The Feminist Gospel: The Movement to Unite Feminism with the Church* (Wheaton, IL: Crossway Books, 1992), p. 208. See also John Jefferson Davis, "Some Reflections on Galatians 3:28, Sexual Roles, and Biblical Hermeneutics," *Journal of the Evangelical*

Theological Society (Summer 1976), 19:202.

[18]Krister Stendahl makes these points in his influential booklet, *The Bible and the Role of Women: A Case Study for Hermeneutics*, tr. Emilie T. Sander (Philadelphia: Fortress Press, 1966), p. 32.

[19]Ibid.

[20]Richard and Joyce Boldrey, *Chauvinist or Feminist? Paul's View of Women* (Grand Rapids: Baker, 1976), p. 33. For the same view see F. F. Bruce, *The Epistle to the Galatians: A Commentary on the Greek Text* (Grand Rapids: Eerdmans, 1982), p. 189; Paul K. Jewett, *Man as Male and Female: A Study in Sexual Relationships from a Theological Point of View* (Grand Rapids: Eerdmans, 1975), p. 142; Longenecker, *New Testament Social Ethics*, p. 75, note 6; and Klyne R. Snodgrass, "Galatians 3:28: Conundrum or Solution?", in *Women, Authority and the Bible*, ed. Alvera Mickelsen (Downers Grove: InterVarsity, 1986), p. 171.

[21]Aida Besançon Spencer, *Beyond the Curse: Women Called to Ministry* (Nashville: Thomas Nelson, 1985), p. 29.

[22]Ibid., p. 37.

[23]Ibid., pp. 133-134.

[24]Ibid., p. 42.

[25]Mary Stewart Van Leeuwen, *Gender and Grace: Love, Work, and Parenting in a Changing World* (Downers Grove: InterVarsity Press, 1990), p. 25.

[26]Ibid., p. 48.

[27]Mary Stewart Van Leeuwen, "The Christian Mind and the Challenge of Gender Relations," *The Reformed Journal* (September 1987), 37:22.

[28]Peter DeJong and Donald R. Wilson, *Husband and Wife: The Sexes in Scripture and Society* (Grand Rapids: Zondervan, 1979), pp. 134-137.

[29]See, for example, Gretchen Gaebelein Hull, *Equal To Serve: Women and Men in the Church and Home* (Old Tappan, NJ: Revell, 1987), pp. 210-211; David W. Diehl, "Theology and Feminism," in *Gender Matters: Women's Studies for the Christian Community*, ed. June Steffensen Hagen (Grand Rapids: Zondervan, 1990), p. 38; R. Paul Stevens, "Breaking the Gender Impasse," *Christianity Today* (January 13, 1992), 36:28; Heine, "Bible," p. 6; McClelland, "The New Reality," p. 66; Oosterwal, "Dialogue," p. 22; and Hayter, *New Eve*, p. 129.

[30]DeJong and Wilson, *Husband and Wife*, p. 137.

[31]Oosterwal, "Dialogue," p. 22.

[32]David M. Scholer, "Hermeneutical Gerrymandering: Hurley on Women and Authority," *TSF Bulletin* (May-June 1983), 6:12.

[33]Schmidt, "Second-Class Citizenship," pp. 13-14.

[34]Ruth Tucker, *Women in the Maze: Questions and Answers on Biblical Equality* (Downers Grove: InterVarsity Press, 1992), p. 124.

[35]Boldrey, *Chauvinist*, pp. 32-33.

[36]Longenecker, *New Testament Social Ethics*, pp. 84, 92.

[37]Don Williams, *The Apostle Paul and Women in the Church* (Ventura, CA: Regal Books, 1977), p. 82.

[38]Boldrey, *Chauvinist*, pp. 55ff., 70; Longenecker, *New Testament Social Ethics*, pp. 80-87.

[39]Boldrey, *Chauvinist*, p. 33.

[40]Longenecker, *New Testament Social Ethics*, p. 92. See Williams, *The Apostle Paul*, p. 86.

[41]Ruth A. Tucker and Walter L. Liefeld, *Daughters of the Church: Women and Ministry from New Testament Times to the Present* (Grand Rapids: Zondervan, 1987), p. 65.

[42]Myrtle Langley, *Equal Women: A Christian Feminist Perspective* (Great Britain: Marshall Morgan and Scott, 1983), p. 48.

[43]Longenecker, *New Testament Social Ethics*, p. 92.

[44]From Berakoth 7.18, cited in Madeleine Boucher, "Some Unexplored Parallels to 1 Cor 11,11-12 and Gal, 3,28: The NT on the Role of Women," *The Catholic Biblical Quarterly* (1969), 31:53. See also Snodgrass, "Galatians 3:28," pp. 168-169.

[45]Letha Dawson Scanzoni and Nancy A. Hardesty, *All We're Meant To Be: Biblical Feminism for Today*, 3rd ed. (Grand Rapids: Eerdmans, 1992), p. 102.

[46]Dorothy R. Pape, *In Search of God's Ideal Woman : A Personal Examination of the New Testament* (Downers Grove: InterVarsity, 1976), p. 202.

[47]S. Scott Bartchy, "Power, Submission, and Sexual Identity Among the Early Christians," *Essays on New Testament Christianity*, ed. C. Robert Wetzel (Cincinnati: Standard Publishing, 1978), p. 58.

[48]Bartchy, "How Much Freedom Can You Stand?" Aurora, IL: European Evangelistic Society, n. d.), pp. 5, 7. Published as a pamphlet, and also as vol. xix, no. 5 of *The European Evangelist*.

[49]W. Ward Gasque, "Response" to Klyne Snodgrass, in *Women, Authority and the Bible*, ed. Alvera Mickelsen (Downers Grove: InterVarsity Press, 1986), p. 190.

[50]Manfred Brauch, *Hard Sayings of Paul* (Downers Grove: InterVarsity Press, 1989), p. 122. See also Bruce, *Galatians*, p. 187; Bilezikian, *Beyond Sex Roles*, p. 277, note 9.

[51] See Bartchy, "Power," p. 58.

[52]Bruce, *Galatians*, p. 187. See Snodgrass, "Galatians 3:28," p. 169, especially note 37.

[53]E. g., Longenecker quotes the prayer thus: "'Blessed be He that He did not make me a boor [i. e., an ignorant peasant or a slave]'" (*New Testament Social Ethics*, p. 33). See also Spencer's reference to "Gentile, slave or uneducated man, woman" (*Beyond the Curse*, p. 64).

[54]Jewish literature does have one version of the prayer that includes a reference to slaves, but it comes from the fifth century A. D., and the rabbi to whom the saying is attributed (Rabbi Aha b. Jacob) is from the early fourth century A. D. This of course is much too late to have influenced Paul. See *The Babylonian Talmud: Seder Kodashim*, vol. 28: *Menahoth*, tr. Eli Cashdan (London: Soncino Press, 1948), section 43b, p. 264.

[55]See Jacob Neusner, *The Rabbinic Traditions About the Pharisees Before 70*, three volumes (Leiden: E. J. Brill, 1971). Neusner identifies and discusses 371 separate stories about or sayings of or allusions to named Pharisees before A. D. 70.

[56]Spencer, *Beyond the Curse*, p. 65.

[57]Tucker and Liefeld, *Daughters*, p. 66.

[58]See H. Wayne House, "Neither . . . Male nor Female . . . in Christ Jesus,'" *Bibliotheca Sacra* (January-March 1988), 145:51, footnote 10, for bibliographical data.

[59]Bilezikian, *Beyond Sex Roles*, p. 126. Bilezikian himself does not press this point.

[60]Bartchy, "Power," p. 58. He says there is "strong support" for the conclusion that Galatians 3:28 "is a baptismal formula which was part of Paul's vocabulary prior to his composition of Galatians" (*MALLON CHRESAI: First-Century Slavery and the Interpretation of 1 Corinthians 7:21* [Missoula, Montana: Society of Biblical Literature, 1973], pp. 129-130).

[61]Longenecker, *New Testament Social Ethics*, p. 32.

[62]Ben Witherington III, "Rite and Rights for Women — Galatians 3:28," *New Testament Studies* (1981), 27:597.

[63]Langley, *Equal Woman*, p. 47.

[64]Bartchy, "Power," p. 58.

[65]Bartchy, *MALLON CHRESAI*, p. 129. McClelland endorses Bartchy's view ("The New Reality," p. 65), as does Sharon Hodgin Gritz in *Paul, Women Teachers, and the Mother Goddess at Ephesus* (Lanham, MD: University Press of America, 1991), p. 83.

[66]Longenecker, *New Testament Social Ethics*, p. 31.

[67]Ibid.

[68]Myrtle S. Langley, "One Baptism, One Ministry: The Ordination of Women and Unity in Christ," *Transformation* (April / June 1989), 6:27; and *Equal Woman*, p. 47.

[69]Bartchy, "Power," p. 58.

[70]Langley, "One Baptism," p. 27.

[71]Longenecker, *New Testament Social Ethics*, p. 33.

[72]House, "Neither," p. 51, footnote 10.

[73]McClelland, "The New Reality," pp. 66, 67.

[74]Roger and Rose Thomas, "It's Not a Man's World," part one, *Christian Standard* (August 3, 1975), 110:12.

[75]Gasque, "Response," p. 189. Italics in the original.

[76]Mary J. Evans, *Women in the Bible: An Overview of All the Crucial Passages on Women's Roles* (Downers Grove: InterVarsity Press, 1983), p. 64.

[77]Ray S. Anderson, "The Resurrection of Jesus as Hermeneutical Criterion," part two, *TSF Bulletin* (March-April 1986), 9:17. "Galatians is normative," says Virginia Mollenkott, in "A Conversation with Virginia Mollenkott," *The Other Side* (May-June 1976), p. 73.

[78]Jewett, *Man*, pp. 112ff.

[79]Kassian, *The Feminist Gospel*, p. 208.

[80]Thomas, "Man's World," part one, p. 12.

[81]Bruce, *Galatians*, p. 190.

[82]Longenecker, *New Testament Social Ethics*, p. 85.

[83]W. Ward Gasque, "The Role of Women in the Church, in Society and in the Home," *Priscilla Papers* (Spring 1988), 2:10. See also Bilezikian, *Beyond Sex Roles*, p. 128.

[84]See Hayter, *New Eve*, p. 146.

[85]Robert K. Johnston, "Women in the Church and Home," *The*

Reformed Journal (June 1978), 28:12-13. Italics in the original.

[86]McClelland, "The New Reality," pp. 67, 71.

[87]Bartchy, "Power," pp. 57-59, 67ff.

[88]Anderson, "Resurrection," part two, p. 17.

[89]Scanzoni and Hardesty, *All We're Meant To Be* (1992), p. 101. In the first edition of this work they state their method thus: "Passages which are theological and doctrinal in content are used to interpret those where the writer is dealing with practical local cultural problems." Only Galatians 3:28 is in the former category (*All We're Meant To Be* [Waco: Word, 1974], pp. 18-19).

[90]Brauch, *Hard Sayings of Paul*, pp. 254-255.

[91]Johnston, "Women," pp. 11, 13.

[92]Langley, *Equal Woman*, p. 56.

[93]Hayter, *New Eve*, p. 146.

[94]Mollenkott, "Conversation," p. 73.

[95]Jewett, *Man*, pp. 145, 147-148. In her foreword to this book Mollenkott affirms, "The liberating vision of Galatians 3:28, not the stultifying first-century actuality, is the ideal to implement" (p. 12).

[96]Longenecker, *New Testament Social Ethics*, chapter 2, especially p. 27; and chapter 5, especially pp. 84-85. See also Longenecker, "Authority, Hierarchy and Leadership Patterns in the Bible," in *Women, Authority and the Bible*, ed. Alvera Mickelsen (Downers Grove: InterVarsity Press, 1986), p. 83.

[97]Bruce A. Demarest, "Analogy of Faith," *Evangelical Dictionary of Theology*, ed. Walter A. Elwell (Grand Rapids: Baker, 1984), pp. 43-44.

[98]E. g., Phoebe (Rom. 16:1-2), Priscilla (Rom. 16:3), Junia (Rom. 16:7), and Euodia and Syntyche (Phil. 4:2-3).

[99]Spencer, *Beyond the Curse*, p. 66.

[100]Evans, *Woman*, p. 65.

[101]Kassian, *Women*, pp. 156-157.

[102]F. LaGard Smith, *Men of Strength for Women of God* (Eugene, OR: Harvest House, 1989), p. 199.

[103]J. David Pawson, *Leadership Is Male* (Nashville: Oliver-Nelson, 1990), p. 67.

[104]"It is important to understand this verse in its context," declare Tucker and Liefeld (*Daughters*, p. 453).

[105]Diehl, "Theology," p. 38.

[106]Snodgrass, "Galatians 3:28," p. 161.

[107]Longenecker, "Authority," p. 83; and *New Testament Social Ethics*, p. 30. That such is "clearly stated" is an exaggeration that begs the question.

[108]Longenecker, *New Testament Social Ethics*, p. 34. He declares that the three pairs in this verse "cover in embryonic fashion all the essential relationships of humanity" (ibid.).

[109]Ibid., p. 51.

[110]DeJong and Wilson, *Husband and Wife*, p. 137. See also Bilezikian, *Beyond Sex Roles*, pp. 126-128; and Longenecker, *New Testament Social Ethics*, p. 33.

[111]Jewett, *Man*, p. 143.

[112]Gritz, *Paul*, p. 83.

[113]Brauch, *Hard Sayings of Paul*, p. 122.

[114]Ibid., p. 254.

[115]Joseph M. Webb, "'There Cannot Be Male and Female,'" unpublished essay, pp. 11, 16.

[116]Ibid., p. 18.

[117]Chatfield, "Women and Men," p. 8.

[118]Austin H. Stouffer, "The Ordination of Women: Yes," *Christianity Today* (February 20, 1981), 25:13.

[119]Boldrey, *Chauvinist*, pp. 48, 70.

[120]Ibid., pp. 46-48.

[121]Tucker, *Women*, p. 124.

[122]Langley, "One Baptism," p. 27.

[123]John Stott, *Involvement, Volume II: Social and Sexual Relationships in the Modern World* (Old Tappan, NJ: Revell, 1984), p. 137.

[124]Peter H. Davids, "Dialogue," *Gospel in Context* (April 1979), 2:17-18.

[125]S. Lewis Johnson, "Role Distinctions in the Church: Galatians 3:28," in *Recovering Biblical Manhood and Womanhood: A Response to Evangelical Feminism*, ed. John Piper and Wayne Grudem (Wheaton, IL: Crossway Books, 1991), p. 154.

[126]Davids, "Dialogue," p. 17.

[127]Boldrey, *Chauvinist*, pp. 45-46.

[128]Witherington, "Rite," pp. 594-595.

[129]Ibid., p. 599. Stephen Clark, a non-feminist, offers the same explanation (*Man and Woman in Christ: An Examination of the Roles of Men and Women in Light of Scripture and the Social Sciences* [Ann Arbor: Servant Books, 1980], pp. 140-141).

[130]Hayter, *New Eve*, p. 135. Clark presents a similar view (*Man*, pp. 144-149).

[131]Faith McBurney Martin, *Call Me Blessed: The Emerging Christian Woman* (Grand Rapids: Eerdmans, 1988), p. 126.

[132]Ibid., pp. 126-131.

[133]Ibid., p. 126.

[134]Ibid., p. 128.

[135]Hayter, *New Eve*, p. 135.

[136]James Hurley rightly says that in Gal. 3:28 "Paul was not reflecting upon relations *within* the body of Christ." Rather "he was thinking about the basis of membership in the body of Christ" (*Man and Woman in Biblical Perspective* [Grand Rapids: Zondervan, 1981], p. 127.

[137]This point is recognized and explained well by F. LaGard Smith in *Men of Strength for Women of God*, p. 204.

[138]I am aware of two non-feminist writers who have understood this point very well. One is F. LaGard Smith (*Men of Strength*, p. 204); the other is J. David Pawson (*Leadership*, pp. 68-70). I am aware of one feminist writer who understands that inheritance is the key theme (Spencer, *Beyond the Curse*, pp. 68-70); but she presses the metaphor far beyond Paul's intention. Her view will be discussed toward the end of this section.

[139]Francis Lyall, *Slaves, Citizens, Sons: Legal Metaphors in the*

Epistles (Grand Rapids: Zondervan, 1984), p. 107.

[140]Ibid., p. 105.

[141]Ibid., pp. 115-116.

[142]Although this is the established norm, the Old Testament refers to a few possible exceptions to it. See Gen. 15:2-3; 1 Chron. 2:34-35; Prov. 17:2.

[143]Lyall, *Slaves*, p. 76.

[144]Ibid., p. 72. Raymond Westbrook agrees (*Property and the Family in Biblical Law*, JSOT Supplement Series, no. 113 [Sheffield, England: JSOT Press, 1991], pp. 74-75).

[145]Westbrook, *Property*, p. 65.

[146]Ibid., p. 143.

[147]Job 42:13-15 "describes an altogether exceptional procedure," says Burton Scott Easton, "Heir," *The International Standard Bible Encyclopedia*, rev. ed. [1929] (Grand Rapids: Eerdmans, 1957), II:1369.

[148]Bilezikian, *Beyond Sex Roles*, p. 126.

[149]Spencer, *Beyond the Curse*, pp. 68-70.

[150]Clark, *Man*, p. 141.

[151]Longenecker, *New Testament Social Ethics*, p. 33.

[152]McClelland, "The New Reality," p. 65.

[153]Webb, "Male and Female," p. 2.

[154]Pawson, *Leadership*, p. 70.

[155]Boatman, "Wondering," p. 8. For another example see Webb, "Male and Female," pp. 18-19.

[156]Snodgrass, "Galatians 3:28," p. 173. See also McClelland, "The New Reality," p. 65.

[157]McClelland, "The New Reality," p. 65.

[158]Bartchy, "Freedom," p. 9. See also Boatman, "Wondering," p. 8.

[159]Smith, *Men of Strength*, p. 203.

[160]Bilezikian, *Beyond Sex Roles*, p. 277.

[161]This view is presented mainly by Spencer, *Beyond the Curse*, pp. 69-71, 134; Hull, *Equal To Serve*, p. 229; and Hull, "Discrimination and Human Rights," in *Applying the Scriptures: Papers from ICBI Summit III*, ed. Kenneth S. Kantzer (Grand Rapids: Zondervan, 1987), p. 342.

[162]See House, *The Role of Women*, pp. 105-106.

[163]See Jewett, *Man*, p. 144; Spencer, *Beyond the Curse*, pp. 66-67.

[164]Pawson, *Leadership*, p. 110.

[165]On page 188 she mentions it as one of the minor "hard passages" but makes no attempt to reconcile it to her egalitarian presuppositions. Some claim the passage is irrelevant because it refers only to women married to unbelieving men (Martin, *Call Me Blessed*, p. 45). Pawson adequately refutes this idea (*Leadership*, p. 63).

[166]Pawson, *Leadership*, p. 70.

CONCLUSION

My goal in this volume has been to analyze the way feminists interpret the major portions of Scripture which they believe provide a positive undergirding for egalitarianism. These include the Biblical teaching on creation and the Fall (Genesis 1-3), the example and teaching of Jesus, and Galatians 3:28.[1] I have attempted to explain the specific feminist interpretations as clearly and as fairly as possible, and I have attempted to show that these interpretations are not justified by the facts and by the standard rules of Biblical hermeneutics.

I believe that the facts and my arguments speak for themselves, and that the feminist interpretations of these Biblical texts are hereby exposed as false. When interpreted according to the principles of sound hermeneutics, there is *nothing* in the teaching about creation and the Fall, *nothing* in the ministry and teaching of Jesus, and *nothing* in Galatians 3:28 that justifies the teaching of egalitarianism with regard to gender roles. Every reader must judge this matter for himself or herself, of course; but conscientious judgment demands that the facts be taken into account and that proper hermeneutical procedures be followed.

If anyone has been patient enough to "persevere to the end," and is actually now reading these words, he or she may be amazed that so much could be written on what appears to be such limited subject matter. I apologize on the one hand if this discussion seems too lengthy. But on the other hand I apologize for not being able to cover all of the nooks and crannies of feminist exegesis on these subjects. Some of the more obscure interpretations had to be passed over so as not to make this work excessively unwieldy. It is difficult to cover everything, because feminism's capacity for producing new and creative interpretations of these texts is truly astounding. This makes it virtually impossible to discuss them all even in a volume of this length.

To analyze and expose the weaknesses of feminist hermeneutics does not in itself prove hierarchicalism to be true. This is especially the case when the discussion is in general limited to Biblical material taken by feminists to be specifically teaching egalitarianism. Nevertheless, in the course of our critique of even this limited scope of feminist exegesis, the sound Biblical roots of the male leadership view have been demonstrated in several ways. This applies especially to our examination of Genesis 2, the content of the teaching of Jesus, and the way other gender texts properly relate to Galatians 3:28.

The next volume, however, will focus mostly on those Biblical texts which do specifically teach a headship-submission pattern for gender roles. While feminists view these as "hard passages" and treat them as exceptions, we shall see otherwise. While the main theme will still be a critique of feminist hermeneutics, it will be made abundantly clear that these texts teach a divinely-intended hierarchical relationship between men and women in the home and in the church.

ENDNOTES
CONCLUSION

[1]Another group of passages which fall into this category are those which speak of actual women who appear to occupy various sorts of leadership positions in Israel and in the early church. A discussion of these will be included in the next volume.

BIBLIOGRAPHY

Aaseng, Rolf E. "Male and Female Created He Them," *Christianity Today* (November 20, 1970). 15:5-6.

Adler, Margot. *Drawing Down the Moon: Witches, Druids, Goddess-Worshippers, and Other Pagans in America Today*, revised ed. Boston: Beacon Press, 1986.

Anderson, Ray S. "The Resurrection of Jesus as Hermeneutical Criterion," *TSF Bulletin*, 2 parts: Jan.-Feb. 1986, 9:9-15; and Mar.-Apr. 1986, 9:15-20.

Archer, Gleason. "Ordination Is Not for Women," *Moody Monthly* (February 1987). P. 8.

Atkins, Anne. *Split Image: Male and Female After God's Likeness*. Grand Rapids: Eerdmans, 1987.

Babylonian Talmud: Seder Kodashim, vol. 28: Menahoth, tr. Eli Cashdan. London: Soncino Press, 1948.

Bartchy, S. Scott. "How Much Freedom Can You Stand?", *The European Evangelist* (n.d.), 19:1-12. Published in pamphlet form.

_____. "Human Sexuality and Our Identity," *Mission Journal* (November 1983). 17:10-14.

_____. "Jesus, Power, and Gender Roles," *TSF Bulletin* (January-February 1984). 7:2-4.

_____ . *MALLON CHRESAI: First-Century Slavery and the Interpretation of 1 Corinthians 7:21*. Missoula, Montana: Society of Biblical Literature, 1973.

_____ . "Power, Submission, and Sexual Identity Among the Early Christians," *Essays On New Testament Christianity*, ed. C. Robert Wetzel. Cincinnati: Standard Publishing, 1978. Pp. 50-80.

Bilezikian, Gilbert. *Beyond Sex Roles: What the Bible Says About a Woman's Place in Church and Family*, 2nd ed. Grand Rapids: Baker, 1990.

Bloesch, Donald. *The Battle for the Trinity*. Ann Arbor: Servant Books, 1985.

Boatman, Charles R. "Wondering About Women," *Christian Standard* (January 6, 1991). 126:7-9.

Boldrey, Richard and Joyce. *Chauvinist or Feminist? Paul's View of Women*. Grand Rapids: Baker, 1976.

Boucher, Madeleine. "Some Unexplored Parallels to 1 Cor 11,11-12 and Gal 3,28: The NT on the Role of Women," *The Catholic Biblical Quarterly* (1969). 31:50-58.

Brauch, Manfred T. *Hard Sayings of Paul*. Downers Grove: InterVarsity Press, 1989.

Braun, Herbert. *"plassō* [etc.]," *Theological Dictionary of the New Testament*, ed. Gerhard Kittel and Gerhard Friedrich, tr. Geoffrey W. Bromiley. Grand Rapids: Eerdmans, 1968. 6:254-262.

Bruce, F. F. *The Epistle to the Galatians: A Commentary on the Greek Text*. Grand Rapids: Eerdmans, 1982.

Cady, Susan; Mirian Ronan; and Hal Taussig. *Wisdom's*

Feast: Sophia in Study and Celebration. San Francisco: Harper and Row, 1989; revision of *Sophia: The Future of Feminist Spirituality* (1986).

Chatfield, Joan. "Women and Men: Colleagues in Mission," *Gospel in Context* (April 1979). 2:4-14.

Christ, Carol. *Laughter of Aphrodite: Reflections on a Journey to the Goddess.* San Francisco: Harper & Row, 1987.

Clark, Stephen B. *Man and Woman in Christ: An Examination of the Roles of Men and Women in Light of Scripture and the Social Sciences.* Ann Arbor: Servant Books, 1980.

Clouse, Bonnidell and Robert G., eds. *Women in Ministry: Four Views.* Downers Grove: InterVarsity Press, 1989.

Cottrell, Jack. *Feminism and the Bible: An Introduction to Feminism for Christians.* Joplin, MO: College Press, 1992.

_____ . *What the Bible Says About God the Creator.* Joplin, MO: College Press, 1983.

Crouch, Owen L. *Not Guilty: Studies in Romans.* Milligan College, TN: published by author, 1987.

Daly, Mary. *Beyond God the Father: Toward a Philosophy of Women's Liberation,* new paperback ed. Boston: Beacon Press, 1985.

Daniel, Eleanor. *What the Bible Says About Sexual Identity.* Joplin, MO: College Press, 1981.

Davids, Peter H. "Dialogue," *Gospel in Context* (April 1979). 2:17-18.

Davis, John Jefferson. "Some Reflections on Galatians 3:28, Sexual Roles, and Biblical Hermeneutics," *Journal of the Evangelical Theological Society* (Summer 1976). 19:201-208.

DeJong, Peter, and Donald R. Wilson. *Husband and Wife: The Sexes in Scripture and Society.* Grand Rapids: Zondervan, 1979.

Demarest, Bruce A. "Analogy of Faith," *Evangelical Dictionary of Theology*, ed. Walter A. Elwell. Grand Rapids: Baker, 1984. Pp. 43-44.

Diehl, David W. "Theology and Feminism," *Gender Matters: Women's Studies for the Christian Community*, ed. June Steffensen Hagen. Grand Rapids: Zondervan, 1990. Pp. 25-50.

Easton, Burton Scott. "Heir," *The International Standard Bible Encyclopedia*, rev. ed. [1929]. Grand Rapids: Eerdmans, 1957. II:1369.

Emswiler, Sharon Neufer, and Thomas Neufer Emswiler. *Women and Worship: A Guide to Non-Sexist Hymns, Prayers, and Liturgies.* San Francisco: Harper & Row, 1974.

Evans, Mary J. *Woman in the Bible: An Overview of All the Crucial Passages on Women's Roles.* Downers Grove: InterVarsity Press, 1983.

Fee, Gordon D., and Douglas Stuart. *How To Read the Bible for All Its Worth: A Guide to Understanding the Bible.* Grand Rapids: Zondervan, 1982.

Fiorenza, Elisabeth Schüssler. *Bread Not Stone: The Challenge of Feminist Biblical Interpretation.* Boston: Beacon Press, 1984.

Fisher, Ronald. "Freedom Within God's Appointments," three parts, *The Restoration Herald* (May/June/July 1989). Pp. 3ff./3ff./4ff.

Fleming, Joy Elasky. "Gender Equality in Genesis 2-3," an unpublished essay. St. Paul, MN: Christians for Biblical Equality, 1991.

Foh, Susan T. "A Male Leadership View: The Head of the Woman Is the Man," *Women in Ministry: Four Views*, ed. Bonnidell and Robert G. Clouse. Downers Grove: InterVarsity Press, 1989. Pp. 69-105.

_____. "What Is the Woman's Desire?", *Westminster Theological Journal* (1975). 37:376-383.

_____. *Women and the Word of God: A Response to Biblical Feminism*. Phillipsburg, NJ: Presbyterian and Reformed, 1979.

Foster, Lewis. "Woman—Where's She Going Today?", two parts, *Christian Standard* (Dec. 11/18, 1988). 123:8-11/9-12.

Gasque, W. Ward. "Response" to Klyne R. Snodgrass, *Women, Authority and the Bible*, ed. Alvera Mickelsen. Downers Grove: InterVarsity Press, 1986. Pp. 188-192.

_____. "The Role of Women in the Church, in Society and in the Home," *Priscilla Papers* (Spring 1988). 2:1-2, 8-10.

Gregory of Nazianzus, "Letter to Cledonius Against Apollinaris (Epistle 101)," *Christology of the Later Fathers*, ed. Edward R. Hardy, "Library of Christian Classics," vol. III. Philadelphia: Westminster Press, n.d. Pp. 215-224.

Grillmeier, Aloys. *Christ in Christian Tradition: From the Apostolic Age to Chalcedon (451)*, tr. J. S. Bowden. New York: Sheed and Ward, 1965.

Gritz, Sharon Hodgin. *Paul, Women Teachers, and the Mother Goddess at Ephesus: A Study of 1 Timothy 2:9-15 in Light of the Religious and Cultural Milieu of the First Century*. Lanham, MD: University Press of America, 1991.

Gundry, Patricia. *Woman Be Free! The Clear Message of Scripture*. Grand Rapids: Zondervan, 1977.

Hagen, June Steffensen, ed. *Gender Matters: Women's Studies for the Christian Community*. Grand Rapids: Zondervan, 1990.

Hauke, Manfred. *Women in the Priesthood? A Systematic Analysis in the Light of the Order of Creation and Redemption*, tr. David Kipp. San Francisco: Ignatius Press, 1988.

Hayter, Mary. *The New Eve in Christ: The Use and Abuse of the Bible in the Debate About Women in the Church*. Grand Rapids: Eerdmans, 1987.

Heine, Ronald E. "The Bible and the Role of Women in the Church," *Christian Standard* (Sept. 24, 1978). 113:6-8.

Hicks, John Mark, and Bruce L. Morton. *Woman's Role in the Church*. Shreveport, LA: Lambert Book House, 1978.

Hopman, Charlene. "The Role of Women in the Church." Cincinnati, OH: an unpublished address, 1976.

House, H. Wayne. "'Neither . . . Male nor Female . . . in Christ Jesus,'" *Bibliotheca Sacra* (January-March

1988). 145:47-56.

_____. *The Role of Women in Ministry Today.* Nashville: Thomas Nelson, 1990.

Howard, Thomas. "God Before Birth: The Imagery Matters," *Christianity Today* (Dec. 17, 1976). 21:10-13.

Hull, Gretchen Gaebelein. "Discrimination and Human Rights," in *Applying the Scriptures: Papers from ICBI Summit III*, ed. Kenneth S. Kantzer. Grand Rapids: Zondervan, 1987. Pp. 333-351.

_____. *Equal To Serve: Women and Men in the Church and Home.* Old Tappan, NJ: Revell, 1987.

_____. "In the Image of God: Women and Men as Social Equals," *ESA Advocate* (November 1990). Pp. 14-15.

Hurley, James B. *Man and Woman in Biblical Perspective.* Grand Rapids: Zondervan, 1981.

Jewett, Paul K. *Man as Male and Female: A Study in Sexual Relationships from a Theological Point of View.* Grand Rapids: Eerdmans, 1975.

Johnson, S. Lewis Jr. "Role Distinctions in the Church: Galatians 3:28," in *Recovering Biblical Manhood and Womanhood: A Response to Evangelical Feminism*, ed. John Piper and Wayne Grudem. Wheaton, IL: Crossway Books, 1991. Pp. 154-164.

Johnston, Robert K. "Biblical Authority and Interpretation: The Test Case of Women's Role in the Church and Home Updated," *Women, Authority and the Bible*, ed. Alvera Mickelsen. Downers Grove: InterVarsity Press, 1986. Pp. 30-41.

_____. *Evangelicals at an Impasse*. Atlanta: John Knox Press, 1979.

Kaiser, Walter. "Shared Leadership or Male Headship?", *Christianity Today* (October 3, 1986). 30:12, CTI supplement.

Kantzer, Kenneth S. "Proceed with Care," *Christianity Today* (October 3, 1986). 30:14-15, CTI supplement.

Kassian, Mary A. *The Feminist Gospel: The Movement to Unite Feminism with the Church*. Wheaton, IL: Crossway Books, 1992.

_____. *Women, Creation, and the Fall*. Westchester, IL: Crossway Books, 1990.

Kessel, Edward L. "A Proposed Biological Interpretation of the Virgin Birth," *Journal of the American Scientific Affiliation* (September 1983). Pp. 129-136.

Knight, George W. III. "Male and Female Related He Them," *Christianity Today* (April 9, 1976). 20:13-17.

Kroeger, Catherine Clark. "Toward an Egalitarian Hermeneutic of Faith," *Priscilla Papers* (Spring 1990). 4:3-7.

_____. "A Plea for Restraint," *Priscilla Papers* (August 1987). 1:1-2.

Kroeger, Richard and Catherine. *I Suffer Not a Woman: Rethinking 1 Timothy 2:11-15 in Light of Ancient Evidence*. Grand Rapids: Baker, 1992.

_____. "Why Were There No Women Apostles?", *Equity*. [An article distributed in duplicated form without a date by Christians for Biblical Equality.]

Langley, Myrtle S. *Equal Woman: A Christian Feminist Perspective*. Great Britain: Marshall Morgan and Scott, 1983.

_____ . "One Baptism, One Ministry: The Ordination of Women and Unity in Christ," *Transformation* (April-June 1989). 6:27-31.

Letham, Robert. "The Man-Woman Debate: Theological Comment," *Westminster Theological Journal* (1990). 52:65-78.

Liefeld, Walter L. "A Plural Ministry Response" to Susan Foh, *Women in Ministry: Four Views*, ed. Bonnidell Clouse and Robert G. Clouse. Downers Grove: InterVarsity Press, 1989. Pp. 112-116.

Longenecker, Richard N. "Authority, Hierarchy, and Leadership Patterns in the Bible," *Women, Authority and the Bible*, ed. Alvera Mickelsen. Downers Grove: InterVarsity Press, 1986. Pp. 66-85.

_____ . *New Testament Social Ethics for Today*. Grand Rapids: Eerdmans, 1984.

Lyall, Francis. *Slaves, Citizens, Sons: Legal Metaphors in the Epistles*. Grand Rapids: Zondervan, 1984.

Martin, Faith McBurney. *Call Me Blessed: The Emerging Christian Woman*. Grand Rapids: Eerdmans, 1988.

McClelland, Scott E. "The New Reality in Christ: Perspectives from Biblical Studies," *Gender Matters: Women's Studies for the Christian Community*, ed. June Steffensen Hagen. Grand Rapids: Zondervan, 1990. Pp. 51-78.

"Men, Women and Biblical Equality," in *Priscilla Papers*

(Fall 1989). 3:11-13.

Mickelsen, Alvera. "An Egalitarian View: There Is Neither Male Nor Female in Christ," *Women in Ministry: Four Views*, ed. Bonnidell and Robert G. Clouse. Downers Grove: InterVarsity Press, 1989. Pp. 173-206.

_____, ed. *Women, Authority and the Bible*. Downers Grove: InterVarsity Press, 1986.

Mollenkott, Virginia Ramey. "The Biblical Basis for Male-Female Equality," a brochure. Albuquerque: Galatians 3:28 Press, n.d.

_____. "A Challenge to Male Interpretation: Women and the Bible," *Sojourners* (February 1976). 5:20-25.

_____. "A Conversation with Virginia Mollenkott," *The Other Side* (May-June 1976). Pp. 21-30, 73-75.

_____. *The Divine Feminine: The Biblical Imagery of God as Female*. New York: Crossroad, 1983.

_____. "Foreword" in Paul K. Jewett, *Man As Male and Female*. Grand Rapids: Eerdmans, 1975. Pp. 7-12.

_____. Letter to the Editor, *Christianity Today* (June 4, 1976). 20:24-25.

_____. *Women, Men, and the Bible*, rev. ed. New York: Crossroad, 1988.

Moule, C. F. D. *The Phenomenon of the New Testament*. Naperville, IL: Alec R. Allenson, 1967.

Neusner, Jacob. *The Rabbinic Traditions About the*

Pharisees Before 70. Three volumes. Leiden: E. J. Brill, 1971.

Norris, Judy. "Jesus, My Lord, Emancipator of Women," *Christian Standard* (Aug. 31, 1980). 115:9-10.

Oosterwal, Gottfried. "Dialogue," *Gospel in Context* (April 1979). 2:22-23.

Ortlund, Raymond C. Jr. "Male-Female Equality and Male Headship," in *Recovering Biblical Manhood and Womanhood: A Response to Evangelical Feminism,* ed. John Piper and Wayne Grudem. Wheaton, IL: Crossway Books, 1991. Pp. 95-112.

Osborne, Grant R. "Hermeneutics and Women in the Church," *Journal of the Evangelical Theological Society* (December 1977). 20:337-352.

Pape, Dorothy R. *In Search of God's Ideal Woman: A Personal Examination of the New Testament.* Downers Grove: InterVarsity Press, 1976.

Pawson, J. David. *Leadership Is Male.* Nashville: Oliver-Nelson, 1990.

Pentz, Rebecca D. "And When the Hour of Birth Came . . . ," *The Reformed Journal* (March 1988). 38:3-4.

_____. "Jesus as Sophia," *The Reformed Journal* (December 1988). 38:17-22.

Pinnock, Clark H. "Biblical Authority and the Issues in Question," *Women, Authority and the Bible,* ed. Alvera Mickelsen. Downers Grove: InterVarsity Press, 1986. Pp. 51-58.

Piper, John, and Wayne Grudem, "Charity, Clarity and

Hope: The Controversy and the Cause of Christ," in *Recovering Biblical Manhood and Womanhood: A Response to Evangelical Feminism*, ed. John Piper and Wayne Grudem. Wheaton, IL: Crossway Books, 1991. Pp. 403-422.

_____ , eds. *Recovering Biblical Manhood and Womanhood: A Response to Evangelical Feminism*. Wheaton, IL: Crossway Books, 1991.

Ruether, Rosemary Radford. *Sexism and God-Talk: Toward a Feminist Theology*. Boston: Beacon Press, 1983.

Russell, Letty M. *Human Liberation in a Feminist Perspective — A Theology*. Philadelphia: Westminster Press, 1974.

Scanzoni, Letha. "The Feminists and the Bible," *Christianity Today* (February 2, 1973). 17:10-15.

Scanzoni, Letha, and Nancy Hardesty. *All We're Meant To Be: A Biblical Approach to Women's Liberation*. Waco: Word Books, 1974.

_____. *All We're Meant To Be: Biblical Feminism for Today*, 3rd ed. Grand Rapids: Eerdmans, 1992.

Schmidt, Ruth A. "Second-Class Citizenship in the Kingdom of God," *Christianity Today* (January 1, 1971). Pp. 13-14.

Scholer, David M. "Hermeneutical Gerrymandering: Hurley on Women and Authority," *TSF Bulletin* (May-June 1983), 6:11-13.

Smith, F. LaGard. *Men of Strength for Women of God*. Eugene, OR: Harvest House, 1989.

Snodgrass, Klyne R. "Galatians 3:28: Conundrum or Solution?" *Women, Authority and the Bible*, ed. Alvera Mickelsen. Downers Grove: InterVarsity Press, 1986. Pp. 161-181.

Spencer, Aida Besançon. *Beyond the Curse: Women Called to Ministry*. Nashville: Thomas Nelson, 1985.

Stanton, Elizabeth Cady, et. al. *The Woman's Bible*, Parts I and II. New York: European Publishing Company, 1895, 1898.

Stendahl, Krister. *The Bible and the Role of Women: A Case Study in Hermeneutics*, tr. Emilie T. Sander. Philadelphia: Fortress Press, 1966.

Stevens, R. Paul. "Breaking the Gender Impasse," *Christianity Today* (Jan. 13, 1992). 36:28-31.

Storkey, Elaine. *What's Right with Feminism*. Grand Rapids: Eerdmans, 1986.

Stott, John. *Involvement, Volume II: Social and Sexual Relationships in the Modern World*. Old Tappan, NJ: Revell, 1984.

Stouffer, Austin H. "The Ordination of Women: Yes," *Christianity Today* (February 20, 1981). 25:12-15.

Swartley, Willard M. *Slavery, Sabbath, War, and Women: Case Issues in Biblical Interpretation*. Scottdale, PA: Herald Press, 1983.

Swidler, Leonard. "Jesus Was a Feminist," *Catholic World* (January 1971). Pp. 177-183.

Thomas, Roger and Rose. "It's Not a Man's World!", two parts, *Christian Standard* (August 3/10, 1975). 110:11-12/7-8.

Thompson, Fred P., Jr. "'Woman: What Manner of Creature?'" *United Evangelical Action* (Spring 1977). 36:33-34.

Torjesen, Karen and Leif. "Inclusive Orthodoxy: Recovering a Suppressed Tradition," *The Other Side* (December 1986). Pp. 14-18.

Trible, Phyllis. *God and the Rhetoric of Sexuality*. Philadelphia: Fortress, 1978.

Tucker, Ruth A. *Women in the Maze: Questions and Answers on Biblical Equality*. Downers Grove: InterVarsity Press, 1992.

Tucker, Ruth A., and Walter L. Liefeld. *Daughters of the Church: Women and Ministry from New Testament Times to the Present*. Grand Rapids: Zondervan, 1987.

Van Leeuwen, Mary Stewart. "The Christian Mind and the Challenge of Gender Relations," *The Reformed Journal* (September 1987). 37:17-23.

_____. *Gender and Grace: Love, Work and Parenting in a Changing World*. Downers Grove: InterVarsity Press, 1990.

_____. "Life After Eden," *Christianity Today* (July 16, 1990). 34:19-21.

_____. "The Recertification of Women," *The Reformed Journal* (August 1986). 36:17-24.

Webb, Joseph M. "The Mailbox," *Christian Standard* (October 2, 1988). 123:13, 22.

_____ . "'There Cannot Be Male and Female,'" unpublished essay.

Westbrook, Raymond. *Property and the Family in Biblical Law*, JSOT Supplement Series, no. 113. Sheffield, England: JSOT Press, 1991.

Williams, Don. *The Apostle Paul and Women in the Church*. Ventura, CA: Regal Books, 1977.

Witherington, Ben III. "Rite and Rights for Women: Galatians 3:28," *New Testament Studies* (1981). 27:593-604.